The Philosophy of Mixed Martial Arts

Mixed martial arts (MMA) – unarmed fighting games permitting techniques derived from a variety of martial arts and combat sports – has exploded from the fringes of sport into a worldwide phenomenon, a sport as controversial as it is compelling. This is the first book to pay MMA the serious philosophical attention it deserves.

With contributions from leading international scholars of the philosophy of sport and martial arts, the book explores topics such as whether MMA qualifies as a martial art, the differences between MMA and the traditional martial arts, the aesthetic dimensions of MMA, the limits of consent and choice in MMA and whether MMA can promote moral virtues. It also explores cutting-edge practical and ethical topics, including the role of gender in MMA, and the question of whether trans athletes should be allowed to compete in the women's divisions.

The contributors to this anthology take down, ground and pound, and submit many essential questions about this fascinating recent development in the culture of sport and spectacle. This is important reading for anybody with an interest in combat sports, martial arts, or the philosophy, sociology, culture or history of sport.

Jason Holt is Professor of Kinesiology at Acadia University, Canada, and author of *Kinetic Beauty: The Philosophical Aesthetics of Sport* (2020).

Marc Ramsay is Associate Professor of Philosophy at Acadia University, Canada.

Ethics and Sport

Series editors
Mike McNamee, University of Wales Swansea
Jim Parry, Charles University, Prague, Czech Republic

The Ethics and Sport series aims to encourage critical reflection on the practice of sport, and to stimulate professional evaluation and development. Each volume explores new work relating to philosophical ethics and the social and cultural study of ethical issues. Each is different in scope, appeal, focus and treatment but a balance is sought between local and international focus, perennial and contemporary issues, level of audience, teaching and research application, and variety of practical concerns.

Sport, Ethics, and Neurophilosophy
Edited by Jeffrey P. Fry, Mike McNamee

Doping in Cycling
Interdisciplinary Perspectives
Edited by Bertrand Fincoeur, John Gleaves, Fabien Ohl

Sport and Spirituality
Edited by R. Scott Kretchmar, John B. White

The Philosophy of Football
Steffen Borge

Kinetic Beauty
The Philosophical Aesthetics of Sport
Jason Holt

Gym Culture, Identity and Performance-Enhancing Drugs
Tracing a typology of steroid use
Ask Vest Christiansen

Coaching, Sport and the Law
A Duty of Care
Neil Partington

The Philosophy of Mixed Martial Arts
Squaring the Octagon
Edited by Jason Holt and Marc Ramsay

For more information about this series, please visit: https://www.routledge.com/Ethicsand-Sport/book-series/EANDS.

The Philosophy of Mixed Martial Arts
Squaring the Octagon

**Edited by
Jason Holt and Marc Ramsay**

LONDON AND NEW YORK

First published 2022
by Routledge
2 Park Square, Milton Park, Abingdon, Oxon OX14 4RN

and by Routledge
52 Vanderbilt Avenue, New York, NY 10017

Routledge is an imprint of the Taylor & Francis Group, an informa business

© 2022 selection and editorial matter, Jason Holt and Marc Ramsay; individual chapters, the contributors

The right of Jason Holt and Marc Ramsay to be identified as the authors of the editorial material, and of the authors for their individual chapters, has been asserted in accordance with sections 77 and 78 of the Copyright, Designs and Patents Act 1988.

All rights reserved. No part of this book may be reprinted or reproduced or utilised in any form or by any electronic, mechanical, or other means, now known or hereafter invented, including photocopying and recording, or in any information storage or retrieval system, without permission in writing from the publishers.

Trademark notice: Product or corporate names may be trademarks or registered trademarks, and are used only for identification and explanation without intent to infringe.

British Library Cataloguing in Publication Data
A catalogue record for this book is available from the British Library

Library of Congress Cataloging-in-Publication Data
A catalog record has been requested for this book

ISBN: 978-0-367-64162-7 (hbk)
ISBN: 978-0-367-64163-4 (pbk)
ISBN: 978-1-003-12239-5 (ebk)

DOI: 10.4324/9781003122395

Typeset in Times New Roman
by Taylor & Francis Books

Jason Holt dedicates this book to Larry Holt, who appreciated MMA for all the right reasons

Marc Ramsay dedicates this book to his Brazilian Jiu-Jitsu instructors and training partners, past and present

Contents

List of Contributors	ix
Acknowledgments	xiii

	Introduction: Weighing In JASON HOLT AND MARC RAMSAY	1
1	Mixed martial arts is not a martial art IRENA MARTÍNKOVÁ AND JIM PARRY	4
2	On the martial arts status of mixed martial arts: 'There are no rules' SARAH MALANOWSKI AND NICHOLAS R. BAIMA	16
3	Loyalty, deference, and exploitation in traditional and mixed martial arts AUDREY YAP AND CHRIS GOTO-JONES	30
4	Violence and constraints in combat sport JOSEPH D. LEWANDOWSKI	43
5	Experimentation, distributed cognition, and flow: A scientific lens on mixed martial arts ZACHARY AGOFF, BENJAMIN GWERDER AND VADIM KEYSER	53
6	Finding beauty in the cage: A utility-based aesthetic for MMA TSZKI CHOW	66
7	An aesthetic apology for MMA JASON HOLT	78
8	The line of permissibility: Gladiators, boxers, and MMA fighters MARC RAMSAY	88
9	Friendship as a moral defense of mixed martial arts DANNY ROSENBERG	105
10	MMA as a path to stoic virtue MICHAEL TREMBLAY	122

11	Ethics of mixed martial arts WALTER VEIT AND HEATHER BROWNING	134
12	Gender, pain, and risk in women's mixed martial arts AUDREY YAP	150
13	Gender and ethics: Thoughts on the case of transgender athlete Fallon Fox NANCY KANE	161

Index   174

List of Contributors

Zachary Agoff is a PhD student at the University of Pennsylvania, USA. His research is primarily on the history of early modern philosophy – viz., early modern metaphysics, ethics, and their intersection. Though much of his time is spent on figures like Descartes and Spinoza, he has strong interests in 'non-canonical' figures, like Elisabeth of Bohemia, Anne Conway, and Peter Sterry. Outside of the academy, Zachary is an avid martial artist, with training in hapkido, eskrima, kickboxing, and judo.

Nicholas R. Baima is Assistant Professor of Philosophy at Harriet L. Wilkes Honors College, Florida Atlantic University, USA. He specializes in ancient philosophy and ethical theory. His work in ancient philosophy has appeared in journals such as *Ancient Philosophy, Phronesis*, and the *Journal of the History of Philosophy*, while his work in ethical theory has appeared in *Ethical Theory and Moral Practice* and the *Journal of Value Inquiry*. He is the coauthor, with Tyler Paytas, of *Plato's Pragmatism: Rethinking the Relationship of Ethics and Epistemology* (Routledge, 2021).

Heather Browning is a research officer in animal sentience and welfare at the London School of Economics, UK. She received her PhD from the Australian National University in Canberra, Australia, with a doctoral thesis exploring some philosophical issues in the measurement of animal welfare. She worked for many years as a zookeeper and zoo animal welfare officer, interested in the application of animal welfare measurement in an applied zoo setting. Her primary research areas are animal welfare, ethics, and consciousness with occasional forays into pop culture and other topics of interest.

Tszki Chow is a PhD candidate in philosophy at Ruprecht Karl University of Heidelberg, Germany. Her main areas of interest include Nietzsche's philosophy, the philosophy of mind, and the philosophy of sport. Besides her academic activities, she has also great enthusiasm for combat sports and martial arts. As an elite sabre fencer, she has participated in the Olympics twice.

Chris Goto-Jones is Professor in Philosophy at the University of Victoria, Canada and Honorary Professor in Asian Studies at UBC; he works and lives on the traditional territories of the Lekwungen peoples. His interests are in East Asian (especially Japanese) philosophy, as well as questions of philosophical practice, therapeutic uses of philosophy, and performance philosophy. He is a certified Mindfulness-based Cognitive Therapist, and has trained in several martial arts over the years, principally Shotokan Karate and Wing Chun. At the time of writing, he is a Research Fellow at the Centre for the Study of Religion in Society.

Benjamin Gwerder's research is on identity and masculinity within the context of martial arts communities, specifically with judoka (judo practitioners). Working within this context, he seeks to better understand embodied knowledge of cultural practices, as well as ways of being within martial arts communities. Through embodying this knowledge, judoka find new ways of living both within and without the dojo.

Jason Holt is Professor of Kinesiology at Acadia University, Canada. His research focuses on topics in aesthetics, philosophy of sport, and philosophy and popular culture. His most recent books are the monograph *Kinetic Beauty: The Philosophical Aesthetics of Sport* (Routledge, 2019) and the literary collection *Poems for Another Time* (Anaphora, 2021).

Nancy Kane teaches kinesiology at the State University of New York, College at Cortland, USA. Her research interests include the study of justice and equity for transgender, non-binary, and gender nonconforming athletes. She is the former Editor-in-Chief of the peer-reviewed *National Dance Society Journal*, and she serves as Vice President of the Lloyd Shaw Foundation for the preservation and transmission of traditional music and dance. She holds advanced degrees in exercise science and dance studies. Kane is a member of the International Society for the History of Physical Education and Sport (ISHPES) and the International Association for the Philosophy of Sport (IAPS). She is the author of *History and Philosophy of Physical Education and Sport* (Cognella, 2020). With a career spanning more than three decades in exercise science and performing arts, she has taught ethics, movement analysis, stage combat, kinesiology, dance, film, and theatre classes in the US and Europe.

Vadim Keyser is a Provost's Award-winning faculty member at California State University, Fresno and liaison between the College of Arts and Humanities and the College of Science and Mathematics (Philosophy Department; Biotech MA Program; and Cognitive Science Program). Keyser's research is in scientific modeling and methodology with a strong focus on technoscience practice (e.g., applied technological systems and computer simulations), in addition to transdisciplinary research on how applied normative frameworks can be used to shape scientific practice.

Joseph D. Lewandowski is an educator, researcher, and author whose current work focuses on sport and culture. The former holder of the Fulbright-Masaryk Distinguished Chair in Social Studies at Masaryk University, Brno, Czech Republic, Lewandowski serves as Professor of Philosophy at The University of Central Missouri, USA. Among his publications in the philosophy and sociology of sport, Lewandowski is most recently the author of 'Between Rounds: The Aesthetics and Ethics of Sixty Seconds' (*Journal of the Philosophy of Sport*), and 'Sport, Trust, and Social Capital' (*Journal of Comparative Sociology*). His next book, *On Boxing: Critical Interventions in the Bittersweet Science,* is under contract with Routledge.

Sarah Malanowski is Instructor of Philosophy at Florida Atlantic University, USA. She specializes in philosophy of cognitive science and biomedical ethics. Her work in philosophy of cognitive science has appeared in journals such as *Frontiers in Neuroanatomy* and *Synthese*, while her work in biomedical ethics has appeared in *Bioethics, Journal of Medicine & Philosophy*, and *Neuroethics*.

Irena Martínková is Associate Professor in Kinanthropology at the Faculty of Physical Education and Sport, Charles University, Prague, Czech Republic, focusing on philosophy of sport and ethics of sport. She is currently Chair of the Faculty Ethics Committee, and Vice-Chair of the European Association for the Philosophy of Sport. She is the author of *Instrumentality and Values in Sport* (Karolinum Press, 2013) and co-editor of *Phenomenological Approaches to the Study of Sport* (Routledge, 2012), and has published numerous chapters and journal articles on sport within the areas of phenomenology, values in sport, Olympism, martial arts, and Eastern thinking. She has cooperated in several international projects and has lectured in many countries; since 2005 she has often been a visiting professor at the International Olympic Academy.

Jim Parry is Visiting Professor at FTVS, Charles University, Prague, Czech Republic, and former Head of the Philosophy Department, University of Leeds, UK. His interests are in sports ethics and social/political philosophy. He is co-author of *The Olympic Games Explained* (Routledge, 2005), *Sport and Spirituality* (Routledge, 2007), and *Olympic Values and Ethics in Contemporary Society* (University of Ghent Press, 2012); and co-editor of *Ethics and Sport* (Routledge, 1998), *Olympic Ethics and Philosophy* (Routledge, 2012), *Fields of Vision: The Arts in Sport* (Leisure Studies Association, 2014), *Ethics and Governance in Sport* (Routledge, 2016), *Body Ecology and Emersive Leisure* (Routledge, 2018), *Experiential Learning and Outdoor Education* (Routledge, 2019), and *Research in PE and Sport in Brazil and the Czech Republic* (UFRGS Press, 2020). He has been visiting professor in Barcelona, Ghent/Leuven, Ancient Olympia, London, Rome, Beijing, and Sochi.

Marc Ramsay is Associate Professor of Philosophy at Acadia University, Canada. His primary research interests are in the philosophy of law. He has written on free expression, legal moralism, liberalism, parental rights, and tort theory. He also practices Brazilian Jiu-Jitsu.

Danny Rosenberg is an Associate Professor in the Department of Kinesiology at Brock University, St. Catharines, Ontario, Canada. His primary research interests are sport and physical education philosophy, sport ethics, sport management ethics, sport history, and sport and ethnicity. He is co-author with the late Joy DeSensi of *Ethics and Morality in Sport Management* (4th ed.) (FiT Publishing, 2020) and has authored or co-authored articles in journals such as the *International Journal of Physical Education; European Journal of Physical Education; Canadian Journal of Sport History; Avante; Journal of the Philosophy of Sport; Quest; Sport, Ethics and Philosophy; Sport in Society; Olympika*; and the *Journal of Sport History*. His works have also appeared as book chapters and in conference proceedings. Dr. Rosenberg is past president of the International Association for the Philosophy of Sport. He holds degrees from the University of Western Ontario and the University of Tennessee, Knoxville.

Michael Tremblay is a PhD candidate in Philosophy at Queen's University, Canada. His work specializes on Ancient Philosophy, especially Stoicism. His current research project includes an examination of how the Stoics used athletic metaphor to help teach students about philosophy, and an exploration of how the Stoics thought athletic training was similar to a philosophical education. Michael is also a competitive martial artist, and his interest in philosophy was first sparked by the

xii *List of contributors*

discussions and concepts he was introduced to while training. He is a first-degree Brazilian Jiu-Jitsu black belt, a former varsity wrestler, and has competed in MMA. His favorite martial art is Brazilian Jiu-Jitsu, a sport which he continues to teach, train, and compete in regularly.

Walter Veit is a naturalist philosopher. With wide-ranging interdisciplinary interests, he studied philosophy, economics, biology, and cognitive science in Australia, the UK, the US, Germany, and Finland, and even worked in the European Parliament for a while. He is currently pursuing a PhD in the History and Philosophy of Science with Paul Griffiths and Peter Godfrey-Smith in Australia. Previously, he has been awarded an MA in Philosophy of Biology and Cognitive Science at the University of Bristol, and a BA in Philosophy & Economics from the University of Bayreuth. He worked at Carnegie Mellon University on meta-science, cultural evolution, and the science of consciousness, and has spent time at the Max Planck Institute for Evolutionary Biology working on the evolution of cooperation.

Audrey Yap is an Associate Professor in the Philosophy Department at the University of Victoria, which stands on unceded Lekwungen territory. She works primarily in feminist philosophy, and has written on epistemic injustice, gendered violence, and gender norms in sport, though she also has research interests in the history of analytic philosophy and the philosophy of mathematics. She has trained in a variety of martial arts and fighting sports over the years, most notably taekwondo (which she now coaches), wushu, and wrestling.

Acknowledgments

Our thanks to everyone at Routledge, especially series editors Mike McNamee and Jim Parry. Simon Whitmore and Rebecca Connor also deserve mention. Thanks also to the contributors for their hard work and insightful discussion. Finally, to MMA fighters themselves, who have given us so much to write about and marvel at, we salute you.

The Editors

Introduction

Weighing In

Jason Holt and Marc Ramsay

It took only a few decades from its birth for the sport of mixed martial arts (MMA) to become a worldwide phenomenon. Indeed, it is the only global sport younger than either of us, the editors of this book.[1] Despite its youthful rise, however, MMA has generated far more controversy than most of its mature counterparts, a sport already more than ripe for philosophical analysis various and serious. Enter this book.

But first, what exactly is MMA? Philosophers in the wake of the later Wittgenstein tend to shy away from definitions, yet the usefulness of at least a working definition should not be ignored. MMA is a combat sport. So too are boxing, wrestling, Muay Thai, and Brazilian Jiu-Jitsu, for starters. But what sets MMA apart is the sheer variety of skills permitted from these other combat sports and more besides. Hence the 'mixed' in 'mixed martial arts'. Despite the name, however, one should be wary of assuming that MMA is a mixture, in any strict sense, of different *martial arts*, especially if we understand martial arts as concerned *primarily* with practical or spiritual matters (e.g., self-defense or character development).[2] Sports can serve such purposes, but that is not their primary purpose, nor does the sport version of martial arts (e.g., karate tournaments) somehow invalidate their primary purposes. Since MMA permits such skills alongside those of more straightforward combat sports, our working definition of MMA is *unarmed fighting games permitting techniques derived from a variety of martial arts and combat sports*.[3] All things considered, 'mixed martial arts' is potentially misleading if not a misnomer. The term 'mixed combat sports' would be more accurate. Short of rebranding the sport, however, we could take 'MMA' to signify mixed martial *athletics*, with its practitioners mixed martial *athletes*, though this too may be too optimistic. By 'MMA', then, we mean at a minimum nominally the sort of open sport fighting seen in the UFC (Ultimate Fighting Championship) and elsewhere. We leave open questions about whether such games should be defined as practices or institutions, by rules or conventions, and so on.

Nicholas Dixon provided the first academic philosophical treatment of MMA in his 2015 paper, 'A Moral Critique of Mixed Martial Arts' (2015). Dixon's treatment of MMA follows up on his earlier call (2001) for a legal ban on blows to the head in professional boxing. While Dixon's call for a legal ban on head strikes in boxing focuses on paternalistic concerns about brain damage, he also emphasizes that in his view boxing is deeply immoral. Fighters intend to harm each other, and audiences come to enjoy those harms. While he is less sure of the brain damage risks in MMA, Dixon insists that the sport shares boxing's key moral failings – fighters violate Kantian respect for persons, treating each other as objects or things to be damaged, and audiences come to enjoy the damage and suffering. MMA is, it seems, morally worse

DOI: 10.4324/9781003122395-1

than boxing because, in MMA, attacks continue of the ground (Dixon 2015: 365). That distinction aside, Dixon has little if anything to say about the particulars of MMA – for him, it is obviously bad and not a subject of further philosophical interest. This sweeping judgment has appeared in non-academic commentary on MMA, most notably the late Senator John McCain's criticisms of early UFC events (Greene 2018). Respectfully, we disagree.

The first half of this volume pursues questions about the classification of MMA, its relation to other martial forms, and its aesthetics. We open with a chapter by Irena Martínková and Jim Parry, who argue that because of its safety precautions and unconcern with moral development, MMA counts neither as close combat nor as a martial art. Sarah Malanowski and Nicholas R. Baima take up this gauntlet, marshalling a distinction from Plato between knacks and crafts to argue that, though usually not practiced as one, MMA is a martial art after all. Following up on how MMA differs from traditional martial arts, Audrey Yap and Chris Goto-Jones infer that because MMA tends to be far less demanding of loyalty and deference from its practitioners, it is less susceptible to the abusive practices that unfortunately sometimes arise in traditional martial arts. As Yap and Goto-Jones see MMA as superior to traditional martial arts in this respect, however, Joseph D. Lewandowski's chapter argues that although MMA shares some of the virtues of other combat sports such as boxing, its comparative openness makes it in some ways inferior to the more tightly constrained martial arts and combat sports. In their chapter, Zachary Agoff, Benjamin Gwerder, and Vadim Keyser take an applied epistemological approach to explore how context affects the stabilization of MMA in different organizations such as Pride, Pancrase, and the UFC. Level changing from epistemology to aesthetics, Tszki Chow's chapter proposes a utility-based aesthetic for MMA, followed by Jason Holt's analysis of what he takes to be four substantial elements in MMA aesthetics: minimalism, pluralism, violence as definitive, and something he calls the empathetic sublime.

The second half of the volume focuses on moral and legal themes, and several of the authors respond to Dixon's moral critique of MMA. Marc Ramsay relates MMA to longstanding concerns about boxing: fighters' knowledge about risks, economic coercion, long-term brain damage, the intent to inflict (or enjoy) suffering, and the comparison with 'voluntary' gladiatorial death-matches. Danny Rosenberg provides a detailed response to Dixon's Kantian criticism of MMA, arguing that MMA is not merely consistent with mutual respect but also conducive to friendship between training partners and opponents. Michael Tremblay contests the claim that MMA lacks traditional martial arts' connection to virtue (or *do*), arguing that, when pursued with appropriate intentions, MMA can facilitate the cultivation of Stoic virtues. Walter Veit and Heather Browning counter Dixon by presenting MMA as a way of satisfying Kantian duties to the self, contrasting what they see as the pursuit of greatness in MMA fights with the arbitrary violence of mere street fights. Audrey Yap uses hostility to (or discomfort with) women's MMA to highlight seemingly contradictory approaches to women's pain and injury – the protective concern about risk and harm applied to would-be women fighters is absent in other activities or sports deemed appropriate for women (even where those activities pose comparable risks of harm). The book rounds out with Nancy Kane's discussion of the rights of transgender MMA fighters, which is presented through a case study of the hostility and disrespect faced by Fallon Fox during her fighting career.

Now for the main card.

Notes

1 For different histories of early MMA, see Snowden (2008) and Adams and Viola, Jr. (2017).
2 See Priest and Young (2014), Allen (2015), and Martínková and Parry (2016). How to delimit martial arts themselves, following Martínková and Parry (ibid.: 144), is itself a 'hard, non-trivial philosophical question'.
3 We take this working definition from Jason Holt's chapter, 'An Aesthetic Apology for MMA', in this volume.

References

Adams, F. and Viola, Jr., B. (2017) *Tough Guys: The Birth of an American Sport*, North Huntington, PA: Kumite Classic.
Allen, B. (2015) *Striking Beauty: A Philosophical Look at the Asian Martial Arts*, New York: Columbia University Press.
Dixon, N. (2001) 'Boxing, Paternalism, and Legal Moralism', *Social Theory and Practice*, 27(2): 323–344.
Dixon. N. (2015) 'A Moral Critique of Mixed Martial Arts', *Public Affairs Quarterly*, 29(4): 365–384.
Greene, N. (2018) 'How John McCain Grew to Tolerate MMA, the Sport He Likened to "Human Cockfighting"', *Slate*, 26 August, https://slate.com/culture/2018/08/john-mccain-ufc-how-he-grew-to-tolerate-mma-the-sport-he-considered-human-cockfighting.html, accessed 15 January 2021.
Martínková, I. and Parry, J. (2016) 'Martial Categories: Clarification and Classification', *Journal of the Philosophy of Sport*, 43(1): 143–162.
Priest, G. and Young, D. (eds.) (2014) *Philosophy and the Martial Arts: Engagement*, New York: Routledge.
Snowden, J. (2008) *Total MMA: Inside Ultimate Fighting*, Toronto: ECW Press.

1 Mixed martial arts is not a martial art

Irena Martínková and Jim Parry

What is a martial art? In the introduction to their fine collection of chapters by a dozen philosophers interested in the martial arts, Priest and Young (2014: 9n) observe that:

> … one philosophical question about the martial arts is how to characterize them. This is a hard and non-trivial question. Should tai chi be included? Should war-gaming? … We do not need to address this issue here, though (and none of the other essays in the present volume do either). We will finesse it by sticking to some paradigm cases.

Our 2016 article on martial categories (Martínková and Parry 2016a), accepted the implicit challenge, and did try to address this hard, non-trivial philosophical question. We criticized several attempts to classify martial practices according to their surface features – techniques, weapons, armed/unarmed, civil/martial, or within a limited context (e.g., Japan). Instead, we proposed a method of differentiating martial practices according to their differing structural purposes.

Lest it be thought that we were thereby seeking to foreclose discussion, or to impose our account on others, we made it clear that we saw it as provisional and open to criticism and revision. We were, however, concerned to argue that some such account is not only useful (to researchers and practitioners) but also essential in gaining an understanding of an activity by bringing it under some description. For how else are we to characterize the nature of an activity? To seek to say something about X necessarily entails describing it in some way, and this involves categorical thinking. Is it useful to be able to categorize something as a martial sport, rather than a martial art or a martial path? We would say yes. And this is not to deny that a particular activity might take different categorical forms. Kendo has been thought of as a kind of close combat (*kenjutsu*), as a kind of martial path (kendo), and as a kind of martial sport. And lest it be thought that we offered this suggestion as if it were complete and finalized, we were careful to indicate that there were many other possible categories than the first five basic categories that we proposed.

Analysis of martial activities into martial categories

Those first five basic categories of martial activities, identified and distinguished according to their differing structural purposes, were close combat, warrior arts, martial arts, martial paths, and martial sports. We used the umbrella term 'martial

DOI: 10.4324/9781003122395-2

activities' in order to avoid the use of the term 'martial art' in a promiscuous way, because this had been a source of criticism:

> The common, everyday meaning assigned to the phrase 'martial arts' is said to include almost any fighting art ... As currently used, it is a term useful for the general public, but not for serious scholars of these systems.
>
> (Donohue and Taylor 1994: 13)

By 'purpose' here we mean the structural purpose(s) of the activity, which describes its character for all possible participants, and thus describes central (and possibly distinguishing) features of various martial activities. The criterion of 'purpose' is suitable for classifying activities since it determines the nature of the activity itself (what the participant is expected to achieve, e.g., victory, self-defense, etc.), the way in which it is practised (whether there are any limitations of techniques), the means to be used (with or without small weapons), its dangerousness (risk of death or serious injury), and its suitability for various kinds of participants (given their specific personal intentions and purposes). Thus, categorization is useful not only for academics, but also for practitioners themselves, who know thereby what to expect from the activity, and what demands will be placed upon them (see e.g., Miller 2008).

The first five basic categories of martial activities are described according to structural purpose, as follows. Close combat and warrior arts both involve real-life fighting with the purpose of overcoming an opponent or defending oneself. However, the purpose of close combat is focused on efficiency – to 'get the job done' or, in the extreme, 'to kill or be killed'. (In the Japanese historical context, these would be the Ninjas.) The warrior arts have a different purpose – that of exhibiting 'honorable' combat, that is, fighting according to a certain style or code. (In the Japanese historical context, these would be the Samurai.) Martial arts and martial paths both have educational purposes, using martial techniques as a means towards the aim of human cultivation; and both involve the learning of 'safetified' martial techniques for people living in a relatively safe society. Martial arts emphasize self-development in terms of the cultivation of character, whereas martial paths follow the aims of philosophical or religious systems. The purposes of martial sports are conditioned by their status as 'essentially competitive' activities, emphasizing victory and rule-adherence. Martial sports have their origins in martial skills, and include a subset of 'combat sports' that usually take the form of one-on-one fighting.

We also identified several minor categories of martial activities according to their structural purposes: martial therapy (whose purposes are health and wellbeing), martial training (fitness), martial games or warrior games (the re-enaction of historical events), martial artefacts, culture, and performance (the celebration of martial activity), martial entertainment and display (the entertainment of spectators and promotion and advertisement of military values and virtues), and gladiatorial entertainment (containing three main purposes – measuring oneself against an opponent in almost close combat, the attraction of a bloodthirsty audience, and the generation of excitement in combat as entertainment). This is a tentative and incomplete list, which does not pretend to be exhaustive or final. (See more in Martínková and Parry 2016a: 156f.)

Objections to categorization

Some people object to the entire project of categorization, for a number of reasons.

Categorization is 'universalistic'

The suggestion is that categorization tries to establish, *per impossible*, categories that capture the eternal essence of martial activities. But this is not how we see the process of categorization, since it is obvious that martial activities have been invented and developed in an historical process that often involves transformations that may be observed, mapped out, and (re)categorized.

Categorization is 'dogmatic'

We do not see this as an exercise in conceptual imperialism – we don't insist on our version – we are open to revisions. We claim merely to be mapping the logical geography of martial activities. We offer it as an *attempt* at categorization. It is a suggestion, a cockshy – it invites the reader to consult her own intuitions, to see if they cohere with ours. And we are ready to consider objections, which may lead to an improved account.

But it's also a challenge: if you don't like it, say why not – maybe you can improve on it. For example, Legendre and Dietrich (2020: 12) complain firstly that there is 'no consensus … on the proper definition of martial arts'. This is true – but if we had to await consensus before proceeding with enquiry, we would never start. There is no agreed definition of 'democracy' – but in political philosophy this disagreement is the *beginning* of enquiry. Again, they say that certain authors 'fail to encompass and account for all manifestations of martial arts' (ibid.), but they give no examples. However, any such failure would simply invite revision of the categories, to account for it. They go on to point out that 'no matter how a practice itself might be *a priori* labeled, the training can sensibly deviate from expectations under the subjective influence of a designated teacher' (ibid.). This is also true, but it is unclear how such a development threatens the idea of categorization. Either the teacher moves into a different mode (category) or he invents another – for us, there is no problem either way.

And here is another challenge: you need categories, too, otherwise you can't say a word about differences between different kinds of martial activities. To identify difference is the first step to categorization; and categorization is the systematic identification of one's research object. Without this, it is impossible to 'operationalize' one's concepts for empirical enquiries. A research object has to be brought under a definite description in order to be identified and studied. This involves categorization. Without this, you literally don't know what you're talking about – and neither do we, your readers.

Furthermore, nor can you do comparative work, unless your comparators' categories accidentally concur with yours.

Categorization is an ontological exercise

Traditionally, following Aristotle, 'a system of categories has been seen as a complete list of highest kinds or genera, [so as to] provide an inventory of everything there is, thus answering the most basic of metaphysical questions: "What is there?"' (Thomasson 2019). However, recent work concentrates rather on category *differences*, than on category *systems*. Work on category *differences* 'tries to draw particular distinctions, especially among our conceptual or linguistic categories, as a way of diagnosing and avoiding various philosophical problems and confusions' (ibid.).

This is precisely our task, as we see it. One such problem/confusion in Western conceptions of 'martial arts' is the deep and significant failure to distinguish martial arts from martial sports (or combat sports). Thomasson's challenge is that those who 'argue for category differences owe an account of the conditions under which two concepts, terms, or objects belong to different categories' (ibid.). This is precisely the aim and methodology adopted by the present authors in their earlier paper (Martínková and Parry 2016a), which seeks to present just such an account.

Categorization is fossilization

It should be clear by now that we do not espouse any categorization that would rule out revision or development, nor that would impose a solution on the description of a particular martial activity in a particular social context. We concur with Waismann, who argued that 'the ideal of correctness is a deadening one, it is vain to set up a language police to stem living developments' (1968: 186). As Bowman puts it,

> Furthermore, any of those involved in taijiquan in any of its different times and places will believe themselves to be either or both learning a martial art, either or both for sport or for self-defence, and/or involved in healthful calisthenics, and/or preserving or changing a culture, and/or involved in a religious or mystical practice. And so on.
>
> (Bowman 2017: 19–20)

However, this way of putting things raises a number of issues.

a   We do not think anyone disputes the suggestion that a martial activity may take different forms. One example is the dispute in Japan over the nature of kendo (sport, or martial path?), or capoeira in Brazil, 'which has been interpreted as an art of defense, a battle dance, a martial art or a kind of "showcase" capoeira for display, etc.' (Martínková and Parry 2016a: 144; see also Talmon-Chvaicer 2008: 2). Bowman objects to the practice of 'defining' *taijiquan* as belonging to one category or another, but still he identifies three categories. We are entitled to ask: how does he manage to identify, characterize, and distinguish these three categories without engaging in categorical thinking?

b   According to Bowman, at least practitioners themselves are able to form and apply categorical thinking to their activity. They can identify whether they are doing this for sport or self-defense, for health or religious expression, etc. (not ruling out the possibility that they might be pursuing more than one of these purposes at the same time). How can they do this, unless they are thinking categorically? 'I'm doing karate as a sport, not as a martial path' requires a self-understanding regarding one's purposes and intentions in participating in the present activity, and this cannot be expressed except in categorical terms. The practitioner must be aware that there are categorical differences between sports and martial paths, which constrain one's actions in participation.

c   This raises the third point: Bowman's characterization is 'voluntaristic', relying on the personal 'beliefs' of the participant. Here we must distinguish between structural purpose (of the activity) and the personal purposes (intentions) of the individual. A farmer might find (personal) life meaning in raising animals for the market. But the (structural) purpose of his activity is raising animals for the market, not making life meanings. One's personal purposes are conditioned by the structure of the activity whose purposes one must pursue, if one is to pursue just that activity.

Once an activity such as a martial art or a martial sport has been established as a relatively stable practice, and can be identified as having been relatively institutionalized and transmissible, this entails that it has been structured so as to address certain values or to achieve certain goals. That is to say, the activity itself has and embodies structural purposes. My personal purposes may be efficiently aligned with these purposes so as to achieve my goals. If I genuinely do feel respect and gratitude to my opponent as co-facilitator of our contest, it is helpful if the activity itself *requires* expressions of respect and gratitude. And if, on occasion, I falter in moral purpose, the activity itself *reminds me* of my moral duty. However, I cannot simply superimpose my personal purposes upon just any set of structural purposes. I would be crazy to think that I was doing calisthenics whilst in a chokehold fighting for my breath, just because I 'believed' it.

This insistence on the reality of structural purpose is important because it provides a direct route to categorization. Our proposal in Martínková and Parry (2016a) was to 'define' martial activities according to their differences in structural purpose.

A note on 'social construction'

There is a position that holds that 'everything' is socially constructed, and that this fact is important. Mathematics, for example, might look as though it presents us with universal truths, but in fact it was socially constructed during a long historical process involving important inventors from Ancient Greek and Medieval Arab worlds. Now, what's important about this? We would say that, whatever interesting and engaging story might be told about the genesis and history of the emergence and development of mathematics, the end product of this process is: mathematics! – as we know it today, and as we try to teach it to our children. They do not need to understand the story to understand the product. So the status of the *product* of social construction is not reliant on the nature of the *process* of its production. I don't need to know that the concept of 'zero' was invented in 5th-century India (or was it earlier, in Mayan culture?), and not brought to Europe from North Africa until the 12th century by Fibonacci (see Matson 2009). Its 'social construction' is irrelevant to its justification, validity, and usefulness.

Something similar is true of martial arts. Our enquiry here is 'synchronic'. Whilst the genealogies of martial activities have their own kind of interest and explanatory power, our categorial enquiries seek to comprehend martial activities *as they are now* – as *products* of their genealogies. Of course, that means that, as things change with future developments and deletions, so will the analysis. But this is the game we are in – continually trying to understand where we are now – and 'now' does not stand still.

Miller's practical approach – 'mindsets'

We note the coherence of our 'categories' approach with what we might call Miller's 'practical' approach. Miller (2008) emphasizes the importance of distinguishing different kinds of combat for practical purposes. He distinguishes between different 'mindsets' that participants must occupy so that they can understand their participation in specific martial situations (such as self-defense, dueling, sport, combat, assault, spiritual growth, and fitness):

> Experience in the dojo is experience in the dojo. Experience in the ring is experience in the ring. Experience on the street is experience on the street. There is some overlap in skills; some lessons transfer. But a black belt in Judo will teach you as much about sudden assault as being mugged will teach you about Judo.
>
> (Miller 2008: 18)

Mindset is always relative to the situation in question. It becomes a problem if practitioners cannot distinguish between the different situations, which could easily happen if the term 'martial art' is not defined, and practitioners fail to think in categorical terms. The practitioner Miller confronts Bowman's 'believers':

> Despite the wide variety of skills and complete incompatibility of the mindsets or strategy, martial artists are often convinced that they are training for all of these things simultaneously.
>
> (Miller 2008: 12)

What is MMA?

So far, we have tried to explain why we use 'martial activities' as the umbrella term for those social practices associated in some way with martiality, and why we think that some attempt to describe 'martial categories' is a desirable step towards understanding those social practices. In this section, we will try to show what this means for an understanding of MMA.

To begin with, we need to identify our object of enquiry. What do we mean by 'MMA'? We mean what everyone means these days – something like: the MMA that you see on TV – cage fighting in the octagon. Khabib Nurmagomedov, Jon Jones, Georges St-Pierre, Ronda Rousey – what those folks do (or rather did). We will take an approach akin to the conceptual technique of exhibition-analysis (see Parry 2019: 6). This approach begins by offering a kind of ostensive definition – definition not by conceptualizing, but by pointing – directly indicating an object in the world. The next stage of the exercise is one of explication – of clarification – of making clearer to oneself (and to others) what one is talking about by providing a conceptual description of the object indicated. So we take it as our task to make explicit what 'MMA' means, as it is more or less implicitly understood and accepted by those who accept that MMA-on-the-TV is a central case of MMA. It seems appropriate to begin to describe such a commonly-accepted conception with a Wiki-definition, which we can then test for adequacy:

> Mixed martial arts (MMA), sometimes referred to as cage fighting, is a full-contact combat sport based on striking, grappling and ground fighting, incorporating techniques from various combat sports and martial arts from around the world.
>
> (Mixed martial arts 2020)

This is a good starting-point, although we will later wish to dispute the adequacy of part of it, and to propose a revision. Let us now consider where MMA is situated in regard to our five basic martial categories. The three most relevant are martial arts, martial sports, and close combat.

Close combat means fighting from immediate distance with an opponent with the purpose of overcoming them or defending oneself. Close combat occurs in real life, often in unpredictable situations, with the aim to 'get the job done' effectively and efficiently. In military contexts, it often boils down to survival – kill or be killed.

Martial arts focus on education, and their purposes include improvement in fighting skills through the acquisition of traditional martial techniques, and the self-development of the individual in terms of morality and character. That is why martial arts emphasize adherence to moral principles and codes of conduct, while also drawing ideas from philosophical, religious or educational systems, albeit often in a rather fragmented way.

Martial sports employ combat techniques with the aim to win a competition. There are both contact and non-contact varieties (for example, boxing and javelin). The contact one-on-one events are usually called 'combat sports' and this entails two opponents trying to overcome each other within the scope of a set of safetified techniques and limited by rules.

MMA and close combat

MMA is sometimes 'hyped' as if it were a kind of close combat, or at least very close to it. But it clearly is not, since MMA fighting is a result of the choices made by competitors, whilst close combat is not: 'The predator mindset is a choice... Self-defense is never a choice. The victim will have to deal with shock and total surprise, the predator won't' (Miller 2008: 11).

Further, the purpose in close combat is to overcome an opponent by any means available, which sometimes may even mean legitimate killing. Close combat is real-life fighting in serious circumstances, such as in the army or police, or in street-fighting. MMA differs in that it has rules that constrain participants' behavior, so that it is less deadly, and more safetified. So, whilst it is true that MMA and close combat do share certain features (for example, their openness to different kinds of techniques from various martial or combat systems and traditions), there are crucial differences. As we have said, unlike close combat, MMA is a practice restricted by rules and by its central purpose: to determine the winner of a sporting contest. And so, while close combat requires use of the most efficient techniques to subdue, defeat or eliminate (kill) an opponent, MMA looks for the most efficient technique within the given rules. In close combat you can fight dirty, whilst MMA does have significant restrictions and constraints.

Thus, the rules of MMA are a function of its institutionalization as a sport. They exist so as to limit the activity by time and space and to restrict its lethality. The rules are there to provide a certain degree of safety, but also the conditions for comparability, that is, the relative equality of means and conditions for engaging with the opponent, which is a precondition for determining the winner of a sporting contest. In close combat, the soldier/fighter looks for an efficient solution in a specific, unique situation. She wants to overcome the adversary as quickly as possible, while being able to use any technique, any weapon, or any item in the environment, for her benefit (sand to throw in the face, a wall to pin the opponent against, furniture to hit them with, etc.). The emphasis for the soldier/streetfighter is on adaptability, and she needs an awareness of the immediate environment (e.g., to guard against the possibility of multiple assailants), and a certain creativity (e.g., to be able to use an element of surprise; in the use of any available means; searching for any kind of advantage, etc.). And so, the outcome of real-life fighting is not 'winning or losing' (as in a sporting competition) but rather 'succeeding' (in defending oneself, or in 'getting the job done') or even simply 'surviving'.

The situation in MMA is quite different from such real-life unprepared situations – MMA is simplified. Of course, the selected techniques need to be efficient with respect to the predetermined time and the emptied space. Participants prepare with respect to how long and where and with whom they are going to compete. The fight starts at a pre-given time – it does not come as a surprise. The octagonal cage for MMA is empty, so that the MMA fighter does not really need to be very much aware of the surroundings (there are no objects lying around presenting a danger or advantage). There is a relative equalization of participants – participation is restricted to one-on-one; there is no one else who might unexpectedly attack; competitors are of similar weight and health status (they have to have a health check); and they are tested for use of prohibited substances. This rule-based and policed equality of opponents is ensured by categories, such as weight (MMA presently recognizes 14 male classes and four female classes), sex (males and females), and age (restricted to adults). Competitors' clothes and equipment (gloves) are pre-defined. MMA rules are formulated by an association or competition organizer, and the application of rules within the competition is overseen by referees. In close combat, however, the fight is often not a fair fight, but rather conditions favor one of the parties. Indeed, parties will actively seek such unfair advantages, to increase the chances of survival or success. There may still remain some restrictions on certain forms of close combat – for example, individual police behaviour in the combat situation may have to be reviewed later to assess whether laws have been broken – but it can also occur anywhere where a person attacks somebody else, often without witnesses, and here anything goes.

Miller has this to say about the difference between the nature of the duel as close combat, and MMA as a sport:

> For close combat it is best if it does not happen at all. Best is to prevent the situation. Contrary to close combat – martial sports and martial arts are activities desired by us, we want to organize them, we value our participation in them, we want them to happen.... Sport is... admirable, to me, because the real goal is to test yourself. For most, it's not about domination but about what they have, what they can do, what they've learned. Mixed martial arts (MMA) is part of a long evolution of taking this concept as far as it can go safely.
>
> (Miller 2008: 8–9)

MMA and martial arts

MMA is sometimes thought to be a martial art. This mistake comes from its very name: 'mixed martial arts'. However, martial arts are educational activities, focussing on cultivation and mastery of the participants, usually in one codified system. So, the availability of more kinds of techniques in MMA also distances it from martial arts, which usually focus on one set of codified techniques (known by name as karate, judo, kendo, etc., or as a particular school), which are polished to be as near perfection as possible. As Lloyd points out,

> This eclecticism operates strictly in the pursuit of effectiveness in competition or combat and with no emphasis on what may be recognized as *budō* or fidelity to an ongoing martial tradition.
>
> (Lloyd 2008: 81)

Similar to MMA, martial arts are usually relatively safetified activities (Martínková and Parry 2016b). Donohue (2005: 10) claims that: '"martial arts" are rather "martially inspired arts" with little or no realistic combat utility in the modern world.' While learners begin with safe techniques, increased mastery may bring more dangerous ones which, however, are not supposed to be used in real life (unless absolutely necessary, for example in close combat situations).

Crucially, in comparison to MMA, martial arts put a much higher importance on values such as cultivation of the whole self, development of discipline, virtues, and morality, rather than on victory, which has overwhelming importance in martial sports (see more in Cynarski 2019; Martínková, Parry, and Vágner 2019). Martial arts also value philosophical or religious ideas, which they partly appropriate into their educational context. For example, martial arts may appropriate some traditional ideas from warrior times to highlight the development of virtues. In kendo, a display of modesty, called *zanshin*, is encouraged by self-restraint from 'an ostentatious display of one's own victory' after a successful strike (Oda and Kondo 2014: 8). This used to be a practical skill in real-life-fighting, because a fighter needed to be ready for any possible continuation of the fight (don't celebrate too early!). In the new educational context of martial arts, *zanshin* helps to promote modesty, thus diminishing overemphasis on the value of victory in competition.

Now, it is not as though MMA cannot *aspire* to such purposes, nor that MMA practice never *contributes* to an athlete's character or moral self-development. The point is that it is not the structural *purpose* of MMA to achieve these ends. As Lloyd again notes, 'The ethos here is a long way from that of the "high" martial arts: the truth of violence is understood in terms or ruthlessness, efficiency, and brutality' (2008: 82).

MMA and combat sports

So, the actual MMA contest is more about the selection of an appropriate technique and its suitable employment against an equal opponent, without a necessity to concentrate on the possible interferences of a real-life situation. That is why the mastery of techniques and their suitable employment comes to the fore. This brings an opportunity to focus more on the mastery of the fighter, while it may also identify more or less efficient techniques, within the context of pre-given conditions. This question was at the origin of MMA – the techniques of which systems are more effective?

This characteristic suggests that MMA sits well amongst sports, specifically combat sports. In sport, human physical skill is being tested (Parry 2019: 6). What makes MMA unique within combat sports is the possibility of using a relatively wide range of techniques. So, unlike boxing, taekwondo, or judo, which are restricted mainly to one single kind of fighting skills (grappling, or striking, or throwing), the 'mixed' character of MMA makes them more dangerous, since the actions of the competitor are more open and harder to anticipate. So, even though the MMA techniques are safetified so that their lethality is limited (e.g., certain moves are not allowed, and parts of the body are protected), the activity itself is still dangerous (whilst still remaining safer than close combat).

The incorporation of the skills of other combat sports into the mix of MMA needs a little explanation. Those skills must be modified, sometimes in subtle ways, if they are to remain effective in the MMA context, since the expected feedback from a foray is less predictable. A boxer can throw punches in a way that does not have to guard against a takedown. A Brazilian Jiu-Jitsu fighter can try some hold without worrying about an elbow to the face. The peculiar fascination of MMA arises partly from the fact that, whilst the skills of other (individual) combat sports are 'prescribed', in MMA there is nothing prescribed. Apart from those techniques that are prohibited, the possibilities are open.

MMA as a 'dangerous sport'

In what does the dangerousness of MMA consist? The dangerousness of an activity (sport) can be determined by different 'risk-of-danger factors' (Martínková and Parry 2017: 83n), among which are: the activity itself, participants, level and quality of organization, and the environment. As seen above, what makes close combat especially dangerous is the unpredictability of the environment and timing, and the number and bodily size and skills of the opponent(s). MMA is much safer than this. MMA has safetified the environment, participants are to be of relatively equal bodily characteristics (through categorization of athletes by weight and sex, and age limitations), and referees ensure the prevention of serious injury and death. It is the activity itself that is dangerous.

According to Russell (2005: 3), dangerous sport can be defined as 'a sport that involves activity that itself creates a significant risk of loss of, or serious impairment to, some basic capacity for human functioning'. MMA is more dangerous than those combat sports that are single-disciplined (i.e., that test just one set of techniques), because of the wider range of possibilities available to competitors, which makes the fighting less predictable. So, even without the most damaging techniques (e.g., head-butting, eye gouging, biting, genital attacks, etc.), many of the skills of MMA come from real-life fighting skills, and there is still quite a high risk of serious impairment of human capacities. This is also confirmed by observers – Thomas and Thomas (2018: 155) report that 'There are no systematic reviews of newspaper or media accounts of fights to assess rates and numbers of injuries or mortality. The few published surveys and case reports markedly understate the worldwide situation.'

Conclusion

'MMA' is a misnomer. Some claim that it is a mix of martial arts, whereas it is really a mix of martial techniques, which are variously deployed in those martial sports that are combat sports (boxing, wrestling, sport karate, sport judo, etc.). It is itself clearly a combat sport in the class of martial sports (although its relative dangerousness leads some to think that it should join boxing as a pariah sport). To be clear, though, we should point out that this chapter is not 'against' MMA. It simply argues that MMA should not be confused with martial arts nor close combat. Whether or not MMA is in some sense a 'desirable' pursuit is a separate question.

So why did who arrive at the designation MMA? We speculate that the reasons for this are multiple. Firstly, it is a result of the general confusion in the West over the term 'martial arts', which is often (mis)taken to refer to a variety of activities in different categories. Thus, for example, martial sports are frequently referred to mistakenly as martial arts, and 'martial arts' movies frequently feature close combat action. This is an example of why we prefer the umbrella term 'martial activities'.

Secondly, 'MMA' is an honorific choice of name that somewhat dignifies the sport, alleviating the negative perceptions and connotations of 'Ultimate Fighting', and profiting from positive association with the noble aspirations of martial arts.

Thirdly, some claim that MMA is in fact a mix of martial arts, but this is a long-distance claim that should be resisted. To begin with, proponents of this idea often fail to distinguish martial arts from martial sports. They can usually be persuaded that they are (really) talking about martial sports (as the Wiki entry evidences) – so the claim fails. Although it might be true that combat sports appropriate some of the techniques of martial arts, and that MMA mixes the techniques of various combat sports, the connection of MMA back to martial arts is a tenuous one. This is partly because the martial arts techniques are modified by incorporation into combat sports, and then modified again by incorporation into MMA.

Our conclusion is that MMA is not a martial art, but a martial sport – specifically, a member of the subset: combat sports. MMA can be described as a dangerous sport, because of its use of mixed techniques, which make fighting less predictable.[1]

Note

1 This chapter was written with institutional support from Charles University, Prague, Czech Republic (PROGRES Q19).

References

Bowman, P. (2017) 'The Definition of Martial Arts Studies', *Martial Arts Studies*, 3: 6–23.
Cynarski, W. J. (2019) 'General Canon of the Philosophy of Karate and Taekwondo', *IDO MOVEMENT FOR CULTURE. Journal of Martial Arts Anthropology*, 19(3): 24–32.
Donohue J. (2005) 'Modern Educational Theories and Traditional Japanese Martial Arts Training Methods', *Journal of Asian Martial Arts*, 14(2): 8–29.
Donohue, J., and Taylor, K. (1994) 'The Classification of the Fighting Arts', *Journal of Asian Martial Arts*, 3(4): 10–37.
Legendre, A., and Dietrich, G. (2020) 'Improving Movement Efficiency through Qualitative Slowness: A Discussion between Bergson's Philosophy and Asian Martial Arts' Pedagogy', *Sport, Ethics and Philosophy*, https://www.tandfonline.com/doi/abs/10.1080/17511321.2020.1730428?journalCode=rsep20, accessed 30 December 2020.
Lloyd, H. M. (2014) 'The Martial Arts as Philosophical Practice', in G. Priest and D. Young (eds.) *Philosophy and the Martial Arts: Engagement*. London: Routledge, pp. 68–86.
Martínková, I., and Parry, J. (2016a) 'Martial Categories: Clarification and Classification', *Journal of the Philosophy of Sport*, 43(1): 143–162.
Martínková, I., and Parry, J. (2016b) 'The Paradox of Martial Arts – Safe Combat', *IDO MOVEMENT FOR CULTURE. Journal of Martial Arts Anthropology*, 16(4): 4–10.
Martínková, I., and Parry, J. (2017) 'Safe Danger – On the Experience of Challenge, Adventure and Risk in Education', *Sport, Ethics and Philosophy*, 11(1): 75–91.
Martínková, I., Parry, J. and Vágner, M. (2019) 'The Contribution of Martial Arts to Moral Development', *IDO MOVEMENT FOR CULTURE. Journal of Martial Arts Anthropology*, 19(1): 1–8.

Matson, J. (2009) 'The Origin of Zero', *Scientific American*, 21 August, https://www.scientificamerican.com/article/history-of-zero/, accessed 30 December 2020.

Miller, R. (2008) *Meditations on Violence: A Comparison of Martial Arts Training & Real World Violence*. Boston: YMAA Publication Center.

'Mixed Martial Arts' (2020) Wikipedia, 30 December, https://en.wikipedia.org/wiki/Mixed_martial_arts, accessed 30 December 2020.

Oda, Y. and Kondo, Y. (2014) 'The Concept of *Yuko-Datotsu* in Kendo: Interpreted from the Aesthetics of *Zanshin*', *Sport, Ethics and Philosophy*, 8(1): 3–15.

Parry, J. (2019) 'E-sports Are Not Sports', *Sport, Ethics and Philosophy*, 13(1): 3–18.

Priest, G., and D. Young (eds.) (2014) *Philosophy and the Martial Arts: Engagement*. London: Routledge.

Russell, J. S. (2005) 'The Value of Dangerous Sport', *Journal of the Philosophy of Sport*, 32(1): 1–19.

Talmon-Chvaicer, M. (2008) *The Hidden History of Capoiera: A Collision of Cultures in the Brazilian Battle Dance*. Austin: University of Texas Press.

Thomas, R. E., and Thomas, B. C. (2018) 'Systematic Review of Injuries in Mixed Martial Arts', *The Physician and Sportsmedicine*, 46(2): 155–167.

Thomasson, A. (2019) 'Categories', in *The Stanford Encyclopedia of Philosophy*, https://plato.stanford.edu/archives/sum2019/entries/categories/, accessed 30 December 2020.

Waismann, F. (1968) *How I See Philosophy*. London: Macmillan.

2 On the martial arts status of mixed martial arts

'There are no rules'

Sarah Malanowski and Nicholas R. Baima

When the Ultimate Fighting Championship (UFC) was first formed, many traditional martial artists asserted that mixed martial arts (MMA) was not a martial art.[1] At first glance it is hard not to meet this sentiment with an incredulous stare – 'martial arts' is in the name, after all. Moreover, the early days of MMA pitted particular martial arts disciplines against each other with the hope of determining what the most effective martial art is. If particular martial arts are competing against each other, how could this competition not be within the domain of martial arts? What about this contest disqualified it from being a martial art in the eyes of these traditional martial artists?

The UFC's early tagline 'There are no rules!' succinctly summarizes all that traditional martial artists found wrong with UFC events: early MMA was marketed as a violent 'no holds barred spectacle', when martial arts are supposed to be centered on discipline, technique, and tradition. Traditional martial artists asserted that the focus on entertainment and lack of technical proficiency at MMA events were antithetical to the spirit of martial arts, and so MMA fighting is not a martial art. With the development of social media and the acceptance of MMA as a legitimate sport, MMA is now more than ever about entertainment, making these early criticisms relevant today.

By drawing upon Socrates' distinction between 'crafts' and 'knacks' found in Plato's *Gorgias*, we clarify the difference between real martial arts (martial crafts) and mere imitation of martial arts (martial knacks). Utilizing this distinction, we examine three reasons why traditional martial artists saw early MMA as martial knack rather than martial craft. We show that (1) MMA is a craft and (2) that it is a craft similar in nature to that of martial arts. In doing so, we argue that MMA is a real martial art, but it is not always practiced as one. Although the spectacular nature of MMA is knack-like, the competitive aspect of MMA has furthered the aims of the craft of martial arts. We conclude by exploring the status of these objections with respect to contemporary MMA.

Crafts, knacks, and martial arts

In order to determine whether MMA is a 'real' martial art, we must first develop an account of what it means to be a real martial art. To do this, we will leverage Plato's account of craft. The craft account basically offers a way of separating practices that aim at goods with internal rational structures – and thus are able to be taught, have experts, and have stance-independent excellences – from those that do not. We think that the craft account is particularly illuminating in this context because of the explicit comparisons that have been made between MMA and things like street fighting,

DOI: 10.4324/9781003122395-3

brawling, and 'human cockfighting' for the purpose of discrediting MMA. MMA has often been criticized for being random, violent show-fighting between aggressive hotheads, which contrasts with what such critics see as the disciplined, restrained sparring between masters that occurs in martial arts. We believe that this perceived contrast between MMA and martial arts maps onto the distinction between crafts and knacks that Plato discusses in his craft account: true martial arts resemble what Plato describes as crafts, while MMA, if the criticism of it holds, resembles what Plato describes as knacks. If MMA is a knack rather than a craft, then this would suggest that MMA is not a real martial art, since martial arts are crafts. Thus, the craft account can be used as a means to distinguish real martial arts from mere imitators.

Crafts

For Plato, crafts (*technai*; singular, *technē*) are rational disciplines that have a characteristic function or activity (*ergon*). As Socrates explains in the *Republic*, 'the function of each thing is what it alone can do or what it can do better than anything else' (353a).[2] By looking at the characteristic activity of something, we can discover its excellence or virtue (*aretē*). The excellence of a thing is the quality, or set of qualities, that allows this thing to do its characteristic activity well (353b–c). The characteristic function of a knife, for example, is to cut; thus, the virtue of a knife is to cut well, which requires that the knife have qualities such as a firm handle and a sharp blade.

Crafts not only have characteristic functions and excellences, they also have experts. A craft-expert isn't merely someone who can perform certain actions well or make certain products; the expert must also be able to correctly explain how her actions relate to the function of the craft. Thus, there is both a practical and a theoretical dimension to craft-expertise. For example, the expert of medicine (a physician) not only has the skill to achieve the aim of medicine (promoting health and minimizing disease and suffering), but she will also understand the nature of health and disease in the body – she will be able to explain why a particular treatment brings about health or minimizes disease.[3]

Crafts and knacks

We can gain further insight into Plato's account of crafts by examining how he distinguishes them from pseudo-crafts, or knacks (*empeiriai*), in the *Gorgias*. Socrates and Gorgias, a famous instructor of rhetoric, are discussing whether rhetoric is a craft. Socrates asks Gorgias what the characteristic activity of rhetoric is (447c–449d). Gorgias says that rhetoric aims at persuading, but not educating, people about matters of justice (454c–455a). Indeed, the rhetorician can persuade non-experts better than an actual expert can (456b–c), and hence there is no need for the rhetorician to actually learn anything other than how to persuade (459b–c).

Socrates doesn't think that what Gorgias has described is an actual craft because it lacks a rational account (454c–455a, 462b–c, 465a, 500e–501b): those who practice rhetoric cannot explain the nature and cause of rhetoric's object (justice); they can only appear to aim at justice. Instead, Socrates argues that rhetoric is a knack, which is done from habit, experience, and memory (462c, 463a, 464c). Socrates argues that knacks are parasitic on actual crafts. For instance, the knack of pastry baking imitates the craft of medicine, the knack of cosmetics imitates the craft of gymnastics, and the knack of rhetoric imitates the craft of justice (465b–c).

In saying that a knack imitates a craft, Socrates means that a knack aims at the appearance of a good that relates to the end of the craft that it imitates. The point of gymnastics (a craft) is to make the body healthy, strong, and beautiful, while the point of cosmetics (a knack) is to make the body *appear* beautiful, but not actually *be* beautiful. Similarly, rhetoric in a law court merely aims at the appearance of justice, not justice itself. Thus, unlike crafts, knacks do not necessarily bring about something good.

In merely aiming at the apparent good of a craft, knacks pander to popular opinion, and since popular opinion fluctuates, knacks lack a rational account: what explains why something is good will change depending on the audience. In contrast, since crafts have goods internal to them – goods that do not depend on the judgment of others – they have a rational structure.

Because knacks lack a systematic account, they cannot be taught in any real sense; instead, they are more or less just a skill one develops a knack for.

Taking stock we see the following:

Crafts

a   Crafts have characteristic activities that determine the excellences of the craft. That is, there are goods internal to the craft.
b   The procedures and activities of crafts are capable of rational explanation and thus can be taught.

Knacks

a   Knacks imitate specific crafts, but aim at external goods rather than goods internal to the craft.
b   Knacks lack rational explanation and thus cannot be taught.

Martial arts and the craft account

In order to determine whether MMA is a craft or a knack, we need to get a grasp on what makes martial arts a craft. If we follow Plato, this will involve examining martial arts' characteristic function. Because there are many types of martial arts, and because the category of martial art is nebulous and has changed over time, the characteristic activity must be somewhat general. The original purpose of martial arts was skill in combat; today, however, martial arts often serve more of a recreational and even a philosophical purpose. Thus, we need an account of martial arts that is general enough to cover the breadth of the concept while capturing what is distinctive about martial arts.

Peter Lorge's work on the history of Chinese martial arts provides us such an account. He defines martial arts as

> the various skills or practices that originated as methods of combat. This definition therefore includes many performances, religious, or health-promoting activities that no longer have any direct combat applications but clearly originated in

combat, while possibly excluding references to these techniques in dance, for example.

(Lorge 2012: 3)

On this definition, martial arts must essentially relate to the 'martial', presumably because fighting is the characteristic activity of martial arts. As Lorge writes, 'at root, martial arts is about skill with violence' (2012: 5). There are many ways to be healthy or to train the mind, but what distinguishes martial arts from these other activities is that martial arts essentially relate to fighting.

Although fighting is the characteristic activity of martial arts, martial arts training certainly involves other aspects, such as physical and mental improvement. Martial arts should improve one in such a way that one is able to perform martial activities well. This would include not only physical abilities, like strength and agility, but also the cultivation of character traits – such as discipline, fortitude, patience, and courage – that will allow one to remain focused, calm, and strategic in a fight. Being skilled in fighting without having the physical and mental ability to execute these skills would be worthless. Since skill in fighting requires the training of both the mind and body, we propose the following three aims of martial arts, with (1) being the characteristic activity.

1 Skill in fighting
2 Physical improvement
3 Character development

With the general function of martial arts outlined, we can begin to distinguish the craft of martial arts from its knack counterpart. Crafts can provide a rational account of how to cause the goods they aim at, while knacks cannot, so the craft of martial arts will not only aim at the three goods listed above, but will also be able to provide a systematic account of how the skills and practices of martial arts cause these goods. As Lorge explains,

> what makes something a martial art rather than an action done by someone who is naturally good at fighting is that the techniques are taught. Without the transmission of these skills through teaching, they do not constitute an 'art' in the sense of being a body of information or techniques that aim to reproduce certain knowledge or effect.

(Lorge 2012: 3–4)

The systematic nature of Jigoro Kano's Kodokan judo provides a useful example of this. Kano (1986) divides techniques into three main categories: throwing techniques, grappling techniques, and striking techniques. Each of these main categories can be broken into subcategories, which can then be further divided. The individual techniques are themselves explicable, and so we end up with a body of techniques that is systemic all the way down. The systematic nature and complexity of Kodokan judo separates it from something that one just does from trial and error and allows the techniques to be explained and taught.

Another way to distinguish martial art as craft from martial art as knack is by looking at the aims of the activity. Martial arts *qua* craft aim at internal goods like mental and physical improvement and skill in fighting, but martial arts sometimes aim at external goods as well. Some common aims of this nature include making money, gaining spectators/popularity, and appearing impressive, tough, or cool. If a particular practice aims more at such external goods, then the practice is a martial knack rather than a martial craft.

Taking stock, we can distinguish martial crafts from knacks in the following ways:

Martial crafts

a   The characteristic activity of martial craft is fighting. The excellences of martial crafts are the cultivation of skill in fighting, as well as the physical and mental development that aids fighting well.
b   Martial crafts have a rational account such that the procedures and activities of the craft are capable of rational explanation and thus can be taught.

Martial knacks

a   Knacks imitate martial crafts by involving fighting, but they ultimately aim at things external to skills in fighting and mental and physical development, such as entertainment, profit, and approval.
b   Martial knacks lack a rational account and thus cannot be taught.

Having outlined the distinction between martial crafts ('real' martial arts) and martial knacks (imitation martial arts), we are now in a good position to examine the question of whether MMA is a martial art.

'No holds barred' MMA and martial arts

As the story commonly goes, MMA as it is known today started when Rorion Gracie came to the United States to teach Gracie Jiu-Jitsu. In order to demonstrate the strength of Gracie Jiu-Jitsu and to increase its popularity in the States, Gracie issued the 'Gracie Challenge', inspired by the Brazilian sport Vale Tudo (Portuguese for 'anything goes'), which pitted fighters with different styles against each other in matches that had very few rules. The Gracie Challenge and Vale Tudo became the inspiration for the UFC when adman Arthur Davie saw an advertisement for the Gracie Challenge and contacted Rorion Gracie about developing a Vale Tudo-style fighting tournament, which led to the first UFC fight in 1993.

The term 'MMA' was not yet in use when UFC 1 was held,[4] and so the genre of fighting seen in the UFC was referred to by a different name: 'no holds barred'. This name accurately captures the Vale Tudo spirit that the original UFC fights were attempting to channel: the only rules were no eye gouging, biting, or groin strikes. Other than that, the matches were completely unstructured – the first UFC fights had no time limits, no scoring, no uniforms, and no referee stoppage unless the fighter's corner asked for it. The final line-up for UFC 1 was chosen in what would now be considered an unconventional way as well: although Davie and Gracie had sent out letters to martial arts organizations in an attempt to find highly trained fighters, most of the fighters they reached out to declined. Davie and Gracie's picks ended up being a mix of men that they knew and men that responded to ads placed in martial arts magazines – that is to say, most were not particularly well-known nor had they proven themselves to be elite within their chosen martial art.

This combination of limited rules and skills made for a violent, but commercially successful first UFC. However, several prominent martial artists were critical of these early UFC events, and worried about what the continuing production of UFC fights would mean for martial arts. Perhaps the most notable critic was Bill Wallace, a full-contact karate champion who was the commentator for UFC 1. Following UFC 3, Wallace wrote:

> After 30 years of practicing martial arts and teaching students the correct way to throw punches and kicks without hurting themselves, I resent guys who throw off-the-wall bogus techniques ... they make a mockery of the martial arts, injuring themselves more than their opponents... As a martial artist, I'm embarrassed to be associated with these people.
>
> (Wallace 1995a: 16)

He also declared that 'the whole event is getting to be a circus' and complained that the commentating 'was a two hour commercial for Gracie's jujutsu'.

We can see in these comments three potential objections to the claim that early MMA is a martial craft and thus a real martial art. One objection holds that MMA fighting aims at things like audience entertainment, spectacle, and promotion of Gracie Jiu-Jitsu – goods that are external to the function of martial arts. The second objection holds that the fighting seen in the UFC lacks skill and technique – the fighters chosen to compete in the UFC are unable to give a rational account of what and why they are doing what they are doing in the cage, and are instead just using moves at random. The third objection is that martial arts involves a commitment to various principles and values which are not reflected in UFC events. If these objections hold, then early MMA would be a martial knack rather than a martial craft.

The spectacle objection

Let's call the first objection the 'spectacle' objection. This objection is based on the idea that the UFC is a spectacle – a visual display that aims at evoking a particular emotion/affect in the audience. If MMA aims at pandering to the crowd in such a way, then it would not have the same aims as martial craft (and, in fact, could not have the same aims as any craft) and thus would not count as a true martial art.

The argument expressed formally is thus:

1 A martial art is a craft.
2 Spectacles are not crafts.
3 Early MMA is a spectacle.
4 Therefore, early MMA is not a craft.
5 Therefore, early MMA is not a martial art.

We defended premise (1) in the first section above: martial arts, like all crafts, have characteristic functions, excellences inherent to those functions, and admit of a rational account. Premise (2) is also based on the discussion in the previous section:

spectacles aim at evoking audience emotion, which is something external to the activity itself. The success or failure of the activity thus depends on the audience's response rather than on the excellence of the activity. The resemblance to rhetoric should be clear here: rhetoric aims at producing a convincing, moving speech – a kind of spectacle of words. Premise (4) follows from (2) and (3), and the conclusion (5) follows from (1) and (4). The crucial premise, thus, is (3), which we examine below.

Regardless of what MMA has become, it does appear that the motivations for creating the UFC were clearly to create a spectacle that would make money and, perhaps, popularize Gracie Jiu-Jitsu. Art Davie, one of the original founders of the UFC, has remarked that, when promoting UFC 1, one of the factors that was considered was whether the UFC should be promoted as a spectacle or a sport: 'I remember sitting in John Milius' office…and we sat around debating that issue. I reminded everybody that I had sold it to Bob on the basis that it was a spectacle. It was designed very much as a spectacle. We did not feel it was a sport' (Gentry 2011: 40). John Milius, a well-known screenwriter and director, was enlisted by Davie and Gracie as a creative director for UFC 1. In order to emphasize the spectacle aspect of the event, the fights needed an enticing stage. Suggestions for additions to the ring included ancient Greek structures, an electrified panel, barbed wire, and a crocodile moat (ibid.: 38). Although these thrilling set-ups never came to fruition, the fact that they were considered in the first place suggests that the event was probably not simply aiming to showcase skill in fighting. The stage that was eventually chosen, the now well-known octagon, was developed after film designer Jason Cusson became the art director for UFC 1. Cusson credits the movie *The Octagon* (1980), a movie about a martial artist (played by Chuck Norris) fighting terrorists, for his inspiration: 'It was just the name of it… I had no martial arts background. The reason there's an Octagon is because of Chuck Norris' (Rossen 2013).

Other aspects of the early UFC fights and their marketing suggest that the aim of MMA at the time was spectacle. Following the bloodiness of UFC 1, the marketing of the second UFC event emphasized the violent, ruleless nature of the match. 'There are no rules!' became the marketing slogan, and the press release for UFC 2 not only highlighted the lack of rules, but also proclaimed that 'each match will run until there is a designated winner – by means of knockout, surrender, doctor's intervention, or death' (Gentry 2011: 72). Giving the UFC the appearance of being a blood sport makes it clear that a major goal of the UFC was to create a sensationalized spectacle (Gentry 2011: 73). UFC 3 continued this trend: following focus group data, it became apparent to the UFC's marketers that most people were not watching the UFC in order to see which martial art was the best – viewers knew little about the technical differences between the martial arts, and were instead simply interested in watching action-packed fighting (Gentry 2011: 82). Marketing for UFC 3 thus adopted a similar strategy as pro wrestling, focusing on highlighting rivalries and personas of the fighters (Gentry 2011: 92). By showcasing competitors who could be colorful performers as well as fighters, UFC 3 was able to raise overall viewership again. Pro wrestling is, of course, all about spectacle, and thus by mimicking the strategy adopted by pro wrestling, the UFC was demonstrating its commitment to making MMA into a spectacle.

This brief examination demonstrates that there is support for premise (3): early MMA was marketed and designed with an eye towards creating a spectacle. Round 1 goes to early MMA being a martial knack, but there are still two rounds left in this fight.

The no technique objection

Let us call the second objection to MMA being a martial craft the 'no technique' objection. This argument maintains that the majority of fighters in early MMA lacked proper martial technique. Because it is a condition of craft-hood that the practitioner be able to give a rational account of how the technique produces the aim of the craft, if it is the case that early MMA fighting lacked technique, then this would suggest that MMA is a knack rather than a craft and thus not a true martial art.

Formally, the argument is this:

1 A martial art is a craft.
2 Crafts involve technical skills.
3 Early MMA lacks technical skills.
4 Therefore, early MMA is not a craft.
5 Therefore, early MMA is not a martial art.

Premise (1) is the same here as it was in the argument above. Premise (2) is based on the idea that crafts involve a rational account: the skills displayed in a craft should be systematic and not something that one just does. We will examine (3) below. Premise (4) follows from (2) and (3), and the conclusion (5) follows from (1) and (4).

A common complaint raised by traditional martial artists in the early days of MMA was that the UFC fighters lacked skills. For example, world kickboxing champion Kathy Long said that '[b]illing these [UFC] events as martial arts competitions definitely makes the arts look bad because of the lack of technique' (Long 1995: 12). And, as we saw in the beginning of this section, UFC 1 commentator Bill Wallace described MMA fighters as lacking proper technique (see also Wallace 1995b: 16n1).

Although it is true that many early MMA fighters had deficient skills, it cannot be denied that MMA competitions as a whole have advanced martial arts techniques and training modalities. By pitting discipline against discipline, early MMA played an essential epistemic role in the development of the craft of martial arts. Stand-up fighters realized that unless they learned how to defend a takedown or how to defend themselves once taken down, they were vulnerable to submissions and ground-and-pound. Wrestlers learned that they needed to develop proper ways to end the competition: without learning submission holds or strikes, taking someone down isn't effective on its own. Submission fighters learned that they needed to develop stand-up fighting techniques or advanced takedown techniques, for if a pure submission fighter cannot take his opponent to the ground, he has no remedy for countering strikes. In essence, MMA competitions helped push martial artists to broaden their skill sets. Martial artists learned the deficits of their particular martial art and then learned the precise ways to make-up for such shortfalls. This is a clear case of MMA advancing the general understanding of the craft of martial arts.

Furthermore, MMA unraveled various myths surrounding martial arts. The rise in popularity of martial arts films in the United States brought with it many illusions about what traditional martial arts was and what it was capable of. As Clyde Gentry III explains,

> If nothing else, MMA competitions laid to rest the stereotypes surrounding martial arts. Martial artists were finally able to throw punches and kicks at their

discretion without any regard for rules germane to their disciplines. The mystique of the black belt, the *dim mak* (death touch), and the lightning-fast kicks that break dozens of boards is a powerful one, often leading followers to believe the performers are deadly. This perception also gives us an unrealistic view of how a real fight unfolds.

(Gentry 2011: 317)

The idea that the martial arts bestow some kind of special power of combat that should only be used in rare circumstances is itself a misunderstanding of martial arts (see Russell 2010). Martial arts, from its origin onward, is about combat, and MMA helped return martial arts to the realistic aspects of combat, at least to some extent.[5] Thus, MMA competitions played two key epistemic roles in the development and health of martial arts: (1) they advanced the technical aspects of martial arts, and (2) they helped eradicate epistemic vice from the martial arts community. Round 2 clearly goes to early MMA being a craft, leaving the final round to decide the fight.

The moral vice objection

The final objection to the craft status of MMA is what we will refer to as the 'moral vice' objection. The idea here is that early MMA promoted moral vices that were contrary to the moral teachings of martial arts. Formally, this objection goes:

1   Moral virtues are essential to martial arts.
2   MMA instantiates and promotes moral vice.
3   Therefore, MMA is not a martial art.

Both premise (1) and (2) are contentious, but we will focus on premise (1) because premise (2) would require a chapter of its own.[6] Premise (1) might be endorsed for two major reasons: (a) because religious, philosophical, and moral principles are core aspects of the martial arts, and (b) because martial arts are crafts, and crafts necessarily aim at good and promote excellent character traits. However, both of these reasons lack sufficient support.

First, one might think certain religious, philosophical, and moral principles are an essential part of martial arts. We saw above that a common complaint levied against the early UFC was that the fighters chosen were not serious martial artists, and some surmised that this was intentionally done so that Gracie Jiu-Jitsu would dominate. However, the absence of skill is more likely attributable to a general disdain for the UFC amongst martial artists. When trying to find competitors for the first UFC, Davie sent letters to people in martial arts organizations, but many people declined, offering 'self-discipline, honor, respect, pacifism and varying Eastern philosophies as valid reasons for not competing in this type of forum' (Gentry 2011: 44–5).

This sentiment is echoed in an opinion letter in *Black Belt Magazine* signed by Tokugawa Yoshimune[7] from Plantation, Florida:

> I am totally disgusted by the hype and egos brought out at the UFC. The goal of most martial artists is peace, harmony, humility, self-improvement, and, of course, to protect what no one has the right to take away – your well-being. The public is being fooled by competitors calling themselves real martial artists, who fight and

act like schoolyard bullies... the martial arts are not for competition, but for personal growth.

(Yoshimune 1995: 8, 34)

These martial artists are not pulling these ideas out of thin air. Embedded in many martial arts are various moralistic teachings. Judo's two core principles, for instance, are maximum efficiency and mutual benefit (Kano 1986). Archery in China is connected to the teachings of Confucius in which the ultimate aim of archery is self-cultivation (Lorge 2012: 38–43). Gichin Funakoshi, the founder of Shotokan karate, preaches that 'the ultimate aim of karate lies not in victory or defeat, but in the perfection of the character of its participants' (1981: 85). Not to mention that if one walks into almost any dojo or reads a popular book on martial arts, one will be told that martial arts is about respect. But are these teachings essential aspects of martial arts, or are they merely associated with a specific iteration of martial arts, practiced in a particular historical context?

Two key pieces of evidence point to the latter. First, this is a very myopic view of what constitutes a martial art, as it ignores practices like Western wrestling, boxing, and fencing, which have no direct association with religion or philosophy (see Priest and Young 2010). Second, from within the perspective of Eastern martial arts, these religious and philosophical teachings were not always present. As Lorge explains with respect to Chinese martial arts,

> It is a modern perspective, both inside China and abroad, that Chinese martial arts is only about self-defense and self-cultivation. This connection to nonviolence is further enhanced by a vastly distorted connection between religion and the martial arts. Martial arts preexisted both religious Daoism and Buddhism and was mostly practiced outside the religious context.
>
> (Lorge 2012: 5–6)

Similarly, many Japanese martial arts see kinship with Bushido (the code of the samurai), but this is problematic because popular conceptions of the samurai are historically inaccurate (see Wert 2019). Moreover, the code found in these popular conceptions is hardly moral. Hence, the moralistic conception of martial arts is thus overly narrow and historically problematic, if not inaccurate. However, as we have argued above, martial arts *does* involve character development as one of its characteristic activities, but we believe it is mistaken to interpret this as *moral* character development, which brings us to our second point about the moral vice objection.

The second reason one may hold that moral virtues are essential to martial arts has to do with the craft status of martial arts that we have defended in this chapter. Crafts aim at something good and involve the cultivation of good skills and traits. From this, one might think that, in learning the craft of martial arts, one must be learning moral virtue, both because crafts must aim at good and because a specific aim of martial craft is character development.

However, although craft-expertise requires the cultivation of certain *ethical* values – patience, discipline, work ethic, perseverance, respect for the craft, etc. – these values differ from *moral* values. Morality picks out a narrow set of norms and values relating to welfare, justice, obligation, right, and wrong (see Williams 1985), and these norms and values are not essential components of all crafts. For instance, although one must develop certain character excellences in order to become an expert cobbler – e.g., patience, precision, hard work, etc. – and though cobbling has a rational structure and aims at producing something good, these are not *moral* character traits nor is cobbling *unconditionally* good. Though it is true that the local character traits one learns through cobbling can, with the right instruction, help one cultivate moral traits, morality is not an essential aspect of cobbling, for one can be an expert cobbler without being a morally good person.[8]

This idea should be all the more apparent when we apply it to the craft of fighting. Why should we expect that a craft centered on striking, choking, and physically controlling another human is necessarily connected to morality? Though it is essential that one develop certain character traits in order to be an expert martial artist – e.g., one must have a certain amount of discipline and fortitude – and though fighting admits of a rational structure and aims at something good, these traits are not *moral* virtues nor is fighting *unconditionally* good. Thus, the moral virtues do not bear an essential relationship to all crafts and certainly do not bear this relationship to the craft of fighting.[9] Martial craft takes round 3.

When we tally the scores as to whether MMA aligns with the craft of martial art, we see that early MMA scored quite well overall. Although the spectacle objection holds merit, the no technique objection and the moral vice objection do not. Thus, early MMA is more craft than knack. But what has become of these objections and the status of MMA in its current form? Though we do not have room to discuss this issue fully, we will conclude in the next section by exploring these concerns with respect to contemporary MMA.

Contemporary MMA, sport, and knack

MMA has evolved significantly since the 'no holds barred' era in three broad ways. First, the technical proficiencies of the fighters have improved and broadened. Competitions no longer pit one style of martial arts against another; rather, all fighters have some familiarity with different styles. In fact, today some fighters could be said to have an MMA style since they have learned multiple disciplines while training at an MMA school. Second, MMA competitions have become more professional. MMA is now on major television networks and fighters can make more money than in the early days. Everything from weigh-ins to post-fight press conferences is now available to fans. The increase in financial opportunities has led to fighters making their training and social persona more professional. Third, MMA has become less of a 'no holds barred' fight and more of a sport. MMA is marketed not as bloody spectacle, but as a display of strategy, technique, and athleticism. MMA coaches and athletes have also become more scientific with their training modalities.

The confluence of these three things has led to the re-emergence of the objections levied against early MMA, though they now differ in interesting ways. With the backing of mainstream media and the prevalence of social media, 'trash talk' has become a central component of MMA culture and broadcasting. Trash talk is seen by some martial artists as antithetical to the spirit of martial arts, since martial arts should be about respect. Chatri Sityodtong, the founder of the ONE Championship MMA promotion, has stated that one of his motivations was to create an MMA promotion that was more in-line with the values of traditional martial arts than the UFC is, and that his approach to promoting fights is to do so 'in the proper way; not in an ugly way but in a positive manner, you know, the martial arts way' (Long 2016). This is the return of the 'moral vice' objection. We have argued above that moral vice doesn't preclude MMA from being a martial art, and those responses still stand in the era of trash talk.

Trash talk can also be seen as a symptom of a larger problem: MMA's focus on popularity and hype-based matchmaking. This is a version of the 'spectacle' objection and just as before, it holds merit today. In fact, the 'spectacle' and 'no skill' objections have been combined and reformulated in a way that creates a novel challenge to the craft-status of martial arts. Greg Downey (2014) argues that UFC fights are 'carefully crafted through constant experimentation with the rules, format, and incentives to better conform to aesthetic standards of what unarmed combat should look like given cultural expectations' (2014: 4). We see that MMA competitors are no longer accused of being unskilled street brawlers; instead, today, Downey argues that the regulation and structure of the UFC aims at producing an 'idealized form of bodily combat that [is] decisive and appear[s] "real"' (2014: 3), thus making MMA 'fights' inherently unrealistic. For example, if there is a lull in action when fighters are on the ground, the referee will stand them back up to encourage more action, but controlling someone on the ground is an effective combat skill and encouraging excitement has little to do with effective martial skill and strategy. Thus, though competitors display athleticism and skill, the skill is aimed at producing a spectacular form of combat, thereby the 'no skill' and 'spectacle' objections have been transformed into the 'not relevant skill' objection: the skills MMA fighters develop are for a form of combat that looks good to viewers, but are not necessarily relevant to *real* fighting.

This 'not relevant skill' objection does endanger the craft (and thus the martial art) status of MMA. If the skills developed in MMA aim more at spectacle rather than excellence at fighting, then MMA will be more knack-like. However, as we argued above, even if the rules of the UFC have been designed to facilitate more spectacular combat, the rise in popularity of MMA has led to epistemic gains in martial arts. Thus, there is still room in MMA for the development of technique and skill in fighting rather than in just the appearance of fighting, but in order to maintain its craft status, MMA must avoid amending its rules for the purpose of appearances.[10]

Relatedly, mastering martial craft requires developing certain character traits such as discipline and patience. However, as Downey notes, these character traits 'pose challenges for the marketing side of the industry, which places a premium on larger-than-life personalities' (2014: 19). Thus, if MMA competitions seek out athletes for their ability to put on fights that appear exciting to the crowd, then MMA is likely to become more knack-like. These fighters likely will not be developing the character-traits of martial arts and thus will not be carrying out the aims of martial craft.

The return and reformulation of these original objections demonstrate how important it is to deal with them adequately. In this chapter, we have utilized Plato's craft account as a framework for addressing them and thus for examining the martial arts status of MMA. In doing so, we have argued that martial arts are craft-like, and that MMA, for the most part, aims at the same goods that martial arts *qua* crafts do and thus qualifies as a real martial art. However, there are some aspects of MMA that are more knack-like. Insofar as MMA wishes to count itself among the martial arts, it should lean into the aspects that make it craft-like, such as focusing on techniques that promote better fighting, and avoid those that make it knack-like, such as pandering to public hunger for spectacle. This is an especially important consideration as MMA continues to grow in popularity and reach a wider audience: if the sport is to maintain its ties to the martial arts, it should avoid practices that aim predominantly at entertainment.

Notes

1 'How can anyone say [the UFC] is a martial arts event, when, in reality, it is just a glorified toughman contest? I have yet to see a display of any martial arts techniques at the event… The ancient martial arts masters are probably fuming over in their graves right now' (Pennenga 1995: 141).
2 See also *Republic* 346a; *Euthydemus* 291e, 301c; *Euthyphro* 13d; *Ion* 537c; *Charmides* 165e.
3 See *Republic* 342d–e, 407d; *Charmides* 170c–171b, 174c; *Apology* 22b–d; *Ion* 537c–538b, 539d–541c.
4 The first documented use of the term appears to be in a review by Howard Rosenberg (1993) of UFC 1, but was not used in promotional material until UFC 7 in 1995, and was not adopted officially by the UFC until 1998 with UFC 17.
5 See the final section for a brief discussion of the ways in which the 'realness' of MMA needs qualification.
6 On moral vice in martial arts, see Roberts-Thomson (2014) and Russell (2014). On MMA and vice, see Dixon (2015) and Weimer (2017).
7 This is likely a pseudonym. Tokugawa Yoshimune (1684–1751) was the eighth shogun of the Tokugawa shogunate. Ironic, given the opinion being expressed, both because feudalism and the samurai are not moral paragons, and the Tokugawa samurai were essentially 'sword-wearing bureaucrats' (Wert 2019, 78).
8 Although we are trying to stay neutral on various interpretations of Plato's view of craft, in denying that crafts are unconditionally good, we are taking an interpretative stance; see Kozey (2019).
9 Nothing we say excludes the possibility that martial arts can lead to moral improvement; we are merely denying that it is an essential aspect of martial arts. Interestingly enough, Brent and Kraska (2013) found that many MMA fighters were motivated to fight and train for the purpose of 'self-actualization'. Thus, even if self-actualization were an essential feature of martial craft, it isn't clear that MMA wouldn't meet this standard.
10 Note that this doesn't entail that MMA must return to its 'no holds barred' rules as there can be legitimate martial craft reasons for restricting the rules in various ways. But it does require that whatever restrictions are implemented can be justified for martial craft reasons, as opposed to simply being more viewer-friendly.

References

Brent, J. and Kraska, P. (2013) '"Fighting is the Most Real and Honest Thing": Violence and the Civilization/Barbarism Dialectic', *British Journal of Criminology*, 53: 357–377.
Dixon, N. (2015) 'A Moral Critique of Mixed Martial Arts', *Public Affairs Quarterly*, 29: 365–384.
Downey, G. (2014) '"As Real as it Gets!" Producing Hyperviolence in Mixed Martial Arts', *Journalism, Media and Cultural Studies*, 5: 1–28.
Funakoshi, G. (1981) *Karate-Do: My Way of Life*, Tokyo: Kodansha International.
Gentry III, C. (2011) *No Holds Barred: The Complete History of Mixed Martial Arts in America*, Chicago: Triumph Books.
Kano, J. (1986) *Kodokan Judo*, Kodokan Editorial Committee (eds.), New York: Kodansha International.
Kozey, E. H. (2019) 'The Good-Directedness of *Technē* and the Status of Rhetoric in the Platonic Dialogues', *Apeiron*, 52: 223–244.
Long, K. (1995) 'Question: What's Missing from the Ultimate Fighting Championship? Answer: Proper Technique', *Black Belt*, 33(5): 12.
Long, M. (2016) 'In Profile: One Championship Founder Chatri Sityodtong', 27 May, https://www.sportspromedia.com/from-the-magazine/in_profile_one_championship_founder_chatri_sityodtong, accessed 16 September 2020.

Lorge, P. A. (2012) *Chinese Martial Arts: From Antiquity to the Twenty-First Century*, Cambridge: Cambridge University Press.
Pennenga, C. (1995) 'UFC Discredits All Arts', *Black Belt*, 33(5): 141–142.
Plato (1997) *Plato's Complete Works*, J. Cooper and D. S. Hutchinson (eds.), Indianapolis: Hackett Publishing.
Priest, G. and Young, D. (eds.) (2010) *Martial Arts and Philosophy: Beating and Nothingness*, Chicago: Open Court.
Roberts-Thomson, S. (2014) 'The Promise and the Peril of the Martial Arts', in G. Priest and D. Young (eds.) *Philosophy and the Martial Arts: Engagement*, New York: Routledge, pp. 19–27.
Rosenberg, H. (1993) '"Ultimate" Fight Lives Up to Name: Television: Pay-Per-View Battle, Instead of Being Merely Gory and Funny, Gets Interesting After the First Two Bouts', *LA Times*, 15 November, https://www.latimes.com/archives/la-xpm-1993-11-15-ca-57200-story.html, accessed 10 May 2020.
Rossen, J. (2013) 'Changing the Shape of Fighting', *ESPN*, 22 May, https://www.espn.com/mma/story/_/id/8515933/changing-shape-fighting, accessed 10 May 2020.
Russell, G. (2010) 'Epistemic Viciousness in the Martial Arts', in G. Priest and D. Young (eds.) *Martial Arts and Philosophy: Beating and Nothingness*, Chicago: Open Court, pp. 129–144.
Russell, G. (2014) 'Practicing Evil: Training and Psychological Barriers in the Martial Arts', in G. Priest and D. Young (eds.) *Philosophy and the Martial Arts: Engagement*, New York: Routledge, pp. 28–49.
Wallace, B. (1995a) 'Ultimate Fighting Championship a Poor Advertisement for the Martial Arts', *Black Belt*, 33(2): 16.
Wallace, B. (1995b) 'Just Say No to No-Holds-Barred Tournaments', *Black Belt*, 33(11): 16, 147.
Weimer, S. (2017) 'On the Alleged Intrinsic Immortality of Mixed Martial Arts', *Journal of the Philosophy of Sport*, 44: 258–275.
Wert, M. (2019) *Samurai: A Concise History*, Oxford: Oxford University Press.
Williams, B. (1985) *Ethics and the Limits of Philosophy*, Cambridge: Harvard University Press.
Yoshimune, T. (1995) 'UFC Sending Wrong Message', *Black Belt*, 33(5): 8, 34.

3 Loyalty, deference, and exploitation in traditional and mixed martial arts

Audrey Yap and Chris Goto-Jones

It is sometimes asserted that mixed martial arts (MMA) lacks the ethical foundations of more traditional martial arts (TMA) – at the very least, this is reflected in the public reputation of each of these fields. However, contrary to this, we argue that the stylistic freedom of MMA might liberate the practice from certain features of TMA that render practitioners vulnerable to exploitation and predatory behaviour. There are many cases of sexual abuse in martial arts (as well as in sports generally). However, in looking at some of these cases, we will note two key features of these environments that contribute to the abuse. First, we have a culture that encourages athletes and students to give over their embodied agency to another, and to behave in deeply deferential ways to their masters and instructors. Often the figure(s) to whom this deference is given are teachers, sometimes from a particular lineage or tradition. The second related feature is that students in such environments often perceive (whether accurately or not) that leaving their school will also mean abandoning a tradition that is meaningful to them; failing to train with that particular person, or leaving a particular school, can mean (or feel like it means) abandoning their martial arts practice altogether.

We argue that one benefit of MMA as a sport practice is its lack of deference to an exclusive tradition and its embrace of multitraditionalism. In MMA, we might find *loyalty* to particular teams, coaches, or training camps, but this falls short of the levels of *deference* built into some systems of TMA. MMA athletes who leave their teams might still face negative consequences but can still be seen as engaging in the same type of practice. This contrast with MMA highlights an important factor with which TMA must contend, namely how particular schools' claims to foster students' personal or ethical development can be reconciled with the conditions of vulnerability cultivated by many traditions. In order to do this, we first note several pertinent differences between traditional and mixed martial arts. Then, considering some well-documented cases of sexual abuse in a traditionally based, though sport-oriented, martial art (taekwondo), we point out how survivors' testimony leads us to identify the key features mentioned above. Finally, we consider the extent to which these features can be found in TMA and MMA respectively, and what this might mean for these practices.

Traditional martial arts and mixed martial arts

The debate about the differences between TMA and MMA is characterized by an ongoing struggle with moving goalposts; while it is relatively clear that MMA refers to

DOI: 10.4324/9781003122395-4

a regulated combat sport epitomized by the UFC and other professional leagues like Strikeforce and Pride, the content and parameters of TMA are sufficiently unclear as to be essentially contested.

For many, the pivot from traditional to mixed martial arts is emblematized by the spectacular iconoclast Bruce Lee, who was famously skeptical of what he called the 'classical mess' of Asian martial arts traditions, which seemed (to him) to emphasize conformity, imitation, and obedience rather than creativity, utility, and efficacy. Lee sought to 'free himself from being bound by the chains of unreasoned beliefs,' not aiming to throw out traditional styles entirely, but working towards the freedom to take what was useful from wherever he found it and to reject what seemed ineffective (Cadwell 2016). That is, Lee's objection was first and foremost to the idea that mastering a specific, exclusive tradition was the best pathway to becoming a superior fighter. He advocated learning aspects of various styles and combining them creatively as needed; indeed, in addition to his early training in Yongchun, we know that Lee also studied Taijiquan, Hongjia, Qinna, Praying Mantis, Southern Mantis, White Crane, boxing, and others.[1] Lee's utilitarian, eclectic and synthetic approach to martial arts became known as Jeet Koon Do, and in many ways set the stage for MMA.

One of the most important legacies of Lee's high-profile intervention has been the emergence of a powerful discourse within the field of martial arts about the primacy of the combat effectiveness of a style or technique as a test of its performative value. That is, at one extreme, the worth of a martial art is to be weighed exclusively by how well its students and masters perform in actual fights. Other possible determinants of value, such as aesthetics, ethics, or self-cultivation, are thus diminished in significance and sometimes ignored altogether. These considerations coincide with ways in which the UFC was initially conceptualized, as contests that would pit one martial arts style against another: Royce Gracie, winner of UFC 1, was initially chosen to represent his family's Brazilian Jiu-Jitsu style precisely because of his small stature. That way, his father noted, it would show that it was the style's superiority, rather than the fighter's physical dominance, to which the victory could be attributed (Cruz 2013).

In recent years, the apogee of this tendency to focus on effectiveness can be seen in accusations that TMA are actually 'fake' martial arts, and that the masters of classical styles are 'frauds'. Perhaps the most public instance of this debate followed the 27 April 2017 contest in Chengdu between MMA fighter, Xu Xiaodong, and Taiji master, Wei Lei. In the end, this much-hyped fight lasted less than 20 seconds: Xu adopts a standard MMA fighting pose, Wei flows gracefully around with arms raised in a mantis-like stance, and then Xu steps in and knocks Wei to the ground – fight over. The video quickly went viral on social media, provoking intense reactions. Many Chinese respondents accused Xu of humiliating Chinese culture, and the Chinese Wushu Association condemned him of 'suspected illegal actions that violate the morals of martial arts' (Campbell 2018). Xu reported that he and his family received death threats. On the other hand, advocates of MMA saw this fight as simply one more nail in the coffin of TMA, exposing 'traditional martial arts snake oil' and fraudulent esotericism. For the *South China Morning Post*, 'it's time to admit most traditional martial arts are fake' (Blennerhassett 2019). Perhaps the most measured response came from *Qianlong.com*, which suggested that the competition demonstrated nothing about the relative merits of TMA and MMA since it focussed attention entirely upon who won a fight when the value of traditional martial arts lies not only in fighting techniques, but also in their culture and spirit ... Traditional martial arts are not only precious cultural heritage for Chinese people, but also a cultural treasure for the whole of mankind. Attention to martial arts should not only focus on the fighting aspect, it should also be directed to the culture.

(Huafeng 2017)

The Xu-Wei incident captures many of the issues in the debate about the fuzzy boundaries between TMA and MMA; it draws clear attention to the idea that a defining feature of TMA is the way that students and masters participate in a specific cultural world, usually identified with East Asia but envisioned as having universal appeal or application. For many, this idea of cultural content means that TMA contain, express, or embody distinctive codes of conduct, philosophies of life, or spiritualities. This sense of TMA neatly sidesteps the problem of whether 'traditional' implies 'classical' or 'ancient' and instead focusses on the ways in which traditions constitute cultural dynamics in the present.[2] Given the fact that many of the martial arts considered 'traditional' today (such as karate, aikido, taekwondo, etc.) actually emerged as so-called 'invented traditions' in the fires of modernity in the Twentieth century, this cultural rather than historical sense of 'tradition' is most helpful (Goto-Jones 2019).

Here, too, the work of Bruce Lee provides us with a useful lens. It was not only the case that Lee was invested in liberating martial artists from a reverential adherence to exclusive lineages, where those lineages were aimed at perfect imitation of a master instead of a technical eclecticism aimed at winning fights. He was also seeking to free the martial arts from cultural nationalism and chauvinism. That is, he wanted to explode the notion that *gong-fu* required or relied upon Chineseness, or Asianness, or maleness – he famously and controversially opened his schools to people of all nationalities, ethnicities, and genders. That is, he effectively cast TMA as exclusive, secretive, and ideologically conservative, and moved MMA towards a form of inclusive, transparent, free-market capitalism.

However, there is an interesting sense in which a contemporary vision of MMA as devoid of cultural norms and values (other than the drive for victory) goes further than even Lee intended. In fact, while Lee wanted to free the martial arts from the technical cages of traditional styles, he remained fundamentally invested in the idea that the martial arts per se should (and must) constitute a philosophical or even spiritual pursuit, with deeply ethical implications. Lee's interest in and advocacy for Daoism and Buddhism is well documented. Indeed, Lee's *Dao of Jeet Koon Do* and his landmark movie, *Enter The Dragon* (1973), were central to the development of a popular discourse tying expertise in the martial arts to spiritual accomplishment (Bowman 2011). So, even though Lee sought to transform TMA into more flexible and effective fighting systems open to participants from any background, his sense of the meaning of the martial arts remained bounded by a 'traditional' vision of philosophical, spiritual, and ethical development. Despite his astonishing technical abilities and his emphasis on combat efficacy, for Lee *gong-fu* retained its traditional meaning: the perfection of character through repeated, disciplined practice.[3]

It is probably for this reason that when we think of MMA today, we're more likely to picture unapologetically unprincipled (yet extremely talented) fighters like Conor McGregor rather than Bruce Lee. Indeed, today, Bruce Lee's Jeet Koon Do emerges as a hybrid form of traditional mixed martial art (TMMA) – being MMA as *gong-fu* – characterized by an integrated quest for ethical uprightness, great technical eclecticism, virtuosity, and effectiveness. In fact, to the extent that Jeet Koon Do has become codified as a style of martial art in itself, it actually becomes the archetype of a sports-oriented or competitive TMA, in which practitioners of the same style compete with each other to demonstrate the effectiveness of their techniques by landing them hard enough to score points. As Martínková and Parry (2016) point out, the accelerating development of traditional sparring into competitive fighting within TMA (what they term 'martial paths' and 'martial arts') might actually create a distinct emergent category, 'martial sports' (or 'combat sports'), in which participants train for the purpose and practice of fighting under tightly controlled conditions that prevent injury. Concerned with purpose rather than style or culture, Martínková and Parry would likely place MMA into the category of martial/combat sports together with any instance of an ostensibly TMA that focusses on competitive fighting. In the schema of the present authors, something like sport-karate or sport-taekwondo occupy a transitional space between TMA and MMA, maintaining at least the trappings of cultural investment and fidelity, maintaining strong elements of stylistic purity, but being unapologetic about the goal of using the art to win fights. As we will see later, our categories of TMA and MMA are really ideal types, between which all concrete instances of schools and clubs are likely to fall.

In the end, it seems plausible that whichever martial arts we include in the category of TMA (Yongchun, karate, aikido, taekwondo, etc.), the function of the modifier 'traditional' is intended to indicate that students and masters are self-consciously participating in semi-ritualized lineage of training and (sometimes choreographed) fighting that is associated with ideas and principles aimed at the perfection of moral character, and often attributed to a founder of that style. Conversely, it seems plausible that fighters placed into the category of MMA are explicitly engaged in diverse training from various styles, teachers, and coaches with the determination to become more effective fighters and to win fights.

Such differences are apparent in the way that different schools market themselves to prospective students. MMA schools might advertise the fighting credentials of their coaches or star fighters, or perhaps the kind of body or physical skills one might obtain by training there. TMA schools often advertise their programs' exclusive lineage and their ability to promote (children's) self-esteem, focus, and discipline. Indeed, this explicit focus on personal development is often a selling point of traditional martial arts training. One of the authors was initially placed in martial arts at the age of seven by a father who thought she was too shy and wanted her to gain some self-confidence. However, the next section will argue that the disciplinary practices that are integral to many traditional martial arts can also help to create an environment in which students are unusually vulnerable.

Sexual abuse in martial arts contexts

It is difficult to know the exact numbers of students who have been victims of abuse by their martial arts instructors, but one US-based study that did news searches found 177 names of coaches convicted of at least one sexual offense between 1989 and 2018, with at least 378 victims (Murphy 2019). Given that these statistics would have required both reporting and conviction, both of which occur in only a minority of sexual abuse cases, we can suppose that the actual numbers are markedly higher.

There have been several high-profile cases of sexual abuse investigations in sports contexts in recent years. USA Gymnastics and USA Swimming had multiple allegations of sexual abuse or misconduct by coaches or team staff which made national and international headlines. But similar things have also happened in taekwondo in both USA and Canada. In Canada, a former Olympic coach was arrested in 2018 for sexually abusing a minor he was coaching (Moon and Syed 2018). Allegations outlined multiple sexual assaults over a period of two years. That same year, several former elite taekwondo athletes brought forward charges, claiming that Steven and Jean Lopez, two of the best known people in American sport taekwondo, had assaulted and abused many women and girls over the years (Starr 2018). Steven Lopez, who has won three Olympic medals in taekwondo, two of them gold, and his brother and coach Jean, are two members of what has been dubbed the 'first family of US taekwondo' (Pucin 2012). Their younger brother and sister are also both former US Olympic athletes. However, the women who brought forward these charges, suing the two older Lopez brothers, the US Taekwondo Association, and the US Olympic Committee, describe ways in which Steven and Jean Lopez used their status and the norms of the sport to victimize young women and subsequently silence them (Fuchs 2018).

Of particular note for our purposes are the plaintiffs' descriptions of how norms of martial arts and of elite sport enabled the abuses. Gabby Joslin, one athlete who trained at the Lopez school in Texas, describes being sexually assaulted by Steven while overseas for a competition. Prior to the assault, her then-coach Jean had told her that he would not be traveling to Germany with the team, though Steven offered to be her coach. She recalled to a reporter that she had thought to herself that she would be able to rely on Steven, since she had been programmed by Jean to have 'blind faith'. This is revealing of the overall pattern of abuse by the two brothers; as described in the lawsuit, 'They used their power and influence – enhanced by the sport's code of obedience – to systematically rape and abuse women and underage girls' (Fuchs 2018).

The organization SafeSport banned Steven Lopez from competition after investigating Nina Zampetti's complaints of sexual abuse against him. Zampetti, describing events that took place when she was between the ages of 11 and 14, outlined both grooming behavior and instances of sexual assault (Armour and Axon 2018). Particularly confusing for Zampetti, as she recalled, were the ways in which a lack of attentiveness to Lopez was treated as a more general kind of disrespect for which martial arts students are often punished.

> Zampetti remembers that when she was around 12 years old [Lopez] called for her as she was walking to a local store; she declined to run to his side. Later, as punishment, he demanded that she hold a headstand position for what she estimates was about five minutes. When he finally let her come up, she started crying uncontrollably. 'I felt like I did something so terribly wrong,' she recalls. 'I felt so humiliated'.
>
> (Starr 2018)

In both Zampetti and Joslin's cases, we see ways in which more ordinary norms of showing respect for an instructor or a coach, and trusting their judgement, were pushed over the line into abuse.

The final feature of these particular cases that we will highlight have to do with the survivors' inability to escape their situation without also leaving the sport. Joslin, for example, noted that she was motivated to train at the Lopez family's school because it was someone's best chance at becoming an Olympian. And her fear of losing that chance was the reason she did not confront Steven Lopez about his initial sexual assault. Similar sentiments are echoed by Heidi Gilbert, another survivor involved in the lawsuit, both about the idea that training with the Lopez family was obviously the best way to be successful in the sport, and that questioning coaches could have significant negative consequences, like being thrown off a team (Fuchs 2018). In these particular cases, one could argue that they would not have had to leave the sport altogether (Gilbert continued on with taekwondo for a while), but at the very least, they would no longer be able to participate in it at their current level. These factors, however, are exacerbated further in contexts in which leaving the school would mean more than a drastic change in their mode of participation, but would mean not engaging in that activity at all.

Loyalty and deference

Giving over embodied authority to a coach or instructor is not unique to martial arts, nor is deference. Most people involved in activities that require significant physical ability have to engage in training that is frequently painful and difficult. Athletes in sports that require significant aerobic capacity might have to wake up earlier and run farther than they might like. Martial arts students who have to perfect their form might have to hold stances with fatiguing muscles. In such cases, younger athletes in particular learn to trust their instructors and perform painful tasks with some faith that they will be somehow beneficial down the line.

Our argument here is not that the kinds of abuses we outline are *unique* to traditional martial arts contexts, but rather that deference to authority is integral to the culture of many traditional martial arts in ways that make students particularly vulnerable to abuse. Doubting or questioning your instructor is typically seen as disrespectful (or even unthinkable) for traditional martial arts students, and can result in punishment. Practices of deference and respect for tradition are normalized, even in schools that do not count themselves as particularly traditional. Such practices might direct deference towards a nation or culture. For instance, some taekwondo schools with no Korean instructors will still have a South Korean flag hanging in the training area to which students bow at the start of practice. The deference might be towards an iconic founder. For instance, aikido schools usually have a portrait of Ueshiba Morihei to which they bow at the start and end of a session. Or the deference might even be towards a set of principles or a code of conduct. For instance, many karate schools start and end each session bowing to the '21 precepts of karate' calligraphy of Funakoshi Gichin (the founder of Shotokan). Iaido classes often start and end bowing to a relic from the home temple of the particular style in Japan.

Practices of deference are also embedded in the ethical principles expounded in different styles and schools. These can vary from somewhat militaristic principles such as self-discipline, honor, and respect for others, to more spiritual and esoteric ideals such as moral uprightness, self-cultivation, and even enlightenment. For example, at the taekwondo school at which one of the authors teaches, instructors often have conversations with younger children about how they can show respect for their parents, and for the teachers in their class. In another author's practice, specific kata (forms) in karate have been presented by senior masters as means to cultivate and purify moral energy. There have been numerous studies on the therapeutic and rehabilitative functions of TMA (e.g., Twemlow and Sacco 1998).

Now the ethical traits that traditional martial arts schools emphasize are typically quite positive. But as Gillian Russell (2010) also notes, the culture of deference cultivated in many martial arts schools can lead to epistemic vices, such as forming beliefs on the basis of inadequate evidence, and a stubborn refusal to revise one's beliefs even in the face of contrary evidence. Russell notes many examples of beliefs that practitioners might hold, about the effectiveness of different kinds of techniques, the history of their style, or the usefulness of particular training methods, that run contrary to history or well-established physiology. Her hypothesis about the origins of this epistemic viciousness points to the same factors that we have mentioned here, such as a culture of deference to teachers, histories, or established practices. Our focus here is on the abuses of power that those deferential relationships enable, rather than the particular beliefs that practitioners might hold, but Russell's point about the dangers of deference remains.

While the possibility of cultivating an unhealthy deference is also a possibility in an MMA context, one distinguishing feature of MMA is that, because of the wide variety of skills required to be an effective fighter, it is common for fighters to be trained by more than one person. Fighters concerned with the expense of training in their sport compared to their pay rate have given interviews in which they break down the high costs of preparation; for instance, even though many fighters have a single school or gym that serves as their base, many of them also have multiple coaches, some of whom will need to travel with them to camps and competitions (Martin 2013). After all, many fighters begin their training in a particular martial art or sport, like kickboxing or judo, and need to supplement their base by improving, say, their ground work or striking. It seems very difficult to be a good contemporary MMA fighter and believe that any one person or style is sufficient to ensure your success. To some extent, irreverence rather than deference is built in to the training regimens and culture of MMA.

With respect to the second point we highlighted in the case study, namely the inescapability of the abuse survivors' situations, martial arts differ. It is difficult to cleanly separate the cultivation of deference from the imposition of the idea that one could not leave the school, but we can at least note a few factors. In the case of TMA, for instance, it is typical for particular styles (or even different organizational units or associations that claim to be part of the same style) to emphasize their unique place in a(n unbroken) lineage, reaching back to a codified set of ostensibly originary, authentic techniques and practices. Indeed, to some extent, these narratives of historical continuity (which are not infrequently modern inventions) comprise the meaning of 'traditional'. Some of the most popular styles of TMA, such as karate, are beset by internal feuds regarding which teaching lineages are 'authentic' and which are somehow 'fraudulent'. A high-profile example might be when Kanazawa Hirokazu split from the Japan Karate Association (JKA) in 1977, founding the Shotokan Karate International Federation (SKIF), and sparking decades of debate about where 'real' Shotokan karate was taught. Students were often actively discouraged from moving between these associations and the (sometimes tiny) technical and performative differences between ostensibly similar practices in each could be rigorously policed. Hence, moving between these associations could mean being demoted one or more ranks. One of the authors has witnessed an accomplished black belt from one being forced to return to white belt in the other because a senior sensei deemed the other association illegitimate.

If remaining within a specific lineage is an important concern for those training in TMA, a corollary of this might be the special status of the 'master' of that lineage in the present. It is well known that terms of respect and honor are frequently deployed in the martial arts, but TMA are often especially ritualistic about terms of address and codes of conduct towards more senior (or more junior) students and teachers. In Japanese TMA, for instance, the *senpai/kōhai* (senior/junior) distinction is often deployed even between students at the earliest stages in their training; the term 'sensei' (teacher/one who has gone before) is usually reserved for blackbelts who are designated teachers; and the honorific '*shihan*' (master) is kept exclusively for senior teachers or, sometimes, for a single individual who is deemed to be the most advanced practitioner in that style. Rather than being the most dynamic or effective fighter in a particular style, the *shihan* is invariably the oldest, most experienced, and most revered teacher, sometimes no longer even able to perform the demanding techniques that he/she is deemed to represent. This kind of hierarchical structure of reverence approximates that found in military and religious organizations, in which seniority carries with it new levels of deference and respect relatively independent of the maintenance or performance of ongoing technical competency. The most senior figures symbolize and embody (and transmit the legitimacy of) an exclusive tradition. The archetype for this quasi-religious figurehead might be *Ōsensei* (great teacher) Ueshiba Morihei, the remarkable founder of aikido; in fact, the *Aikikai* (the home of traditional aikido today) is presided over by the hereditary grandmaster of aikido known as the *Dōshu* (Master of the Way). The current *Dōshu* is Ueshiba Moriteru, *Ōsensei*'s grandson.

On a more practical level, in towns of a decent size, there will often be several martial arts schools practicing similar styles, that are not affiliated with each other. It is not unusual for students, particularly children, to change schools for a variety of reasons, such as incompatible schedules, or moving to a different part of town. Although this is not always without consequences, for more popular martial arts students might have several different options for continuing their practice in a recognizable way at a different venue. Such options might shrink as one becomes more committed to a certain narrative of the tradition in question, or as one advances in levels, as we saw in the taekwondo cases above: the individual athletes could certainly have trained elsewhere and still have been doing taekwondo, albeit not at the level at which (or with the trajectory) they would need in order to be competitive.

In sport-oriented martial arts such as taekwondo or judo, countries have national-level teams, for which many athletes aspire to qualify. Their best chance to excel is generally by making the team and training with other high-level martial artists under accredited coaches; as in many other niche sports, there is an ever-narrowing pyramid. By contrast, in high level MMA, there are many gyms with the capacity to train professional athletes, though they might be scattered around the country. And even in cases where athletes are criticized for leaving a team that trained them for some time, there is no sense that they have left the sport, or are no longer MMA practitioners. For example, when then-head coach Duane Ludwig left Team Alpha Male in Sacramento to return to his former home in Colorado, one of Team Alpha Male's star athletes, T. J. Dillashaw, chose eventually to go with him. Dillashaw's departure caused a significant rift between him and his former teammates, with Dillashaw being banned from training at the gym in the future (Mindenhall 2015). Still, while people might have criticized Dillashaw for a lack of loyalty to his former team, he was still clearly an MMA fighter, and leaving his team was in no way a violation of the norms, practices, or conventions of the sport.

For MMA as well as many other sports, including sport martial arts, changing schools or training centres, or supplementing one's training elsewhere, is often seen as a normal part of an athlete's progress. For example, an athlete might start their training at a small program with a primarily recreational focus, but need to move elsewhere when they start becoming more skilled, or more interested in competitive training. Some instructors might frown on this practice, or see the student as disloyal, but we can primarily understand this decision in terms of the student's progress as an athlete. Indeed, they might be seen as disloyal precisely because they have decided to prioritize their own training wants over their loyalty to a particular instructor or school. So, such decisions are vulnerable to criticisms of various kinds, but are not, in and of themselves, reflections of a student's lack of dedication to their practice. Indeed, a change of schools in the service of their own progress is often seen as a reflection of their dedication to their practice or their sport. Their development in MMA is tied to the constant endeavour to train with and defeat better and better fighters, rather than to perfect a specific set of 'authentic' techniques.

In contrast, TMA, or less sport-focused martial arts, will often take a very different view of students' decisions to change schools. Rather than being motivated by the prospect of a more challenging fight per se, students of TMA are as likely to decide to change schools in order to participate in more authentic traditions or to train under more revered teachers. Practitioners often aspire to train at their style's *honbu dōjō* (head dojo), which is likely to be in Asia, where they might envision a more direct line of transmission, probably from the oldest and most senior teachers of that style. In some cases, students of TMA might also become disillusioned by the emergence of controversies about the legitimacy and authenticity of their school or style, and therefore seek an alternative with less disputed traditional credentials. For example, one of the authors has taught students who left a successful university karate club to join a private karate dojo (in the same style) in the same city because they gradually came to believe that the university club's emphasis on kumite, free sparring, and competition was overshadowing the traditional teachings, values, and philosophy of Shotokan.

The implications of these different forms of participant motivation and mobility in TMA and MMA have serious implications for their marketing in contemporary societies, which in turn impacts public perceptions of these related fields, which then reinforces and encourages changes in practices between TMA and MMA institutions (McNamara 2008).

Towards ethical embodied practices

This chapter has not attempted to make a clean distinction between traditional and mixed martial arts with regard to their ethical content – indeed, it is likely that such a rigid distinction on these grounds would be impossible – but we can at least note that martial arts practices range between two ideal types or potentialities. On the one hand, we have MMA as exemplified by the eclectic skills and techniques we see in the octagon, and in fight leagues such as the UFC, building on training in a variety of gyms. On the other hand, we have traditional martial arts such as aikido, karate, and taekwondo that are mostly contested in exclusive tournaments and practiced in particular lineages, dojos, or dojangs. But most contemporary martial arts fall somewhere between the two, with differences in the extent to which they emphasize a combative or sport aspect, a link to a particular culture or established tradition, or ethical principles of some kind or other.

Our chapter here is not meant to claim that MMA is ethically superior to TMA, all things considered, despite the appeal of such a counterintuitive conclusion. In fact, the lack of ethical focus in contemporary MMA often contributes to a negative public image. For example, the cult of celebrity in MMA, where some extremely famous and highly paid fighters have well cultivated 'bad boy' images, is not something we think TMA should try to emulate in any way.[4] Title fights are often heavily marketed by pointing to rivalries between fighters; promotional videos will show opponents trash talking each other or even getting into altercations outside the ring. Colby Covington, for example, frequently disparages his opponents with racist comments without being sanctioned by the UFC (Kussoy 2020). This arguably only adds to the appeal of watching him fight people like Kamaru (The Nigerian Nightmare) Usman, since a fighter's overconfident or offensive persona often helps to sell tickets, both to those who want to see them win and those who want to see them taken down a notch. Presenting as ethically cavalier, repugnant, or ruthless is a marketable MMA asset.

Interestingly, the behavior of modern MMA superstars has drawn criticism from a person sometimes credited as one of the sport's founding fathers. Frank Dux, on whose life the movie *Bloodsport* (1988) was based, writes with disdain about the conduct of modern MMA fighters as 'undisciplined, hedonistic, episodic' as well as 'brutish, backstabbing, petty and intrusive' (Dux 2017). Dux contrasts the culture of modern MMA with a culture that elevates honourable conduct, self-discipline, and a military bearing. This military emphasis is also present in one of Dux's examples intended to argue that MMA does not live up to its reputation for effectiveness. In this account, some US Special Forces personnel asked their civilian trainer, a traditional martial artist, about incorporating MMA methods into their training. This ended with an arranged match between the traditional martial artist and a respected professional MMA fighter, in which the traditional martial artist won the match by violating the rules of sport (he shoveled dirt into the MMA fighter's mouth). Dux credits this to the 'mindset of a warrior' overcoming sports training.[5] But it is notable that the explicitly militaristic characteristics he points out help to create a culture of unquestioning obedience among both soldiers and martial artists. And it is precisely that culture that we are pointing to as increasing the potential for abuse.

The discipline, honor, and deference that Dux point to are hallmarks of many types of martial training. Indeed, in most kinds of physical skill training, it is inevitable that you will need to defer to a teacher or coach to some extent. After all, in learning any kind of physical skill, it is very likely that you will have to do something that is counterintuitive, such as stepping or carrying your hands in a different way, or physically painful, like holding a position to build strength and endurance. In that sense, most physical practices do require a person to give over their embodied agency to a teacher to some extent. So we are certainly not arguing that deference is a wholly negative practice or something that should be eliminated from martial arts entirely. It seems ineliminable from any kind of high-level physical training that the student will have to defer to a coach that is presumably more knowledgeable than they are about how they will achieve their goals.

What we do want to say, though, is that on the flip side of the celebrity and press conferences, in the resistance to the superstar MMA culture, we also have traditions whose practitioners are extremely vulnerable to abuse. In practice, this means being careful not to assume that traditional martial arts practice will necessarily make people ethically good, or that students are safe even in those environments with an explicitly ethical focus. Traditional martial arts schools may be places that more frequently emphasize codes of conduct, even if they do not have the monopoly on ethical training that one sometimes finds in marketing materials for such dojos or studios. That said, if your priorities include ethical self-cultivation it is unlikely that you would choose to train in MMA rather than TMA. However, the contrast between the privileging of discipline and self-cultivation as a selling point and the dangerous potential of certain kinds of deferential environments creates a dilemma for TMA that is less of a problem for MMA. TMA claims to be the ethical field, while MMA does not, and yet the very practices that inculcate ethical principles in students create a potentially dangerous culture of deference that can easily be abused.

Notes

1 Romanization of Chinese terms is inconsistent and often confusing in the literature. Out of respect, here we utilize the Pinyin (system developed and recognized by the Chinese government in 1950s) rather than the Wade Giles system (developed by the Englishmen Thomas Wade and Herbery Giles at Cambridge University in the 1890s, at the peak of Victoria colonialism). Hence, 'Yongchun' rather than 'Wing Chun', 'Taijiquan' rather than 'Tai Chi Chuan', 'Hongjia' rather than 'Hung gar', 'Qinna' rather than 'Chi Na', and *gong-fu* rather than 'kung fu'. Where other authors have used different romanizations for martial arts, we quote them in their original and provide the Pinyin at the first appearance of the term in this chapter.
2 This is consistent with the meaning of 'tradition' deployed in the work of Hobsbawm and Ranger (1992).
3 Indeed, in an interview with *TIME Magazine* in 2018, the Abbot of Shaolin temple, Shi Yong Xin, seems to channel Bruce Lee's character from *Enter The Dragon* when he argues (in response to the Xu-Wei fight), that *gong-fu* 'can't be compared to MMA because its true essence is spiritual rather than simply physical, bringing not superpowers but inner peace' (Campbell 2018).
4 An intriguing 'bad boy' exception in TMA might be the famous case of Mas Oyama (Ōyama Masutatsu), the founder of Kyokushin karate – the first style of full contact, fight-oriented karate. After training with Funakoshi Gichin (founder of Shotokan) and Miyagi Chojun (founder of Gōjūryū) in the late 1940s, Oyama is reputed to have challenged (and defeated) numerous US servicemen in occupied Japan. After a mountain retreat, he became a national karate champion and founded Kyokushinkai in the 1950s. Oyama's style was (in)famous for emphasizing harsh physical conditioning, breaking techniques, and full-contact sparring; very strict and traditional in some ways, Oyama's style emphasized practicality, effectiveness, and victory. There are many stories of Oyama challenging and defeating masters of other styles in combat to promote Kyokushinkai. Yang Yun-ho's film, *Fighter in the Wind* (2004), was based on Oyama's life.
5 Ironically, this type of move would have been better suited to the villain of *Bloodsport* (1988), Chong Li, than to its protagonist, based on Dux himself.

References

Armour, N. and Axon, R. (2018) 'Two-Time Olympic Taekwondo Champ Steven Lopez Banned by SafeSport for Sexual Misconduct', *USA Today*, 8 September, https://www.usatoday.com/story/sports/olympics/2018/0, accessed 21 May 2020.

Blennerhassett, P. (2019) 'It's Time to Admit Most Traditional Martial Arts Are Fake and Don't Actually Teach You How to Fight', *South China Morning Post*, 24 October, https://www.scmp.com/sport/martial-arts/kung-fu/article/3034175/its-time-admit-most-traditional-martial-arts-are-fake, accessed 21 May 2020.

Bowman, P. (2011) 'The Fantasy Corpus of Martial Arts, or, the Communication of Bruce Lee', in D. S. Farrer and J. Whalen-Bridge (eds.) *Martial Arts as Embodied Knowledge: Asian Traditions in a Transnational World*, Albany: State University of New York Press, pp. 61–96.

Cadwell, L. L. (2016) 'In Pursuit of a Passion', in J. Little (ed.) *Bruce Lee: The Tao of Gung Fu*, Tokyo: Tuttle Publishing <ebook version>.

Campbell, C. (2018) 'Meet the Chinese MMA Fighter Taking on the Grandmasters of Kung Fu', *Time*, 8 November, https://time.com/5448811/mma-kung-fu-xu-xiaodong/, accessed 21 May 2020.

Cruz, G. (2013) 'Rorion Gracie and the Day He Created the UFC', *MMA Fighting*, 12 November, https://www.mmafighting.com/2013/11/12/5043630/rorion-gracie-and-the-day-he-created-the-ufc, accessed 21 May 2020.

Dux, F. (2017) 'The Difference between Traditional Martial Arts and Mixed Martial Arts', *Artvoice*, 15 February, https://artvoice.com/2017/02/15/difference-traditional-martial-arts-mixed-martial-arts/, accessed 19 May 2020.

Fuchs, J. (2018) 'Terror in Taekwondo', *Sports Illustrated*, 5 September, https://www.si.com/olympics/2018/09/05/taekwondo-us-olympics-steven-lopez-jean-lopez-sexual-misconduct-lawsuit, accessed 3 October 2020.

Goto-Jones, C. (2019) 'Bushidō and Philosophy: Parting the Clouds, Seeking the Way', in B. W. Davis (ed.) *The Oxford Handbook of Japanese Philosophy*, Oxford: Oxford University Press, pp. 307–329.

Hobsbawm, E. and Ranger, T. (eds) (1992) *The Invention of Tradition*, Cambridge: Cambridge University Press.

Huafeng, Q. (2017) 'A Ridiculous Competition', C. Surtees (trans.), *Beijing Review*, 'Are Traditional Martial Arts Really So Weak?', 18 May, http://www.bjreview.com/Lifestyle/201705/t20170513_800096086.html, accessed 4 October 2020.

Kussoy, H. (2020) 'UFC Fighters Slam Colby Covington as "Racist"', *New York Post*, 24 September, https://nypost.com/2020/09/24/ufc-fighters-slam-colby-covington-as-racist/, accessed 4 October 2020.

Martin, D. (2013) 'John Cholish Explains How Much It Costs to Be a UFC Fighter', *Bleacher Report*, 23 May, https://bleacherreport.com/articles/1649483-john-cholish-explains-how-much-it-costs-to-be-a-ufc-fighter, accessed 20 May 2020.

Martínková, I. and Parry, J. (2016) 'Martial Categories: Clarification and Classification', *Journal of the Philosophy of Sport*, 43(1): 143–162.

McNamara, J. D. (2008) 'The Effect of Modern Marketing on Martial Arts and Traditional Martial Arts Culture', *The Sport Journal*, 14 March, https://thesportjournal.org/article/the-effect-of-modern-marketing-on-martial-arts-and-traditional-martial-arts-culture/, accessed 21 May 2020.

Mindenhall, C. (2015) 'Banned from Team Alpha Male, TJ Dillashaw Feels Urijah Faber "Threw Me under the Bus"', *MMA Fighting*, 13 October, https://www.mmafighting.com/2015/10/13/9514451/banned-from-team-alpha-male-tj-dillashaw-feels-urijah-faber-threw-me, accessed 1 May 2020.

Moon, J. and Syed, F. (2018) 'Toronto Police Charge Former Canadian Olympic Coach with Multiple Sex Assaults of Taekwondo Student', *The Star*, 3 May, https://www.thestar.com/news/gta/2018/05/02/toronto-police-charge-four-time-canadian-olympic-coach-with-multiple-sex-assaults-of-taekwondo-student.html, accessed 22 April 2020.

Murphy, W. F. (2019) 'Investigating the Incidence of Sexual Assault in Martial Arts Coaching Using Media Reports', *Digital Investigation*, 30: 90–93.

Pucin, D. (2012) 'The Lopezes Are the First Family of U.S. Taekwondo', *Los Angeles Times*, 19 May, https://www.latimes.com/sports/olympics/la-xpm-2012-may-19-la-sp-oly-taekwondo-lopez-20120520-story.html, accessed 22 April 2020.

Russell, G. (2010) 'Epistemic Viciousness in the Martial Arts', in G. Priest and D. Young (eds.) *Martial Arts and Philosophy: Beating and Nothingness*, Chicago: Open Court, pp. 120–144.

Starr, A. (2018) '4 Accusers Sue Taekwondo Champion Brothers for Alleged Sexual Abuse', *NPR*, 4 May, https://www.npr.org/2018/05/04/608454710/4-accusers-sue-taekwondo-champion-brothers-for-alleged-sexual-abuse, accessed 17 April 2020.

Twemlow, S. and Sacco, F. (1998) 'The Application of Traditional Martial Arts Practice and Theory to the Treatment of Violent Adolescents', *Adolescence*, 33(131): 505–518.

4 Violence and constraints in combat sport

Joseph D. Lewandowski

Banned in New York State until 2016, widely decried in popular media as a predatory blood sport, and criticized in the philosophy of sport as a morally unjustifiable and 'prolonged mutual assault' (Dixon 2015), there is much that is claimed to be wrong with the professional sport of mixed martial arts (MMA). More recently, important philosophically informed attempts to defend MMA against such moralizing critiques have also begun to emerge (Weimar 2017; Kershnar and Kelly 2020). Yet with an almost exclusive focus on violence, rights, and consent, such discussions tend to obscure, or so I want to suggest in this chapter, other important considerations of the nature of combat sport skills and violence, and the normative difficulties of *mixing* martial arts in the ways that MMA does. In MMA, the 'constitutive skills' (Torres 2000) needed to excel – the variously combined skills of striking, grappling, submitting, etc. that are defined and enabled by the minimalist rules of the sport – are *constitutive violent skills*. Indeed, when properly understood, MMA, like all combat sports, is a form of rule-constituted skilled violence – a point I should like to develop further here.[1] A focus on the 'immoral' violence in MMA disembedded from the constitutive rules of the sport loses sight of the unique nature of combat sport violence and overlooks the crucial problem of combat sport hybridity in MMA. In what follows, I shall seek to characterize more fully the precise nature of combat sport violence, as well as address the challenges of properly constraining such violence in a uniquely hybrid combat sport such as MMA. What's 'wrong' with MMA, as we shall see, is not the skillful forms of violence that constitute the sport but rather the constitutive rules that poorly constrain it.[2]

To develop such an argument, I draw on work in rational-choice theory. Most generally, I seek to extend relevant aspects of Jon Elster's constraint theory into the philosophy of sport. More specifically, I use such an analytical theory to sketch a philosophically robust account of the nature and functioning of constraints, skills, and violence in competitive combat sport. From the standpoint of a constraint theory of combat sport, the central claim to elaborated here is that MMA in its current form is a sport constituted by violent skills that are sub-optimally constrained by the sport's constitutive rules.[3] As I hope to demonstrate, in what ways and to what extent combat sport violence is constitutively constrained – how, that is, the rules of combat sport define and enable maximally skillful, creative, and yet relatively safe matches – is especially elusive in an athletically hybrid and physically perilous sport like MMA.

The argument is organized as follows. I begin with a brief summary of Elster's constraint theory; I then go on to outline a constraint theory of sport, and briefly contrast that theory with a related position in the philosophy of sport, namely, Suits's

DOI: 10.4324/9781003122395-5

discussion of sport as games. In the core section of the chapter, I develop a constraint theory of combat sport and combat sport violence, and apply that theory in a critical discussion of MMA. I conclude with a summary of the argument, as well as some reflections on what, from the standpoint of a constraint theory of combat sport, may in fact be *right* about MMA and combat sport more generally.

Ulysses and the Sirens: towards a constraint theory of sport

In the most general of terms, constraint theory is Jon Elster's unique attempt to develop, from within methodological individualism, a conception of rational action that is thick enough to capture the relationship between limits on human action (constraints) and the choices that can be made within such limits (preferences and courses of action). Although it has many dimensions and applications, the seeds of constraint theory can be found in Elster's *Ulysses and the Sirens* (1984), where he argues that all human action is the result of two successive filtering devices:

> The first is defined by the set of structural constraints, which cuts down the set of abstractly possible courses of action and reduces it to the vastly smaller subset of feasible actions. The second filtering process is the mechanism that singles out which member of the feasible set shall be realized.
>
> (Elster 1984: 113)

What makes Elster's thinking unique is that he is interested in not merely the rationality of individual preferences and choice-maximizing action but also: (a) the role that constraints play in shaping those preferences and choices; (b) the fact that many constraints on human action are not merely structurally pre-filtered but can themselves be reflexively selected by individuals; and (c) the forms of choice and action, such as creative and skillful action, wherein these two filters are not successive but interactive.

Now, the mythological hero Ulysses is Elster's model of a constraint theorist in action. For in his encounter with the Sirens, structural constraints (technological limits that require Ulysses travel by boat and not, say, airplane or helicopter) and elective constraints (stopping up his rowers' ears and having himself lashed to the mast of the ship) interact and creatively enable what would have otherwise been an impossible course of action. Put in Elsterian terms, Ulysses' own reflexive reduction of his feasible set (choices of constraints) frees him to safely hear the call of the Sirens (a choice within and enabled by those very constraints). In Elster's more recent study, *Ulysses Unbound* (2000), he attempts to characterize more fully this interaction of choices of constraints and choices within constraints in an analysis of creativity and constraints in the arts, where artists bind (and often seek to unbind) themselves in various ways. In this study as well Elster provocatively suggests but does not develop the relevance of constraint theory for the philosophy of sport (Elster 2000: 281). Thus let me briefly summarize Elster's thinking about art, before extending that thinking to sport.

In his constraint-theoretical account of art, Elster argues that artistic creation is 'guided by the aim of maximizing aesthetic value under constraints' (ibid.: 200). In art, the philosophically interesting constraints are not so much objectively given or 'hard' constraints such as technical or physical limitations but, rather, 'soft' constraints or conventions – those 'restrictions that constitute a specific genre' (ibid.: 190). On Elster's account, the soft constraints or conventions in the arts are best understood as constitutive rules. Adhering to them, like adhering to the rules of chess, does not merely normatively regulate artistic endeavors; it defines such behavior as a *specific kind* of artistic endeavor. Yet, Elster is no mere formalist. His analysis concedes that sonnet writers, if they are to be skilled composers who achieve anything of aesthetic value or excellence, cannot simply adhere to or unintentionally 'embody' their chosen constraints. Following the rules is simply not enough: the point of writing a sonnet, Elster suggests, is to write one well or in a maximally excellent way *within* the binding constraints of sonnet-writing.[4]

In many respects such is the case with competitive athletes as well. They, too, are engaged in a more or less complex practice aimed at what I characterize as constitutively constrained maximization (Lewandowski 2007). In competing in a particular sport, athletes, like artists, have elected their soft constraints and deliberately adopt the constitutive rules of a specific sport. Being bound by the rules of tennis is what it means to play tennis and be a tennis player. Of course, *how* one plays and competes – the quality of the choices and the skillfulness and creativity of the moves one makes – within those binds/rules is what makes one a better or worse tennis player. In this regard we can say Roger Federer is Shakespearean in his athletic realization of constrained maximization in the sport of tennis.

The basic Elsterian argument by analogy being introduced here is simply that, at least at one level, all competitive sports are athletic genres in which individuals strive to achieve constrained maximization. The inverse of such a striving would be something like engaging in sport (or art) as a leisure activity or recreational hobby where the only objective would be something akin to 'constrained diversion'. Drawing a distinction between the chosen pursuit of constrained maximization and that of constrained diversion does not necessarily imply that there are any essential differences between a competitive athlete and a recreational player, or between athletic action and mere play. Instead, from the rational-choice perspective I am developing here, such a distinction simply makes explicit the relative potential for increasing constitutive skill and creativity in each case. Like the accomplished sonneteer, the competitive athlete's committed maximizing orientation toward the constitutive rules of his or her sport characteristically enables skill levels and forms of creative action that are difficult if not impossible to realize in the pleasure-maximizing activity of constrained diversion. As it turns out, in competitive athletics, less (constraints that bind) typically fosters more (excellence in skill and creativity within those constraints).

Now to be sure, there is no need to push this preliminary analogy between constrained maximization in art and constrained maximization in sport too far. Important distinctions should be preserved. The orientation athletes adopt in relation to the rules of their chosen sport is not identical to that of artists in relation to the conventions of their chosen genre. Artists often self-consciously seek to violate or reject the conventions of their genre by subverting or exceeding them. This is evident in much contemporary art. Competitive athletes, by contrast, must endeavor to maximize their creativity and constitutive skill levels within existing constraints.[5] The relative constitutive quality of constraints/rules in competitive sport, on the one hand, and conventions in art, on the other hand, are also quite different. While we might view the recent history of postmodern art, literature, and theatre as having eliminated (or exceeded) all conventions, there is a reason we do not have a similar historical vocabulary for postmodern sport. Though it often seems that anything goes in postmodern poetry, what counts as playing tennis remains playing by the rules that constitute tennis (even if/when those rules are modified). And what counts as playing excellent tennis remains an individual's athletic ability to maximize his or her tennis-playing constitutive skills and creativity in the course of a tennis match.

The general point to be drawn from this difference in the nature of constraints in sports and the arts is that the relationship between constitutive rules and constitutive skills and creativity appears to be decisive for competitive sport ways that it is not for art (or play). What introducing constraint theory to sport makes explicit is that in competitive sport constraints (constitutive rules) are determinative for enabling the pursuit of constrained maximization of skill and creativity. Constitutive skills are dependent upon constitutive rules. To put the matter in the terms of constraint theory, where a certain number of the right kinds of constraints obtain, more possibilities to achieve constitutively skilled excellence exist. Of course what makes for the 'right kind of constraints' in competitive sport is an essential, if open, question. This is particularly the case in combat sport, which, unlike many other sports, is constituted by violent skills that, improperly constrained, risk the safety of the athletic participants and threaten to undermine the activity *qua* sport – I shall take up precisely this point in the next section.

But before doing so, it should be acknowledged that the kind of rational choice theory of sport I am proposing here is not without a well-known antecedent in the philosophy of sport. In fact, two core elements of game playing singled out by Bernard Suits in his 'The Elements of Sport' (1995) are consistent with aspects of a constraint theory of sport. Specifically, constraint theory shares with Suits a conception of the rules of sport as constitutive rules. It also shares with Suits a general sense that game playing entails that game players adopt a certain attitude as game players toward those rules – or what Suits helpfully describes as 'the lusory attitude'. Athletes can be defined, at least in part, as individuals who take up a lusory attitude vis-à-vis constitutive rules: They choose their constraints or knowingly accept constitutive rules 'just so the activity made possible by such acceptance can occur' (Suits 1995: 11).

Yet in 'The Elements of Sport' Suits makes clear that his purpose 'is to define *not well-played games*, but games' (ibid.: 10, my emphasis). A constraint theory of competitive sport should thus be viewed as a supplement to Suits' thinking. That supplement could be summarized as follows: in competitive sport, the function of constitutive rules and the lusory attitude (choices of constraints) is not merely to make game playing possible but also to make for well-played games by enabling choices within those constraints that maximize constitutive skills and creativity. Put differently: a constraint theory of sport is not merely an attempt to define the conditions of the possibility of sport. It is also an attempt to scrutinize the constitutive conditions of sport that make for more or less creative and skill-maximized sporting competitions. As we shall see directly, this applied focus offers a critical analytic tool with which to understand sport constituted by the constrained violence of athletic combat.

What's wrong with MMA? Constitutive violent skills and sub-optimal constraints

At a distance, combat sport might seem an unlikely candidate for an account of constraint theorizing informed by rational choice theory. The martial arts typically conjure up images far more Hobbesean than Elsterian. In many combat sports it is not the rationality of constrained maximization but rather an unbound state of nature that appears to prevail. The sport of MMA, both in the popular imagination and in the philosophy of sport, would seem to find itself on the extreme end of this kind of irrationality and immorality – a kind of Hobbesean war of 'all against all' in octagonal form, as it were. Indeed, unlike, say, boxing or wrestling, MMA is defined by an almost unconstrained admixture of striking, grappling, and submissions. Nearly every form of holding and striking is allowed, with the exception of stomping, knees and kicks to the head when an opponent is down, eye gouging, fish hooking, rabbit punching, head-butting, blows to the groin, and hair pulling – to highlight most of the notably short list of impermissible moves; for that very reason MMA is considered a paradigmatically depraved case of violent sport (Dixon 2015).

This is surely unsurprising. The interdisciplinarity of MMA, which makes it unique among combat sports, has, as is well-known, historical origins in the violent anything goes *pankration* of ancient Greece. But while the ancient Greek amateur sport of *pankration* combined the skills of two combat sports (boxing and wrestling), the contemporary professional version of *pankration* blends boxing and wrestling with a broad array of other combat sports, including, among others, karate, judo, kickboxing and, most prominently today, Muay Thai and Brazilian Jiu-Jitsu. With so many fighting styles at play, a casual observer of MMA competitions is likely to see a 'sport' that frequently amounts to little more than a random and incoherent series of Hobbesean bloody clashes.

This intuitive sense that 'something is wrong' with MMA stems, or so I would like to suggest here, from the many combined forms of violent striking, grappling, and submitting simultaneously on display in an MMA competition. In MMA the constitutive violent skills of many combat sports are adeptly fused (and confused) in the flow of competition. And that, precisely, is what I want to argue is the problem with the sport: with its hybridized fighting and minimalist approach to constitutive rules, MMA bouts often blur the line between violence and *combat sport violence*. Indeed, it is that distinction, and MMA's complex hybridity – in particular, its unhappy fusion of the constitutive violent skills but not the constitutive rules of Muay Thai and Jiu-Jitsu – that demand further scrutiny.

The term 'violence', broadly construed in the sense of physical harm, characteristically denotes injurious actions limited and motivated solely by arbitrary and idiosyncratic factors, such as emotions, prejudices, threats, circumstances, and so on. Violence is this sense is 'thin'; that is to say that violence is little more than unconstrained assault. Violence in this regard would include activities like gang attacks, road rage incidents, and bar brawls. Such 'anything goes' violent encounters are in fact paradigmatic of *rationally unbound action*. From the standpoint of constraint theory, they lack precisely the interaction of constitutive rules (constraints) and embedded and embodied individual choices and actions (pursued within those constraints) necessary to maximize creativity and skill. Or, to put the matter in Suits' terms, violence per se lacks the lusory attitude. Combat sport violence, in contrast, is lusorily 'thick'; that is to say that combat sport violence is non-arbitrarily constituted by the adoption of shared binding constraints (rules) of the competition and the skillful and creative moves enabled by such constitutive constraints. In short, the violence peculiar to combat *sport* is not violence per se but rather *constitutively skilled violence.*

To capture the core distinction being made here we need only consider the difference between the skilled execution of a left jab-right cross-right leg kick combination in an

MMA bout with the haphazard throwing of a 'haymaker' and a flailing kick in a bar brawl. The latter combination, regardless of whether it lands or not, cannot be said to be a constitutive skill, as there are no mutually binding constraints (or lusory attitudes) that constitute the activity of bar brawling as such. Of course one might be a 'good' bar brawler in the limited sense of having prevailed in numerous random anything goes encounters, but that success is itself an arbitrary outcome in no way defined and made possible by the (non-existent) constitutive constraints/rules of bar brawling. The difference between violence and combat sport violence, then, turns on the presence or absence of constitutive constraints and concomitant constitutive violent skills defined and enabled by those constraints.

As a complex hybrid combat sport, MMA frequently vacillates between these two types of violence. Indeed, the complex hybridity of MMA poses genuine challenges to devising constitutive rules that make the violence in it *constitutively skilled*. Put differently, the central difficulty lies in adequately constraining the myriad violent skills that are permitted to be creatively *mixed* in the course of MMA competition.

To see this one needs look no further than the prominent role that Muay Thai and Jiu-Jitsu forms of combat play in MMA. These two combat sports have largely replaced boxing and wrestling in the modern version of the *pankration*. As a hybrid sport that combines stand up and ground combat, it no surprise that MMA athletes train extensively and seek to excel in both Muay Thai and Jiu-Jitsu. Known as the 'art of eight limbs', Muay Thai entails stand up fighting constituted by the constrained use of fists, elbows, knees, and legs (shins). In consistently utilizing eight striking surfaces, it is far more effective – and physically devastating – than mere western style boxing or other eastern martial arts, such as karate or judo. The constitutive rules of competitive Muay Thai – which among others include no striking when the opponent is down, no grappling, tackling, or choking, the mandatory use of specially padded gloves (6–10 ounces in weight, depending on the competitors' weight class), and five-round matches consisting of 3-minute rounds with 2-minute rest periods between rounds – clearly indicate an attempt to constrain the combat in ways that make it both compelling and relatively safe. Indeed, the sport of Muay Thai contains constitutive constraints that aim, however imperfectly, to maximize violent skill and creativity in the use of 'eight limbs' and minimize risk of injury in competition.

But when introduced and practiced in the hybrid sport of MMA, the constitutive rules of Muay Thai proper largely melt away. MMA fighters do not wear Muay Thai gloves. Instead, they wear 4-ounce grappling (open-fingered) knuckle pads. MMA fighters are permitted to take down, mount, and repeatedly strike (with fists, elbows, and forearms, but not knees or feet) a downed (and often semi-conscious) opponent – a gruesome practice known as 'ground and pound' that has no correlate in Muay Thai. Additionally, MMA rounds are 5 minutes in length, and offer competitors only a 1-minute rest period between rounds. Championship MMA contests are mandatory (and non-title main event bouts are typically) five-round fights – thus 10 minutes longer than standard Muay Thai contests. In other words, MMA contains within it a sub-optimally constrained version of Muay Thai – one that endangers competitors and, in the practice of 'ground and pound', clouds the distinction between the 'thin' violence of unbound action and the 'thick' combat sport violence of constitutively bound skills articulated here.

The matter of MMA's impoverished version of Muay Thai is compounded with the widespread use of Jiu-Jitsu in MMA. For, just as Muay Thai has largely come to overshadow boxing in today's version of the *pankration*, so too has Brazilian Jiu-Jitsu appropriated a large part of what was once wrestling's exclusive domain. When blended with Muay Thai in this way, the complex choke holds and python-like submission maneuvers of Jiu-Jitsu, which are designed to cut off the flow of oxygen and dislocate limbs, make MMA even more problematic from the vantage point of constraint theory. For while the constitutive rules of Jiu-Jitsu forbid striking of any kind (indeed, the penalty for striking in competitive Jiu-Jitsu is immediate disqualification), in MMA the sport is fused with Muay Thai in a way that makes certain combat sequences difficult to distinguish from an arbitrary 'anything goes' assault.

One often sees this in a three-phase combat sequence distinct to MMA. In the initial encounter, which begins with both fighters on their feet, Muay Thai style stand up fighting (punching and striking with fists, elbows, knees, and shins) leads to a knock down. In a furious second phase, the downed and semi-conscious fighter is mounted by his opponent and set upon with all manner of fists, elbows, and forearms – 'ground and pound' moves, as noted above, which are *not* permitted in Muay Thai or Jiu-Jitsu – or any other combat sport, for that matter. In the final phase of the sequence, a bloodied and nearly defenseless man or woman is brutally choked unconscious or otherwise painfully submitted in a Jiu-Jitsu hold. In this kind of disturbing sequence the line between violence and the constitutive skilled violence of martial art all but dissolves. In mixing but not adequately constraining the fusion of Muay Thai and Jiu-Jitsu in MMA, constrained maximization via constitutive violent skill and creativity can quickly degenerate into little more than a bar brawl pummeling.

Conclusion: what's wrong – and what's right – about MMA

From the standpoint of the constraint theory of sport outlined here, in this chapter I have sought to highlight the extent to which minimalist constitutive constraints (rules) play an outsized role in MMA and the kind of violence peculiar to the sport. I argued that in contemporary MMA the safety of competitors and the excellence of competition in skilled violence is often undermined by sub-optimal constraints: the sport fuses many forms of martial art, but does not preserve enough of the constitutive rules that define and enable the skill and creativity peculiar to those individual martial forms. Indeed, as I sought to demonstrate, certain phases of MMA competition, such as combat sequences that fuse Muay Thai, 'ground and pound', and Jiu-Jitsu in poorly constrained ways, illustrate that when it comes to the constitutive constraints of combat sport, less is in fact not always more. On the contrary, what is paramount in combat sport is the right kind of constraints – ones that maximize violent skill and creativity and at the same time seek to minimize, to the extent possible, physical harm and injury resultant from unconstrained violence. Normatively speaking, that is to say, I've argued that what's wrong with MMA is that its competitive matches lack the right kind of constraints – the optimal tightness of bounds, to borrow a phrase from Elster – needed to consistently and adequately preserve the distinction between violence and combat sport violence.

Now, this failure to create an optimal tightness of constitutive rules is of course not unique to competitive MMA. It is in fact a challenge for professional and amateur boxing (Lewandowski 2007, 2015) and combat sport more generally. With respect to combat sport competitions, the solution would seem relatively straightforward:

combat sports – MMA in particular – need a thorough rethinking of the rules that constitute their competitions. In the hybrid case of MMA, such a rethinking would begin by addressing the need to reintroduce some of the many constraints of the individual martial arts blended within the sport – for example, by prohibiting any striking of and permitting only grappling with a downed opponent. In essence, such a revision of the constitutive rules of MMA would have the effect of prohibiting all 'ground and pound' maneuvers. The introduction of additional constitutive rules may very well profoundly alter the familiar flow of MMA competitions. But tightening, as it were, the bounds of action permitted in an MMA bout would help to preserve MMA as a combat *sport*.

Of course a constraint theory of combat sport need not confine itself to analyses of combat sport competitions and constitutive rule reformation. One might also look beyond octagon competitions and *in the gym* to examine combat sport sparring to see what may be right, as it were, about MMA. Indeed, although a treatment of combat sport sparring has hitherto eluded the philosophy of sport – and remains beyond the scope of the present inquiry – I would argue that sparring constitutes a normatively fertile subgenre of combat sport research.[6] Thus in closing let me briefly highlight the normative potential of this under-analyzed practice of combat sport training.

In-house sparring, in which athletes spar with other members of their gym or club, is a central part of the routine of all combat sport athletes; and in fact, competitive combat sport athletes spar far more frequently than they compete. Sparring occupies a complex midpoint between an actual fight and a simple series of individual drills. Under the watchful eye of a good trainer, in an in-house sparring session constraints and choices interact in ways explicitly intended to mutually expand and sharpen constitutive violent skills possessed by *both* fighters.[7] Such a sparring session is a dynamic attempt at constrained maximization of skill and creativity tempered by and realized through the trainer's (and fighter's) tightening (or loosening) the constraints of the spar. In MMA, weaknesses in striking or grappling are addressed through additional constraints on who is selected for sparring – a strong wrestler to help improve an adept stand-up fighter's ground game, for instance – and what sparring participants are permitted to – or must – do in the course of the spar, such as throwing only jab-kick combinations or repeatedly defending takedown attempts without using counter-strikes. In contrast to the heat of sub-optimally constrained MMA competitions in the octagon, to be effective, sparring in the gym must be a mutually respectful and highly cooperative practice.

In-house sparring, that is to say, is a form of reflexive social cooperation (Lewandowski 2007, 2015) – a joint 'we' endeavor in *honing* constitutive skills and creativity *cooperatively*. As every fighter knows, the value of sparring is not reducible to instrumental ends – one doesn't 'win' or 'lose' an in-house spar. Indeed, in such sparring constitutive skilled violence is doubly constrained – by the additional constraints of the spar (as imposed by the trainer) and the fighters' shared commitment to mutual betterment, rather than victory. To be sure, in combat sport competitions one fights with an opponent. But in combat sport training/sparring one 'works', as the saying goes in the gym, with a *partner*. In-house sparring sessions are thus a form of 'co-labor' or 'teamwork'; they are shared cooperative endeavors aimed at mutual enhancement. In-house sparring cultivates a profoundly co-operative ethos. In this regard it would not be an exaggeration to say that there is a kind of moral grammar to combat sport sparring. Hence what just may be right about MMA and combat sport more generally discloses itself most fully not in competitive venues but rather in the gym – in the unique and complex forms of teamwork combat sparring sessions both demand and promote.

Notes

1 Of course one might question such a generalization and argue that a combat sport such as fencing is not violent, but that would be misguided, especially with regard to sabre. Indeed, even in foil and epee, the central task of competitive fencing is to utilize skilled violence to land blows ('touches' that often deeply bruise one's opponent) with what amounts to a modified lethal weapon.
2 Thus the focus here is on the intersection of violence and rules in MMA. But for a helpful discussion of the ways in which MMA athletes negotiate the spectacle and physical experience of violence in their sport, see Andreasson and Johansson (2019).
3 For a related discussion of constraint theory and boxing, see Lewandowski (2007).
4 To be sure, in the history of art there are numerous exceptions to Elster's generalization about the pursuit of excellence within binding constraints. In fact, self-consciously violating the rules of sonnet-making, for example, is a way to play, as it were, with existing constraints in an effort to expand (or reject) what counts as excellence in sonneteering. I address this point – and contrast it with the pursuit of excellence in competitive athletics – briefly in what follows.
5 Of course there would appear to be obvious exceptions to this generalization. Consider snowboarding, for example. Here is a case where a new athletic genre – a new set of constitutive constraints – emerges. But such an exception, which is itself parasitic on existing constraints, only highlights the extent to which the pursuit of excellence in competitive sport – even new and hybrid sports – remains necessarily embedded within constitutive constraints of one sort or another.
6 Dixon (2015) implicitly acknowledges a similar point when he admits that MMA sparring is not subject to his moral critique.
7 Of course in-house sparring sessions that take place in the lead up to a competitive match have a somewhat different air about them. Such sessions are characteristically more intense, and the aims and benefits of the spar are deliberately weighted on the side of the athlete who has an upcoming match. But even in such cases, the practice of sparring remains mutually (if not equally) beneficial, and demands high levels of reflexive social cooperation and mutual respect to be effective. Perhaps the only case in which sparring may not entail reflexive social cooperation and mutual respect in the manner characterized here can be found at the more privileged economic levels of professional combat sport, where training camps in preparation for a marquee fight have the budget to bring in paid sparring partners from another gym/club. In such cases, the sparring 'partner' becomes merely an *employee*.

References

Andreasson, J. and Johansson, T. (2019) 'Negotiating Violence: Mixed Martial Arts as a Spectacle and Sport', *Sport in Society*, 22(7): 1183–1197.
Dixon, N. (2015) 'A Moral Critique of Mixed Martial Arts', *Public Affairs Quarterly*, 29(4): 365–384.
Elster, J. (1984) *Ulysses and the Sirens*, Cambridge: Cambridge University Press.
Elster, J. (2000) *Ulysses Unbound*, Cambridge: Cambridge University Press.
Kershnar, S. and Kelly, R. (2020) 'Rights and Consent in Mixed Martial Arts', *Journal of the Philosophy of Sport*, 47(1): 105–120.
Lewandowski, J. (2007) 'Boxing: The Sweet Science of Constraints', *Journal of the Philosophy of Sport*, 34(1): 26–38.
Lewandowski, J. (2015) 'Teamwork as Reflexive Social Cooperation', *Journal of the Philosophy of Sport*, 42(1): 43–49.

Suits, B. (1995) 'The Elements of Sport', in W. J. Morgan and K. V. Meier (eds.) *Philosophic Inquiry in Sport* (2nd Ed.), Champaign, IL: Human Kinetics, pp. 8–15.

Torres, C. (2000) 'What Counts as Part of a Game? A Look at Skills', *Journal of the Philosophy of Sport*, 27(1): 81–92.

Weimar, S. (2017) 'On the Alleged Intrinsic Immorality of Mixed Martial Arts', *Journal of the Philosophy of Sport*, 44(2): 258–275.

5 Experimentation, distributed cognition, and flow

A scientific lens on mixed martial arts

Zachary Agoff, Benjamin Gwerder and Vadim Keyser

Over the past 50 years, mixed martial arts (MMA) has seen a stark shift from being publicly perceived as an obscure, controversial, and gladiatorial combat experiment to a more recognizable, respectable, and professional sport. This shift in public perception is certainly not insignificant, and is deserving of deeper philosophical attention. What is the 'stabilizing' process of a given sport – in this case, specifically MMA? What sorts of structures and mechanisms are at play during this process? Here, we argue that recent insights in scientific experimentation (of all places) can clarify these sorts of questions, particularly in the contemporary development of MMA.

Recent work in the philosophy of experimentation (Keyser 2017, 2019) has argued that scientific knowledge stabilizes in a given physical context and it is *distributed* through the context. The stabilization amounts to developing new things, never seen in nature, as well as manipulated things in nature. Keyser's account attempts to clarify *how* things are stabilized in scientific contexts. We apply this framework of experimental *stabilization* to the development of mixed martial arts. We show that technique development, flow states, and the sport of MMA itself stabilize.

We proceed in three broad steps. First, we flesh out an account of experimental/epistemic stabilization in the philosophy of experimentation. There, we introduce a key conceptual term, 'intervention systems', to discuss *how material components organize* to respond to contexts. We apply intervention systems to techniques in MMA. In the second section, we describe 'agency' by showing that the stabilization concept, combined with 'distributed cognition', has interesting implications about the *distributed location* of a martial technique within a fighter. We describe the neuroscience of flow states in light of Bruce Lee's representation of a technique 'throwing itself'. We make some 'far-out' conclusions, like: not only is one's effectiveness as a fighter distributed through components that are beyond self-reference, but a given technique is delivered absent of self-reference. In our final section, we apply our general framework to the stabilization of material conditions and representation in MMA. By considering relevant historical developments in the material conditions from Pancrase to Pride to the UFC, along with a host of particular, recent examples from the sport, we argue that the multiple aims of MMA organizations are satisfied by striking a certain balance between the excitement of fans, the safety of fighters, and traditional martial arts philosophical principles, while also exhibiting remarkable degrees of fluidity in context. We discuss, in particular, how the context of the COVID-19 pandemic impacts the representational content of the spectator.

DOI: 10.4324/9781003122395-6

Stabilizing intervention systems: from science to martial art

Keyser (2017, 2019) argues that scientific knowledge occurs through various types of stabilization processes. First, material stabilization occurs in different scientific settings or contexts – whether in a laboratory or in the field. Keyser (2017) coins the term 'intervention systems' to describe the rearrangement of causal conditions for specific *scientific purposes*. Causal conditions in a laboratory are manipulated for a purpose – e.g., to develop repeatable, reproducible, and reliable results. Sometimes these stabilized results do not exist in nature, even though it is instructive of natural processes (Keyser 2019). This kind of material stabilization can occur in field settings, too. By observing animal behavior with camera crews and drones, we may shape the very behavior that we wish to reveal.[1] Intervention systems consist of *arrangements* of material 'things'. Protocols for experimental procedure guide the re-arrangement process. Additionally, how the arrangement is manipulated and the details of scientific procedures are both dictated by the goals of the scientists – prediction, explanation, creation of technology, etc. The parallel between scientific practice and martial arts practice is striking.

A given martial art is itself an intervention system, or is reducible to multiple intervention systems. Each system contains arrangements of processes – i.e., techniques. The arrangements matter for *specific goals* of the practitioner, but also the *material context of practice*. For example, one can effectively implement bobbing and weaving head movement with a major forward tilt in a boxing match – take for instance, the seamless head movement of Dwight Muhammad Qawi.[2] Vary the boxing context slightly – where the opponent throws diagonal, upward shovel hooks, and the bobbing and weaving becomes ineffective. In fact, we see something similar in the match between Overeem and Ngannou, where ducking movement was, unfavorably, intercepted with a looping uppercut. *Vary the context* to the use of knees or front kicks to the head, such as the one used by Anderson Silva against Vitor Belfort's forward-ducking head position, and the defensive technique becomes highly ineffective. But add the effective arrangement of lateral wrestling takedowns or Muay Thai defense, and a new *interaction-effect* is stabilized. That is, each technique stabilizes with others in order to produce an effective response to a given context. Interestingly, the *range* and consistency of a technique is determined by both context and goals. For instance, head movement can be stabilized in an MMA context within three dimensions, based on evaluating multi-technique risk. Ducking and weaving are effective if used sporadically, rather than consistently, thus ensuring safety from shovel hooks, front kicks, and knees. But similarly 'pulls' – characteristic of stepping back and slightly slipping or sometimes leaning back – while effective for getting out of the way for looping punches and roundhouse and front kicks, put one's hips in a dangerous position for takedowns. In general, slips can lead one's momentum toward well-timed roundhouse-kicks, and often require an interaction with elbow covers toward the slipping direction. Imagine a *range* of techniques and their various interactions with other techniques. Now imagine that two fighters are altering their ranges by studying other fighter ranges. The range is often decided by *local material conditions* – e.g., which fighter one is facing at that time, rather than general conditions. For instance, Stipe Miocic implemented wide weaving against Frances Ngannou as a clear modification learned from the Overeem fight. This is where 'studying a fighter' amounts to co-stabilizing technique ranges between both fighters.

Experimentation, cognition, and flow 55

A given range of techniques is intertwined with important *procedural representations*. (A lab scientist is presented with a set of material things to manipulate, and a set of material procedures for *how* to manipulate.) We propose that this is why it is so difficult to learn a martial art – i.e., the complexity of material stabilization coupled with procedure – all embodied in the fighter. For instance, I can learn a punch from a YouTube tutorial – e.g., one of Elvis doing karate – by pausing the video at every frame and mimicking the body position. But I will miss key *procedural cues* that can only be applied through kinesthetic learning. For example, what is the diaphragm contraction before and after hip torque? Interestingly, depending on which martial art one practices, arrangements and procedures can vary, even for a similar technique.

Arrangements and procedures are not the full story. The second part of Keyser's (2017, 2019) 'stabilization' amounts to a co-stabilization or coherence between material practice and representation. Representations respond to material organization by adjusting representational content; and through representation, the plan to control, manipulate, and vary material components is achieved. There is a feedback loop between representation and material organization. This is where we can apply how *representational principles of a given martial art control, manipulate, and vary material organizational components*. For instance, *judokas* – i.e., practitioners of judo – develop representational stability by practicing kata. Kata are patterned forms that represent combative throws that are utilized in competition. A *judoka* will repetitively practice kata, making their performance in competition second nature. But kata are also a reflexive way for the judo community to iteratively improve an individual's practice. That is, kata are represented and evaluated by the judo community in order to intervene in an individual's practice, for the purpose of improvement. This process of iterative representation and technique manipulation allows a *judoka* to stabilize in a chaotic, competitive context. The story is similar in mixed martial arts, though the fighter might not practice movements as traditional as a *kata*. Still, it is through the habitual practice of certain movements that representations stabilize and become usable in competition. The practice of judo adds a fascinating dimension to representationally-led material stabilization – that it can be internal as well as external. That is, representational repeatability is not only to form a stable response to external chaos; it is also for the purpose of controlling inner chaos. Inner control through representation is not often discussed publicly in MMA. We discuss inner and outer control of chaos shortly, but for now it is important to note that representations determine how a fighter sees themselves. This often has to do with general representational elements from the sport itself. In judo, there is often an implicit representation of a *judoka* as born rather than made; and along with other representational elements influences fighter psychology, even in very different contexts. For example, even in a relatively egalitarian culture with progressive gender dynamics, certain traditional martial arts representational elements can be invariant even within the cultural context – e.g., those of biology and masculinity, and being a martial artist vs. becoming a martial artist (Kavoura et al. 2017). Issues of internal and external representation need more access. An interesting issue here is that self-representation amounts to representation within a larger context, where both are co-dependent – e.g., who I am as a *judoka* is determined by the evolution of judo context, and yet, judo context is at least partially produced by the sum of its physical practice. Representations, both internal and external, can *determine the dynamical movement through one's material practice.*

It is important to point out that our stabilization model has its own simplification. Because material organization is already entangled with procedural representations, this means that representational and material components are intertwined within a continuous scientific process. The idealized model helps us to understand key slices in this scientific process. For example, in a given scientific practice we can map out the precise relations between which material components produce a change in representation, and which scientific goals change how experiments and procedures are implemented. Simply, understanding the process of stabilization allows philosophers of science to track *how* a particular scientific practice is evolving in terms of material organization, procedure, greater physical context, models, and scientific and social goals. The total process of stabilization includes all of these components. Keyser (2017) describes the goal of stabilization as often reducing to repeatability, reproducibility, and reliability. But these are just some of the goals of scientific practice. In the next section, we apply the framework of stabilization to MMA practice.

Agency in stabilization

In the previous section, we described the stabilization that occurs between representation – both external and internal – and material conditions. We acknowledged the idealization of modeling this stabilization. An exact model would take into account the ontological entanglement between material conditions and representational elements. But such a model would produce vagueness and ambiguity when describing a particular adaptation in technique or evolution in martial art. However, there is a place for something like vagueness and entanglement within our account. We briefly describe a type of interaction in the martial arts, where vagueness is informative about agency. Earlier in the discussion we implicitly referred to martial artists practicing techniques or representing procedures, external circumstances, and self-images. But this is misleading because it locates the *agency* of representation, practice, and action, solely within the martial artists – while influencing conditions are external. We present a *distributed cognition* model of stabilization, where the agency is distributed throughout the total set of interactions and information that composes the greater context of martial arts practice.

Giere (2006) describes the process of science as analogous to distributed cognition. That is, multiple agents, instruments, and technology work together in order to attain knowledge. In distributed cognition, it is not accurate to say that a scientist figures something out by using an instrument or technological tool. Rather, the total system of 'interactions' produces a given epistemic goal (Giere 2006: 103). We can think of this simply as multiple system components, each with autonomous, and possibly overlapping, function, co-producing an epistemic goal. Likewise, the process of stabilization is distributed throughout material components (e.g., scientists, instruments, lab setup, etc.) and representational components (e.g., models and procedures).

This can be applied to the martial arts, generally, and MMA, in particular, in many ways. The clearest way is that a fighter's technique, effectiveness, and actions are co-produced by the team, training regimen, particular fighting organization's rules, audience, etc. Small modifications in the *total distributed system* – e.g., fighters switching organizations, changes in training teams, or altered press conference interactions – can have large impacts on a fighter's performance. This may be why consistency in regimen develops as a major background – there is the awareness that *one small detail can*

Experimentation, cognition, and flow 57

destabilize the fighter phenomenon. The model of judo is helpful here because it adds a temporal dimension to distributed cognitive practice. Not only is a fighter co-produced within dojo practice, but that fighter is also the distributed production of the surrounding community over a dynamical time scale. In other words, an individual's practice is distributed over the evolution of judo practice. This is an important epistemic lens to add to MMA. We see the strong dynamical representation of BJJ practitioners – where the focus is on tradition and lineage. But often, an MMA fighter is not discussed within the larger cultural and temporal system that co-produces them.

A more interesting way that distributed cognition can be applied to martial arts is in non-self-referential agency during a fight. In *Enter the Dragon* (1973), the famous line is '[W]hen there is an opportunity, I do not hit – it hits all by itself'. We acknowledge that doing the philosophy of martial arts is really just focusing on the finger that is pointing at the moon (Hanh 1991). Yet instead of a finger, it is a highly complex model of scientific practice. But just as in scientific classification, the qualia slip by; so, too, in analysis of technique stabilization, with a bunch of academic wordiness, we miss those mysterious components that fuel the embodied practice of martial arts. One such mysterious component corresponds exactly with what Bruce Lee was alluding to with the aforementioned quote: the 'flow state'.

Neuroscientifically, flow states are operationalized with the necessary conditions of clear goals, unambiguous and immediate feedback, and exact correspondence between skill and challenge (Mao et al. 2016). Phenomenologically, flow eliminates any friction between knowledge of technique and bodily performance, creating a sense of clarity that blends the environment with the individual's actions. Neuroscientifically, flow states result from the interaction between a developing list of components:

1 Sport-specific corticospinal commands (Cheron 2016), including karate (Moscatelli et al. 2016);
2 Excitability of primary motor cortex and supplementary motor area – with important measures of control of force and sense of effort (Toma and Lacquaniti 2016) but also potentially motor creativity (Cheron 2016);
3 The frontoparietal attention network (right lateral frontal cortex and right inferior parietal lobe) (de Sampaio Barros et al. 2018).

An important neuroscientific observation has been that the frontoparietal attention network is often 'anticorrelated' (ibid.) with the default mode network (Fox et al. 2009; Greicius et al. 2003), specifically with the dorsal MPFC, shown to be involved in self-referential tasks – i.e., explicit representations of the self (Gusnard et al. 2001). Additionally, ventral MPFC activity is reduced in the context of attention-demanding cognitive task performance (ibid.). This is interesting because the ventral MPFC is involved in processes that incorporate 'emotional-biasing signals' (or markers) into decision-making processes. These are just the starting points in evaluating self-reference and representation in flow states. But the conclusions suggest that not only is sense of self reduced in the flow state, but so is complex emotional-biasing. This might make sense of Bruce Lee's insistence that the strike hits by itself. Our interpretation here is that a *given technique is a production of the various neurophysiological flow state components, but lacks a determinate self-representational element*. To combine it with our previous statements: not only is one's effectiveness as a fighter distributed through components that are beyond our self-reference, but a given technique is delivered absent of self-reference.

To see how distribution works in practice, there is an applied martial arts concept that has at least one of its origins in Bruce Lee's Jeet Kune Do: i.e., 'interception'. Interception amounts to an instantaneous anticipation response, and requires heavy attentional access in a flow state. It also requires motor creativity. How does one 'know' when to counter a jab with a slipping lead uppercut? The question does not make sense. On the distributed cognitive model, the knowledge is distributed among the corticospinal, motor cortex, frontoparietal network, among other physiological features. *One neither knows nor acts; it acts.*

It is important to note that the modern-day 'flow state' concept has a history of thought (Krein and Ilundain 2014). In Zen Buddhism there are experiential states where the distinction between subject and object disappear (Suzuki 1976). But there is a more relevant discussion of the integration between body and mind in 'body's learning', where there is an integrated wholeness of action, which gives rise to the freedom of movement, called 'stillness in motion' (Takuan 1986). The important point is that previous philosophical traditions have characterized the distributed, yet integrated nature of movement.

Stabilization at many scales in mixed martial arts

The role of stabilization has been characterized in terms of usability. Scientists' aims determine the usability of a given stabilized system – a system stabilizes relative to the purpose of those creating the system. It has also been noted that this process of stabilization occurs contextually, and features of the context determine the sorts of systems that are stabilized. In this section, we turn our attention to MMA, utilizing the general framework of experimentation to discuss its historical and cultural development. In particular, we focus our attention on the development of MMA by observing the development of dominant MMA organizations. We demonstrate that in observing certain shifts in the material conditions of each organization, certain features of the events change to meet the desired ends of the organizations. In this way, the development of MMA is similar to that of science: material conditions are manipulated such that the developed system might satisfy the aims of those creating the system. The conditions go from unusable chaos to stabilized and coherent systems.

We begin by developing the analogy between a scientific experiment and MMA by considering the analogous elements. This involves identifying certain features of MMA that align with certain features of experimentation. We focus on those discussed in the previous sections: material conditions, representation, usability, context, and stabilization.

There are a variety of elements that constitute the set of material conditions in mixed martial arts. In the previous section, this was roughly applied to the implementation of technique and how representations change those techniques; but we need to broaden the scope to discuss MMA stabilization. We saw in the case of experimentation, that the material conditions include a given physical context (e.g., a laboratory), measurement and observation apparatus, the inferences developed by scientists, the methods and techniques of scientists, and the physical products that result in the construction of some new causal process. In MMA, we take the (non-exhaustive) list of material conditions to be:

1   The particular rule set adopted by the particular organization,
2   The permissible gear that is utilized in a particular fight,
3   The particular techniques that are deployed in a particular fight, and
4   The particular modes of spectating.

While this is obviously not a complete list, it will be sufficient for our purposes. Let us consider each individually.

The particular rule set adopted by the particular organization

Rule sets stabilize in unique ways from organization to organization. In Pancrase, the rule set stipulated that closed fist strikes and elbows to the head were impermissible, while it was also stipulated that stomps and knees on downed opponents were permissible. In Pride, however, the rule set stipulated that closed fist strikes to the head and stomps were permissible, while elbows were not. And finally, in the UFC, the rule set stipulates that stomping is impermissible, while closed fist strikes and elbows to the head are – with the exclusion of downward elbows to the top of the head (Association of Boxing Commissions and Combative Sports 2018).

Interestingly, these conditions will stabilize differences in technique implementation. For instance, the UFC's *initial* permissibility of headbutts has since transitioned – headbutts being permissible at the earliest iteration of UFC rules, while later being ruled out as impermissible. The permissibility of headbutts resulted in a counter for close-quarter Greco-Roman clinches, as well as Thai clinches. But upon a change in rules, the headbutt counter was, sometimes ineffectively, substituted for 'dirty-boxing' counters. There are various martial art forms of 'dirty boxing', one being, *panantuken*, in Filipino martial arts, introducing close-quarter combat tools like: elbows, tight hooks, and lower-level knees. We say that these counters are sometimes ineffective because it can be difficult to generate proper torque for the techniques when body control is maximized. Nonetheless, notice here that rules as boundary conditions set templates for techniques. The elimination of headbutts eliminates options for striking counters to clinches, so 'dirty-boxing' becomes a repeatable, reproducible, and, sometimes, reliable option. Nonetheless, rules set the *boundary conditions for the stabilization of general techniques*. However, this needs amending.

The malleability of rule sets creates an even more interesting scenario. In the UFC, there is currently no rule preventing side-kicks to the knees, often referred to as 'oblique' kicks. The jarring motion, stoppage, and hyperextension that this technique creates is highly dangerous – with fighters like Robert Whittaker suffering tendon injuries. The technique was rarely used, even though its popular history extends all the way to Bruce Lee's discussion of its comparability to a sticking jab – with an emphasis on its damage (*Longstreet*, 1971). But the technique is now on the rise in terms of reproducibility, often used in Jeet Kune Do's spirit of interception, and other times as a forward-shifting stomp. It is the vagueness of boundary conditions that has stabilized an effective and potentially dangerous technique. So, as the sport of MMA continues to evolve and develop, the cases of vagueness will likely stabilize into a stipulated set of determinate rules. What becomes of the 'oblique' kick remains to be seen. The following amendment, then, is sufficient: rules set the *boundary conditions for the stabilization of general techniques and these boundary conditions can be vague, creating potentially dangerous, yet effective stabilizations of borderline techniques.*

The permissible gear that is utilized in a particular fight

The specific gear that is permissible in a fight stabilizes alongside other material conditions of the fight, like the techniques that are utilized and the sorts of martial systems that can engage in the sport of MMA. This becomes evident when considering the implementation of different sets of gear across different organizations. Pancrase, for instance, did not permit the use of gloves. As we saw earlier, Pancrase also did not permit closed hand strikes to the head. It is unclear which came first, the (im)permissibility of gloves or the (im)permissibility of closed hand strikes to the head. However, whichever came first, the two stabilized together. In ruling out gloves, closed fist strikes to the head would reasonably be disallowed, for concerns over fighter safety and fight longevity. A slight tilt of the head to meet the oncoming punch can absolutely devastate a bare hand. Risk of injury would then be high, and the longevity of fights would be compromised. Likewise, if closed fist strikes to the head were ruled out before a decision was to be made around the (im)permissibility of gear, then the decision would come quite easily. If closed fist strikes to the head are not permissible, then no gloves would be *necessary*.

Of course, decisions around what gear is permissible also influences the sorts of martial systems that can engage in MMA. In disallowing gloves, Pancrase did not encourage traditional boxing systems to engage in MMA – it actually limited the degree to which mixed martial arts was truly *mixed*. So, the (im)permissibility of *gear determines the scope of inclusivity in* mixing *martial arts*. Later iterations of MMA organizations, like Pride and the UFC, permitted the use of gloves. And since then, boxing, kickboxing, and Muay Thai have become something of essential elements to the toolkit of an MMA fighter.

The particular techniques that are deployed in a particular fight

In a chaotic context, like a fight, deployable techniques stabilize with each other. Consider again how the *judoka* trains in kata for stabilization in competitive contexts. In training kata, the *judoka* internalizes and memorizes certain cues and movements. Thus, when a competitor transitions from kata to *randori* – i.e., live sparring – or from *randori* to competition, the *judoka* has internalized possible responses to certain movements of their opponent. The pull on the gi's sleeve, or the shifting of the opponent's hip can be felt in a *randori* session or competition, and it instinctively elicits particular reactions that have been internalized through repetitions of kata. Of course, feeling an opponent's style in the context of *randori* or competition is significantly different from feeling a partner's static movements in kata. Nonetheless, in internalizing kata, the *judoka* internalizes specific techniques in response to specific opposing movements. Some techniques are suitable as responses to particular movements of the opponent. So, the movements of the two *judoka* in a competitive context stabilize *together*. For (an albeit grossly oversimplified) example, let us say that a person x and a person y are both *judoka* that practice kata. X practices techniques a and c, and c is particularly useful in countering technique b. Y practices technique b, as b is particularly useful in countering technique a. When the two compete, the deployment of their techniques *stabilize*. Technique a from competitor x elicits response b from competitor y, which in turn elicits response c from competitor x, and so on. We thus maintain that ce*rtain movements and techniques in live, competitive judo stabilize together*. The same is true for MMA.

In consistently training particular techniques, an MMA fighter internalizes the movements for use in a chaotic context. In practicing certain boxing combinations, wrestling offense and defense, and grappling techniques, along with repetitively training cage awareness, and the angles of squaring off with an opponent, the deployable techniques between two fighters *stabilize relative to one another*. This is ultimately what makes MMA so particularly interesting. The scope of possible techniques is wide. So, any two fighters, and the techniques that they deploy, stabilize uniquely.

Competing in judo and competing in MMA have relevant differences in methodology. In judo, one needs either an *ippon* (full-point), two *waza-ri* (half-points), or to submit or pin the opponent during *ne waza* (ground grappling) to win the match. There are a limited number of ways to achieve these ends. However, in MMA, the competitive context is more fluid and complex. One can win via decision, knockout, submission, or through penalties. And the means to which any of these forms of victory can come vary widely, largely depending on one's ability to dominate and control the style of their opponent. For instance, one fighter may specialize predominantly in grappling, while the other could specialize in a whole variety of similar or different styles. They could specialize in boxing, kickboxing, various styles of grappling or wrestling, or some unique blend between some or all of these modes of combat. Whereas in judo both competitors have relatively similar means (i.e., throw, submit, or pin the opponent), MMA competitors have to not only dominantly express their particular mix of martial arts, but also do so relative to the unique blend of martial arts represented in their opponents.

This is why training camps are so particularly relevant. The representation that a given fighter develops (along with their team) of their opponent during training camp either does or does not stabilize the techniques deployed relative to their opponent. The fundamental point here is simple. But it becomes more nuanced: *representation in training camp determines the set of techniques that stabilize in a fight*. Tony Ferguson, for instance, would model his training camp for a fight against Khabib Nurmagomedov significantly differently than he would a training camp for a fight against Justin Gaethje. And in so doing, Ferguson would be internally stabilizing a set of techniques that might be effective against Khabib's particular style, but not Gaethje's. *Both fighters represent their opponents in some way that determines the set of techniques that stabilize in the fight*. And while this principle applies to combat sports other than MMA, like boxing, kickboxing, wrestling, or judo, MMA has a significantly wider range of possible ways for the set of techniques to stabilize. These representations can be more or less accurate, and are temporally extended, insofar as fighters develop and change. So, when two fighters enter the octagon, they are (at least partly) testing whether the given representations that they have internally developed of their opponent, and the particular responses they developed relative to those representations, stabilize in a more chaotic context. If they do not, then they will likely be dominated (unless they are particularly strong at improvising); if they do, then they stand a better chance in the fight. So, an MMA fight ultimately *involves the realization and stabilization of certain internal representational content developed through extensive training and visualization*.

The particular modes of spectating

Spectating is a central aspect of the process of stabilizing other material conditions, like rule sets. This is particularly evident when considering the sort of usability that MMA organizations seek for their events – viz, profit. So, rule sets and other material conditions need to stabilize in a way that maximizes those ends. Also, different modes of spectating stabilize the ethical representational content of the spectator. This is clear in the recent UFC events during the COVID-19 pandemic. The more intimate atmosphere, where each strike lands with audible thuds as the respective corners yell instructions, yields different ethical representational content than the usual crowd filled arenas. Let us handle these two theses separately.

Excitement, safety, and stabilization

A given experiment is deemed successful if and only if the experiment stabilizes in the correct terms of usability. This is also the case in MMA. For MMA organizations, like Pancrase, Pride, and the UFC, the success of a particular event is evaluated (at least partly) in terms of profit margins. So, these organizations seek to establish a certain sort of stabilization in the material conditions that results in positive-economic value. Interestingly, the economic conditions can depend on factors that have ranges of uncertainty. This is similar to Keyser's (2017) discussion of uncertainty ranges in scientific measurement outcomes. That is, over a series of experiments, instead of an accurate and precise value, small variations in experimental conditions will produce variable measurement outcomes. So, the scientist is left with a range of uncertainty for a given phenomenon. In scientific practice, these ranges are difficult to track and control because they depend on arrangements, not only in relevant variables, but also in countless other uncontrollable variables. Economic value can depend on a multitude of uncertainty ranges. For example, fan excitement over a series of fights can produce an uncertainty range. That is, it is not clear how dynamics of fan excitement change with small changes in conditions. Fan excitement might or might not be fueled by an absurd press event. But something that seemingly should produce an increase in fan excitement, does not. For example, a fight that is not based in trash-talking or absurdity, but only in pure technique might not generate as much excitement. Excitement is also evaluated as a *contrast between prospective excitement and retrospective evaluation*. Adesanya vs. Romero, for some fans, had such a pattern: prospective excitement and retrospective disappointment. This contrast or discrepancy can be damaging to the anticipation of future cards.

Of course, another element that goes into the evaluation of an event is the degree to which the fighters are kept safe. This is connected to the previous point about excitement. The fights need to be exciting, in that the fighters cannot *not* be at risk, but the fighters also should not *really* be at risk. MMA is not truly gladiatorial – nobody seeks the serious injury or death of an opponent. The financial or economic usability of MMA events indeed depends (in part) on the repeatability of those events. And if the fighters were to be disposable, insofar as they were not kept safe, then that repeatability would ultimately be undermined. Here, there is a fascinating intersection between scientific representations and a given philosophy of sport. Recent discussion of CTE in the popular spotlight has had the effect of fighters speaking out about the phenomenon – e.g., Georges St-Pierre (Willis 2017). This public discussion is influencing the representation of what it means to be an MMA athlete or a martial artist. Specifically, the representational focus is on repeatability of fighting as 'health', and repeated destruction as the opposite. Of course, the nature of the sport is dangerous, and accidents certainly do happen, just as they do in any other sport. However, the representational push seems to be that of a new perspective on health and recovery.

Experimentation, cognition, and flow   63

Ethical representation of MMA during the COVID-19 pandemic

There has recently been a major shift in the spectatorship of UFC events. In the wake of COVID-19, the entire sporting calendar received a shock, and virtually all sporting events were cancelled. The first sporting organization to re-emerge in the context of the pandemic was the UFC, which put on a number of spectator-less events with remarkable success, in terms of exposure to the virus. Nonetheless, the representational content of the spectator has changed, though perhaps to an indeterminate degree. In this subsection, we will look more closely at the effects of going spectator-less.

In the previous section, we considered the remarkable balance that MMA organizations have to strike between excitement and safety. The fights need to be exciting; however, also safe. Here, we first consider the excitement component, then consider how the representation of the safety of the fighters has shifted in the context of the pandemic, concluding that ethical representations and judgements stabilize uniquely in varying contexts of spectating.

If a cage match happens and no one is there to see it, is it exciting? The current pandemic situation has produced an unusual contextual effect – i.e., no attendees during fights. Initially, it might seem like this has no impact on the general phenomenon of excitement – promotional videos and backstories are still just as high-quality and the fights themselves have no noticeable difference, in terms of athletic performance. But there is something unusually eerie about the contrast. It might even be that the emptiness of the arena is not the context that spoils excitement, but rather it is the overall physical context of the pandemic. The future of the pandemic might create new contexts that stabilize new norms for fan excitement. For our purposes, it is interesting to consider that the material conditions of a given fight, and how one evaluates a given fight are at least partially determined by slippery uncertainty ranges like that of fan excitement. Without the fans present, it becomes unclear, socially, how exciting the fight truly is. Moving forward, MMA organizations like the UFC will continue to experiment and seek stability for their desired ends.

It is not only the excitement of events that is affected by the absence of spectators in the pandemic, but also the way in which fights are ethically represented by the remote spectators. We maintain that watching an MMA fight can, and often does, involve ethical representations and judgements, and these representations and judgements are affected by certain modes of spectating.

The results of fights – especially when they are decisions – can often be described in terms of fairness. If a fighter was represented by fans as clearly dominating, yet they lose, the fans represent the result as 'unfair', or perhaps even 'unjust'. This is an ethical representation. Ethical representation and judgement also enters into spectatorship around particular behaviors of the athletes – both in and outside of the cage. Inside, fighters can garner questionable reputation for regular sketchy behavior, like eye pokes and brushes; outside, fighters can often develop representations as ethically questionable characters. How does this connect with the pandemic? First, there is the obvious possible ethical judgement or representation of the UFC storming ahead and hosting events, which obviously depends on a whole host of other representational judgements that one has made (e.g., the degree to which the virus is a threat).

But this is quite a broad example. What about the *act* of spectating? How can ethical judgements play *into* spectating MMA during the pandemic? Consider Anthony

Smith's fight against Glover Teixeira, which occurred toward the beginning of the UFC COVID reboot. The fight was brutal. Smith was largely dominated for the entire time, and suffered immense damage throughout. At one point, Smith crouched over and picked something up off of the canvas, handing it to the referee – his teeth. Even still, Smith's corner did not throw in the towel, nor did the referee make a stoppage. Following the event, multiple commentators questioned the ethics of the fight. Who was to *blame* for the excessive brutality? What is presupposed within this sort of question is an *ethical representation of the fight*. When we spectate fights, we can often develop ethical representations, and can judge whether the fight is ethical or not. In the cases of fights in front of live audiences, spectators have a way to voice their ethical concerns. They can shout and chant for the referee or corner to end the fight. However, in the case of spectator-less fights, no such voice is possessed by the spectator. The distinction between live spectatorship vs. observation at home is interesting. At home, the audience can either continue watching or choose to turn the fight off. We make no argument over what one should do. We only note that spectating can involve an ethical representation, and the judgement that goes along with it is influenced by the context of spectatorship – in this case the remoteness of spectating. Nonetheless, it is clear that *ethical representation and judgement does stabilize uniquely within varying contexts of spectating.*

Conclusion

We have here argued for an extended analogy between the development and nature of mixed martial arts and certain features of scientific experimentation. First, we developed Keyer's (2017, 2019) account of epistemic stabilization. We then argued that the process of stabilization in martial arts influences the agency of the martial artist. In stabilizing, the martial artist stabilizes a technique for possible deployment in a chaotic environment. Finally, we explored a variety of ways in which the sport of MMA stabilizes. We argued that stabilization occurs within at least four components of mixed martial arts: the adopted rule set, the permissibility of certain gear, the particular techniques that are deployed, and the representational content of both fighters and spectators.

Notes

1 The more extreme example is how material conditions of captivity reshape animal behavior. For an unusual example see 'Gray Parrots Separated at Zoo After Swearing a Blue Streak' (2020).
2 For reference: 'Evander Holyfield Misses About 10 Consecutive Punches vs Muhammad Qawi' (2015).

References

Association of Boxing Commissions and Combative Sports (2018) 'Unified Rules of Mixed Martial Arts', https://www.dli.mn.gov/sites/default/files/pdf/official_unified_rules_MMA.pdf, accessed 2 October 2020.
Cheron, G. (2016) 'How to Measure the Psychological "Flow"? A Neuroscience Perspective', *Frontiers in Psychology*, 7: 1823.
de Sampaio Barros, M. F., Araújo-Moreira, F. M., Trevelin, L. C., and Radel, R. (2018) 'Flow Experience and the Mobilization of Attentional Resources', *Cognitive, Affective, & Behavioral Neuroscience*, 18(4): 810–823.

'Evander Holyfield Misses About 10 Consecutive Punches vs Muhammad Qawi' (2015) YouTube, 16 October, https://youtu.be/OgH6WyIUlMQ?t=4, accessed 2 October 2020.

Fox, M. D., Zhang, D., Snyder, A. Z., and Raichle, M. E. (2009) 'The Global Signal and Observed Anticorrelated Resting State Brain Networks', *Journal of Neurophysiology*, 101(6), 3270–3283.

Giere, R. N. (2006) *Scientific Perspectivism*. Chicago: University of Chicago Press.

'Gray Parrots Separated at Zoo After Swearing a Blue Streak' (2020) *Associated Press*, 30 September, https://apnews.com/article/wildlife-archive-b13335d5e7af11ef9afbbab0382d8fc2, accessed 2 October 2020.

Greicius, M. D., Krasnow, B., Reiss, A. L., and Menon, V. (2003) 'Functional Connectivity in the Resting Brain: A Network Analysis of the Default Mode Hypothesis', *Proceedings of the National Academy of Sciences*, 100(1): 253–258.

Gusnard, D. A., Akbudak, E., Shulman, G. L., and Raichle, M. E. (2001) 'Medial Prefrontal Cortex and Self-Referential Mental Activity: Relation to a Default Mode of Brain Function', *Proceedings of the National Academy of Sciences*, 98(7): 4259.

Hanh, T. N. (1991) *Old Path White Clouds: Walking in the Footsteps of the Buddha*, Berkeley: Parallax Press.

Kavoura, A., Kokkonen, M., Chroni, S. 'A.', and Ryba, T. (2017) ' "Some Women Are Born Fighters": Discursive Constructions of a Fighter's Identity by Female Finnish Judo Athletes', *Sex Roles*, 79 (3–4), 239–252.

Keyser, V. (2017) 'Experimental Effects and Causal Representations', *Synthese*, Special Issue: Models and Representation, 1–32.

Keyser, V. (2019) 'Artifacts and Artefacts: A Methodological Classification of Context-Specific Regularities', in J. R. S. Bursten (ed.) *Perspectives on Classification in Synthetic Sciences: Unnatural Kinds*, New York: Routledge, pp. 63–77.

Krein, K. and Ilundain, J. (2014) 'Mushin and Flow: An East-West Comparative Analysis', in G. Priest and D. Young (eds.) *Philosophy and the Martial Arts: Engagement*, New York: Routledge, pp. 139–164.

Mair, V. (trans.) (1990) *Tao Te Ching: The Classic Book of Integrity and the Way*, New York: Bantam Books.

Mao, Y., Roberts, S., Pagliaro, S., Csikszentmihalyi, M., and Bonaiuto, M. (2016) 'Optimal Experience and Optimal Identity: A Multinational Study of the Associations Between Flow and Social Identity', *Frontiers in Psychology*, 7: 67.

Moscatelli, F., Messina, G., Valenzano, A., Monda, V., Viggiano, A., Messina, A., Petito, A., Triggiani, A. I., Ciliberti, M. A., Monda, M., Capranica, L., and Cibelli, G. (2016) 'Functional Assessment of Corticospinal System Excitability in Karate Athletes', *PLOS ONE*, 11 (5), e0155998.

Takuan S. (1986) *The Unfettered Mind: Writings of the Zen Master to the Sword Master*, W. S. Wilson (trans.), New York: Kodansha International.

Toma, S., and Lacquaniti, F. (2016) 'Mapping Muscles Activation to Force Perception during Unloading', *PLOS ONE*, 11(3), e0152552.

Suzuki, D. T. (1976) *Essays in Zen Buddhism* (2nd Series), New York: Samuel Weiser.

Willis, O. (2017), 'Georges St-Pierre on CTE: Some Fighters Started the Same Time as Me, and They Aren't the Same', *The Mac Life*, 26 October, https://themaclife.com/featured-posts/georges-st-pierre-on-cte/, accessed 2 October 2020.

6 Finding beauty in the cage
A utility-based aesthetic for MMA

Tszki Chow

The aesthetic categories of movement that interest us in combat sport might include strength, speed, power, efficacy, and so on, and their corresponding forms of beauty (e.g., grace and dramatic elements) may vary between categories. It is true that the functional qualities of movement have drawn philosophers' attention, due to the fact that much athletic movement is supposed to be purposive. However, the concept of utility, which is also an aspect of functionality, is seldom considered as an aesthetic category or a form of beauty in philosophy of sport, although it has been discussed for a long time in many other philosophical areas. My main questions in this chapter are that of whether the theory of utility may give us some insights into an aesthetics of MMA and that of whether utility of purposive technique as such can be aesthetically appealing in an MMA setting.[1]

In my experience, there were indeed occasions in which I, as an elite sabre fencer, was affected aesthetically merely by the practical and beneficial use of technique by my opponent. For example, in one match, my opponent and I both advanced quickly towards each other. At the last moment of her full lunge, I went to her right-hand side and took her blade with a tierce parry (she was right-handed). The distance was so close, and the move was so quick that I was sure I would take the touch. During my riposte, however, she suddenly squatted down (which is not a usual move in sabre fencing) and took my blade with a quinte. I could not react and she got the point by her counter-parry riposte. After this touch she led 14:13 and needed only one more point to end the match. Despite the points being so close that I should have been nervous and angry, I found her technique gorgeous and could not help but give her a hug. My first and immediate impression had been of the beautiful use of the move. The feeling of beauty even overwhelmed my will to win. Besides this, I have had similar experiences when watching other bouts. I have taken aesthetic pleasure from some ordinary or even ugly techniques just because of how well they worked, whereas some good-looking techniques did not interest me.[2]

Admittedly, one of the main factors in me experiencing the above aesthetic appreciation is that I am a fencer. I know well what is going on on the piste and I understand the rationale behind the techniques. I am able to judge whether a technique is useful or not. On this account, judgments of utility require the use of our faculty of reasoning and corresponding knowledge, which is also, I claim, the case for viewing utility as aesthetically pleasing. The more one knows about the setting of a sport, the more one takes pleasure in its movements. The use of a movement in combat sport can be attractive in itself. It may, for example, give us aesthetic pleasure to witness a successful technique when its completion rate is relatively low, due to the uncertainties

DOI: 10.4324/9781003122395-7

about things like the rival's movements and reactions. The uncertainty rate varies between types of sports, as does the completion rate. For instance, a running technique seems to be easier to be completed or successfully performed in a race compared to an MMA striking technique with a combination of punches, kicks, and elbows. It does not mean that the running technique is easier, but rather that there are more factors in an MMA bout which influence the use of any given technique. A technique is useful only if it can be first completely performed. The use of technique seems to be more difficult in MMA, which has relatively fewer constraints on skills, than it is in other more restrictive combat sports, such as judo or karate.

In this chapter, I am going to show on what basis utility of technique can be aesthetically appealing. The first three sections will serve as preliminaries for the analysis. In the first section, an overview of the discussions in aesthetics about utility and its alleged antithesis, disinterestedness, will be presented. We will see that the view of aesthetic experience as disinterested trivializes the aesthetic value of sport as such. In the second section, I am going to examine Hume's theory of utility and address some counterarguments. The third section will show that the objects of aesthetic appeal related to functional qualities are movement and performance. Having settled the foundation, the analysis will proceed according to three questions: (1) What does the utility of technique actually mean in MMA? (2) In which way is utility perceptible in the game? (3) How is utility (a non-aesthetic value) 'translated' into beauty (an aesthetic value)?

Utility and disinterestedness in aesthetics

The concept of utility in ancient Greek was originally related to the concept of good in the non-moral sense. An object is good if it contains material or spiritual values. For example, a useful object, a desired goal, a virtue, and an ability are all good. A person can also be signified as good according to their performance, ability, or works. A warrior who has killed a lot of enemies in war is thus considered to be good, as they are useful. From this view, utility as such pleases us naturally. However, the concept of good gained a new meaning under the influence of philosophy following Greek antiquity. The term 'good' has thus turned ethical and aesthetic, where good, moral, and beautiful were originally often considered to be one. Consequently, utility parted with the concept of good and its implication of beauty.

Plato locates the source of good and beauty in a metaphysical reality, whereas Aristotle, who agreed with Plato in claiming that an object's form causes its beauty, denied the existence of that form in some other realm. For both of them, an aesthetic experience arises from a kind of contemplation of the form in different contexts. The functional quality plays no significant role in aesthetics. In the middle ages, philosophers introduced the ideas of proportion, light, color, and symbolism to address the question of beauty. Plato and Aristotle certainly had a great influence on the views of those philosophers, but the discussion of beauty shifted from a mere aesthetic issue into a matter of religion. Augustine of Hippo and Pseudo-Dionysus the Areopagite considered platonic ideas to be the ideas in God's mind, which meant that all beautiful things participate in the beauty of God, who Himself is the origin of the beautiful. In contrast, Thomas Aquinas conformed to Aristotle's ideas and argued that we take aesthetic pleasure through the activity of contemplation of an object's form as it exists in the empirical world.

In the subsequent development of the term 'aesthetics', it became more important than the term 'beauty'. A lot of new aesthetic notions, such as grace, taste, and the sublime, were coined in that period. One of the most popular notions then to emerge is that of disinterestedness,[3] which denotes originally the attitude of non-egoistic ethics – i.e., a moral act is an act that does not involve self-love or any selfish motivation – and non-instrumentalist theology – i.e., God should not be the means for satisfying human needs. Anthony Ashley Cooper, 3rd Earl of Shaftesbury, is the first philosopher who brought this terminology into the field of aesthetics. According to him, judgments of beauty, moral good, and divinity are all made by a special faculty, the faculty of taste. For him aesthetic contemplation is an objective contemplation of the (platonic) form of beauty which is God Himself. Such contemplation is free from empirical subjectivity and hence also free from any self-interest. Francis Hutcheson also believed that perception of beauty, just like perception of moral good, does not involve any personal advantage. For him one immediately feels if an act is morally good or if an object is beautiful, no matter whether this act or this object is beneficial for oneself. According to Edmund Burke, beauty is independent from the ideas of proportion, fitness, and perfection. On this account, aesthetic appreciation is absolutely disinterested; it does not require any perception of utility of the object. Besides that, the aesthetic principle of disinterestedness was also supported by some German philosophers, notably Kant, Schopenhauer, and the early Nietzsche. Briefly speaking, the source of aesthetic experience should not involve any egoistic interest or personal will – for Nietzsche, the distinction between subject and object in aesthetic reality had fallen away completely – and the ground for aesthetics is taken to be absolutely independent from any functionality-aspect. Accordingly, aesthetic value is an intrinsic quality of the observed object or the immediate, unconditional, independent perception of that object itself.

This view has been also adopted in philosophy of sport. For example, Mumford (2013) differentiates between partisan and purist ways of watching sport. According to him, the partisan way is a common but basically non-aesthetic way of watching sport, in which the spectators are looking for victory of their favored team. In contrast, a purist is indifferent to which side attains victory and thus 'watches sport for its own sake' and 'takes pleasure in seeing the sport played well' – which is the aesthetic way of experiencing sports (ibid.: 7). The former can be seen as being in a state of self-interest and the latter in a disinterested state.

Despite their disinterested attitude, Mumford tries to establish victory as a necessary condition for the aesthetic feature that purists admire in sport. His argument is grounded in the hypothesis that humans invent sport for the purpose of providing themselves with better aesthetic experiences of movement – for instance, running fast is aesthetically appealing. In order to see someone run fast, people set up contests, and to push athletes to run faster, they set up more rules and obstacles (ibid.: 8–9). In trying to attribute intrinsic value to the game itself, Mumford has, instead, effectively marginalized if not abolished its value altogether. Having gained an intrinsic value, the game is not just a game having the purpose of victory, but becomes valued merely as a performance, like a drama, indeed an artwork. Is it still sport? It is hard to tell. But there is no doubt that Mumford's purist's way of watching sport threatens to trivialize the aesthetic value of sport as such. For, if this way of watching sport is in reality even possible, his purist can potentially see any movement as aesthetically appealing, regardless of whether the perceived object is sport or not. On top of that, it also undermines the purposiveness of technique in the game: MMA fighters are neither just fighting in the game, nor are they merely striving to be the strongest, but they are fighting *for* victory – notice that to be the strongest fighter does not necessarily lead to gaining the victory.

The theory of utility and its counterarguments in aesthetics

In contrast to the theory of disinterestedness, the aesthetic theory of utility claims that an object's appearing fit for its assumed purpose may cause aesthetic pleasure.[4] On this account, perception of beauty is dependent on perception of the object's practical and beneficial use for a specific purpose. David Hume is one of the most important philosophers who clearly defends this idea.[5] For him, it is not our reasoning but our faculty of taste that tells us what is beautiful and what is virtuous by giving us 'the sentiment of beauty and deformity, vice and virtue' (Hume 1988: 294): beauty and virtue give us delight and satisfaction, ugliness and vice give us pain and uneasiness. On this account, moral and aesthetic sentiments are both generated by the taste which we have learned from our experience. Regarding beauty,

> if we consider, that a great part of the beauty, which we admire either in animals or in other objects, is deriv'd from the idea of convenience and utility, we shall make no scruple to assent to this opinion. That shape, which produces strength, is beautiful in one animal; and that which is a sign of agility in another. The order and convenience of a palace are no less essential to its beauty, than its mere figure and appearance [...] From innumerable instances of this kind, as well as from considering that beauty like wit, cannot be defin'd, but is discern'd only by a taste or sensation, we may conclude, that beauty is nothing but a form, which produces pleasure, as deformity is a structure of parts, which conveys pain [...].
> (Hume 1960: 299)

In addition, he defines usefulness as 'a tendency to a certain end; and it is a contradiction in terms, that anything pleases as means to an end, where the end itself no wise affects us' (Hume 1988: 219). It follows that one is only pleased by a means if its end interests one. The interest here is neither self-love nor self-interest, but rather an interest in others. That is to say, if I find a quality of a person appealing (it conveys the idea of easiness to me), it is because I am interested in its great use for the happiness of society and the wellbeing of its members, due to my 'sympathy' (ibid.: 221). In this context, usefulness is no longer considered with reference to the self, but to others. This pleasure, as it is generated by the faculty of taste, has also aesthetic implications.

One may immediately have doubts about the dependence of beauty on usefulness, as a lot of things that appear to be useful are not aesthetically appealing. For example, my computer, which I am now using to write this chapter, is not appealing to me. Likewise, some beautiful things have no specific purpose and thus no utility, as for example *The Last Supper* by Leonardo Da Vinci.[6] To these questions, Hume did try to give an answer. According to him, both the utility of an inanimate object and the utility of a person pleases us, but the sentiments directed to them differ in strength. The beneficial qualities of an object are essentially based on its fitness for its assumed purpose and those of a person (their 'social virtue') are based on usefulness to the public. The sentiment directed to social virtues is mixed with 'affection, esteem, approbation, &c.'

(Hume 1988: 213), whereas the sentiment directed to the object's fitness is much weaker. Therefore, social virtues have 'a natural beauty and amiableness' and must 'take hold of some natural affection' (ibid.: 214). According to this view, I find my computer not aesthetically appealing because my sentiment directed to its utility is too weak. Although it does please me, that pleasure is not sufficient to cause in me strong aesthetic appreciation. Similarly, Hume might argue that the form of *The Last Supper*, including the use of figures and the combination of colors, convey the ideas of warmth and comfort, for instance, which strongly pleases me (though this pleasure is still weaker than that of a social virtue). I grant that Hume's account leads to other theoretical problems, which, however, will not be discussed here.

Utility of technique: movement and performance as objects of beauty

A (physical) technique can be a single movement or a series of movements. No matter how simple the technique is, it is the result of the cooperation of different body parts and is constrained by rules and setting. Movements or techniques can thus be examined from different aspects, such as the body and conventions, to name two examples. Jason Holt's (2020) five-level analysis provides a framework for the analysis of movement in sport aesthetics.[7] According to his framework, the analysis of utility of technique seemingly belongs to the second and the third analysis levels, which he calls the levels of movement and performance respectively. At the second level, the object of beauty is sporting movement. The analysis of movement usually needs to provide some conditions to constrain the ways of performing the movement so that it is aesthetically appealing. For, as Holt points out, movement itself is not sufficient for aesthetic appreciation. In other words, the aesthetic property, say grace, is dependent on other properties, such as precision – a *precise* movement may be *graceful* in part because of its precision. At the third level, the object of analysis is performance that comprises movements. The concept of performance thus represents a collective view of different individual movements, whose aesthetic appeal is hidden behind the unity of movement, since '[t]he beauty of a sport performance or an artwork can reside in how it all comes together, in how it just jells' (ibid.: 9). That is, aesthetic appeal is dependent on what the movements as a whole present to us. Just like, at the second level, a movement itself may not be sufficient for aesthetic appeal (grace) without another condition being met (precision), a sheer achievement of performance is hardly beautiful without further necessary conditions – not just any performance is beautiful, but a *difficult* performance, say, can be. To understand the achievement of performance and its realizing conditions is to understand the same setting and the rules that constrain athletes' behaviors. For this reason, knowledge is often required as a basis for aesthetic judgment.

It is clear that utility should be analyzed at the level of movement and performance, but it is still unclear if there is any immediate relation between functional and aesthetic qualities. Barry Allen (2013) tries to show a possible relation between effectiveness of movement and aesthetic qualities in martial arts. MMA and other martial arts are certainly different, but his explanation of the dependence of aesthetics on effectiveness in martial arts gives us some insight into the question about how these two properties may correlate with each other in MMA. For Allen, sport and martial arts movements are both expressly purposive. The former expresses the intention to win, the latter the intention of violence. For this reason, their beauty in both cases is dependent, which means the main aim of the movements is competitive effectiveness, not beauty. Allen believes that the 'aesthetic quality of martial arts movements comes from their purposiveness, their instrumental effectiveness. Aesthetic quality is a by-product of real efficacy' (ibid.: 250) The validity of this thesis depends on the assumption that intentionality and effectiveness (as well as adequacy) are all being expressed – and hence perceivable – in movements, and their expression makes those movements aesthetic appealing. He also adds one more property, namely the eloquence of movement, to the aesthetic appeal of martial arts, arguing that 'true speed and power come with eloquence, when the many movements become one beat, one corporeal melody beautifully performed – if, that is, something so violent can be beautiful at all' (ibid.: 251). It follows that efficacy comprises intentionality, effectiveness, and eloquence, which are all necessary – perhaps even sufficient – for the aesthetic appeal in martial arts.

Allen makes the interesting further point that in martial arts, beauty is based on the expression of its external, instrumental value (violence). But how important is the role of intentionality, which at the same time implies purposiveness, in his framework? First of all, Allen's use of the term 'intentionality' is vague. It seems it has nothing to do with consciousness, nor does it refer to the intention of the agent (in the traditional sense of the theory of agency by, for example, Donald Davidson), which makes an action intentional and also makes the movement ascribed to the agent their action, but it indicates a kind of intention of the movement pattern in itself or intention of the body itself. Is such an intention an intention at all? What contents of the state of intention make the intention expressive, if the state is unconscious? If all bodily movements can simply be ascribed to an agent as their intentional actions, we will see that we cannot distinguish what they intend to do from what they do but do not intend to do. For instance, suppose an MMA fighter is off balance and instinctively extends their arm to steady themselves and thereby knocks down the opponent. Is this an intentional action and is this *his* intentional action? In this example, it appears that, if anything does, the agent does not intend to knock down the opponent and thus it is hard to see this movement as their intentional action (it can be their action though). Setting aside these theoretical problems, we still encounter a crucial problem: is an observer able to perceive the difference between an action of unconscious competence (i.e., an eloquent action) and an action of conscious competence, so that they are pleased by the former but not, or not in the same way, the latter? Allen's framework seems to set the content of an unconscious mental state as perceivable from a third-person perspective. But obviously we do not perceive unconscious (or even conscious) mental states of another person. Assuming that a person lifts up their hand, can we tell whether they did it with or without consciousness? My point is that the qualitative difference between a conscious act and an unconscious act is not obvious enough to mark their difference in appearance. Lastly, it is true that effectiveness is comparable to the concept of utility, but, in my opinion, it fails to emphasize the aspect of particularity as utility does – this point will be discussed in the following section. In other words, effectiveness only shows the functional aspect of an object *itself*, but lacks the aspect of being *for* someone.

In contrast to Allen, Cordner (1984) argues against considering functionality (mainly efficiency) as a sufficient source of aesthetic value (grace). He gives different examples to show that there is no dependence between grace and functionality. Finally, he proposes a theory of harmony and unity of being, and concludes

[t]he mistake of that functionalist view was to suppose that those elements of a display could be isolated as constituting the content of a judgment of grace. When we register a display as graceful, those elements, if present, are absorbed into a total harmony of being, the perceptual criteria of which are the effortlessness and easiness of the display.

(Cordner 1984: 311–12)

First of all, the purpose of this chapter is neither to argue that utility is sufficient for grace, nor to prove that the only type of aesthetic property in sport is grace, but rather to provide another view on the functional aspect in sport aesthetics and provide an explanation for some specific phenomena in our sport experience. The theory of utility suggests that utility itself may be aesthetically appealing for the observer and thus constitute already a form of beauty in sport, provided that the observer in question has sufficient knowledge about the sport setting.

Utility as fitness and usefulness: grounding aesthetic interest in MMA

The concept of utility can be generally divided into two functional concepts: fitness and usefulness. To say that something is fit means that it seems to have some qualities which make that thing fit for its assumed purpose. Take a tent which is made for extreme weather and is heavier and has more tent poles and stakes, which give it more resistance against high wind; this tent seems to be fit for its purpose. However, usefulness is different from fitness, as there is something which is fit for its assumed purpose but not useful for its user. The tent made for extreme weather appears to be fit for its purpose, but it can be useless for its user, when, for example, the tent is too heavy for them, of if they never go camping in extreme weather. Contrarily, a lighter tent, which is also intended for extreme weather but is perhaps less fit for that purpose, can be useful for someone just because it is lighter. In this case, the light tent may not be fit for its purpose but may still be useful for its owner in a different context. Therefore, being useful and being fit are two radically different concepts. When an object is held to be useful, it is held to be useful *for* someone; but when we say that an object is fit (for its purpose), its possessor and the particular context may be irrelevant.

In addition, the concept of fitness is more general in terms of its abstraction from concrete context, for the fitness of an object can be tested against objective criteria, regardless of any particularities and individualities. An FIE (*Fédération Internationale d'Escrime*) sabre fencing mask, for instance, can be tested in industry (or in weapon control before fencing starts) in accordance with some general measurements (1600N resistance, level of electric conductivity, etc.). If it passes all tests, it will get the quality stamp that means it is fit to be used by any sabre fencer in any FIE competition. By contrast, usefulness is a concept which refers to a particular individual with particular intentions in a particular context (the qualified sabre mask is useless for an MMA fighter in their sport).

The utility of an MMA technique can be evaluated through these two aspects correspondingly. All techniques, such as punches and kicks, are developed as means for the purpose of defeating the rival. Can the fitness of a given technique be tested regardless of particular context, just like the sabre mask in the industry? It seems it can, or as least it seems that we assume it can. Unless the MMA fighters accept the general fitness of some techniques, they will not repeatedly learn and practice them in training. A particular combination of movements is chosen exactly due to the assumption that this combination is fit for defeating one's rival. On this account, all techniques, especially those which are generally practiced, turn out to be fit in themselves. In other words, the concept of technique implies the concept of fitness. However, if all techniques are supposed to be fit in themselves, fitness has no more bearing on their aesthetic effect, as the techniques which cause and those which do not cause our aesthetic appreciation are both fit. For these reasons, the quality of being fit to its assumed purpose cannot be the sufficient determinant of the utility-based aesthetic for MMA. In spite of that, this aspect cannot be simply ignored, as it, especially as a tendency to an end, forms the general purposive character of the technique, which usefulness may not.

In contrast, usefulness can only be judged as it is actualized in a particular context, and it depends on numerous variables, for example on the abilities of the agent performing the technique and the abilities of another participant on whom it takes effect. Grappling techniques seem less useful for a proficient MMA striker to fight against a good MMA grappler, but the same grappling technique can be useful for the grappler or for a striker who wrestles with another striker. Furthermore, the physical condition of a fighter is not always at the same level. Injury may affect the usefulness of technique, for instance. Besides that, timing and distance also have influence on usefulness. Bad timing and bad distance happen when, say, a striker throws a combination of punches, elbow, kicks, and knees too late or out of range. Sometimes bad timing or wrong distance may even result in illegal moves (e.g., a kick to the groin area of the opponent because of mistiming). Certainly there are other elements affecting one's judgment of usefulness of techniques, but I am not going into those in detail here. The point I want to make clear here is that the level of usefulness varies due to changes in given circumstances.

But this clarification seems insufficient, for it may lead to the misunderstanding that only the last technique (if any) with which the agent defeats their opponent – that is to say, the finishing move, if there is one – is strictly useful. All the other previous techniques and actions in the match would then seem not useful, even if they contribute significantly to the victory or one of them is actually the main cause of victory, despite technically not being the final blow. For example, suppose a fighter has already hurt their opponent badly with a previous strike, so that the opponent loses his balance at the last confrontation and finally loses. Defeating the opponent should, therefore, be considered a process composed of various moves and a series of confrontations between two fighters. Thus, a better way to analyze the general purpose of combat techniques is to consider the fight as a continuous process – the level of performance rather than movement – over a period of time. It follows that every action is supposed to tend to that end and is performed to give its agent a greater chance of winning. If a technique satisfies this purpose, then it is useful (and not just fit). A greater chance here means gaining advantage or control over the opponent, for example, by landing a significant strike.

The problem of intention: perception of utility

Regarding usefulness, the intention of the agent seems to have its influence too, as a thing is useful for a person if it can do what they want. Having to consider the intention behind an action would make this analysis more difficult. First of all, besides the assumption that fighters intend to win by doing the things they do, an action can have more than one intention. Besides the primary intention of defeating the opponent, a technique can be motivated by other intentions as well: irritating the opponent, hurting their arm, showing that one is more skillful, preparing for the next technique, and so on. An action is always 'multi-intentional'. On top of that, a good combat sport athlete actually does not intend in the match as much as one may think. It is not like choreographed fight scenes in films where one has at the very beginning a blueprint for the next ten moves, much less all the moves to follow. The fact is rather that, most of the time, the athlete just sees and reacts in a fraction of a second without any clear and solid decision-making process, and these fast reflexes are exactly the point of training. In this sense, most of the actions of the athlete are arguably not intentional actions at all (though they are conscious). Furthermore, there are also other cases like match-fixing. In a fixed fight, at least one of the competitors performs his techniques not for the sake of winning the match but merely to give the appearance of trying to do so.

The example of reflex may not really challenge the principle of intention, as one could argue that the original intention of a fighter is still to defeat their opponent. This intention is already internalized by long-term training and exactly those reflexes imply the extreme concentration originating in the will to win. As for the other examples, the problem lies in the fact that access to subjective mental states and motivations is restricted only to their possessor. As a consequence, one can hardly claim someone knows the real intentions and motivations of an agent only by observation and can hardly judge whether something is really useful for them in terms of their intentionality. Nonetheless, the consideration of intention may not be proper in the context of aesthetics, as, for instance, an artwork can be interpreted separately from its artist's intentions. The intention of a musician, for example, who plays the violin only for money and actually hates playing, lowers neither the quality of his music nor the aesthetic interest of his audience. The good intention of a bad cook to cook something delicious does not make my steak tastier. Similarly, the intention of the competitors makes their actions neither more beautiful nor uglier, because their actions are separately conceived by the spectators from a third-person perspective. Therefore, such intention is not sufficient to affect the aesthetic interest of the spectators. But in what sense can we talk about utility of technique if intention and motivation of the agent do not play any role?

Utility is understood spontaneously, an idea generated in or conveyed to the mind of the spectator. That is the reason why it does not necessarily refer to any actual state of the agent's intention, but is a kind of immediate intelligible perception by the spectator: it *seems* practical and beneficial for that fighter in that situation. This conveyance becomes possible only when there is a sign or a symbol which indicates the completion or the successful effect of the technique on another participant, such as (on the agent's side) scoring a clear point or takedown, a celebratory gesture, or (on the opponent's side) losing balance, being taken down, becoming unconscious, and so on. Without such an intelligible sign – sometimes in the form of color commentary in the case of broadcasted fights – it is difficult for causal spectators to guess or understand what is happening and they thus cannot enjoy to the same degree watching the game. Therefore, instead of the intention of a competitor, it is the series of moves and 'sign of completion' that determine perception of utility in knowledgeable spectators. Focusing only on the qualities of movements (strength, speed, etc.) leads to hiding the competitive context determining utility and sometimes subsequent beauty in MMA. Perception of the qualities of a technique (strength, speed, etc.) alone does not determine the aesthetic pleasure of the spectators, as we can imagine that a powerful but useless technique does not excite spectators so much as a powerful, useful technique. Utility, on the contrary, provides the ground for the aesthetic state.

Setting and significance: 'translating' utility into beauty

For Hume, one is only pleased by a means as such if its end pleases one as well. In this view, a technique pleases the fighter who performs it because their own victory pleases them. It seems to make sense, but do the spectators have an interest in the victory of a fighter in such a way that they also have an interest in his technique? According to Mumford's two ways of watching sport, the spectators, regardless of whether they are partisan watchers or purists, do have an interest in the match's outcome in different ways. But how can I explain my (extreme) example at the beginning of this chapter? Does the victory of my rival please me, a participant of the game who wants to win over that rival, so that their technique is aesthetically appealing for me? It seems not. To answer the question of its source of appeal, I have to assume that the functional quality of a technique alone is aesthetically pleasurable, provided that it is understood within a sport setting.

First of all, there are different levels of utility which can be appealing. The practical and beneficial use of an object may please us, but will hardly cause in us feelings of beauty, just as Hume said. The concept of utility in general and as concerning the utility of tools in everyday life is differentiated from that of the aesthetic of MMA (and other combat sports) in meanings and significance. The former normally cannot stimulate our awareness in daily life until the tool suddenly does not function anymore, whereas the latter stimulates our awareness only when the technique suddenly functions. For example, the utility of a cell phone and even its existence does not come into one's awareness, when one is using it to call someone. Only until it is broken and no longer functions, does one become aware of it and its function. In Heidegger's terms (1990: 95–102), the mode of encounter has changed. According to him, a piece of equipment (*ein Zeug*), such as a well-functioning hammer, is related to us (as *Dasein*, 'there-being') normally in a trouble-free manner. The Being of such equipment is readiness-to-hand (*Zuhandenheit*) for its user, who is not normally conscious of the equipment. Only when it is broken and does not function, its mode of Being shifts into a temporary un-readiness-to-hand (*Unzuhandenheit*) and finally to mere presence-at-hand (*Vorhandenheit*), in which the malfunction interrupts the user's activity and it presents itself to the user as a thing (*ein Ding*). A thing is something which is removed from its equipmental-practical context. On this account, the concept of utility or the concept of function is a kind of setting or the context of our activities in everyday life, where we presuppose, without awareness or conscious experience, that all equipment is well-functioning.

The setting in MMA is different. Spectators and athletes do not presuppose that every technique functions in the cage as well as it is supposed to in training or in theory. In MMA, the number of unsuccessful attempts is usually much greater than that of successful attempts due to, for example, the opponent's resistance or one's own limited ability. A match is in fact a process full of numerous confrontations between two athletes with unsuccessful attempts, ridiculous movements, failures, missed opportunities, bad timing, not finding one's rhythm, equipment failures, and so on. It will often take an MMA fighter a round or two to find their rhythm and try out different techniques. These are potential obstacles to performing techniques practically and beneficially to their ends. A useful technique implies overcoming these obstacles, which brings the technique immediately into our awareness and gives us pleasure. Its completion indicates the highest use of physical and cognitive abilities of the agent and overcoming all uncertainties in its particular context. Only observers who understand the setting sufficiently can 'translate' utility into beauty. In an extreme situation, even an ugly technique can cause our aesthetic appreciation.

Notes

1 In this chapter, the term 'aesthetic' is understood in the beauty-centric sense, i.e., the aesthetic as beauty. On this account, the aesthetic theory of utility, which will be established below, is a theory about beauty.
2 Admittedly, my example only represents my subjective view as a sabre fencer, but this kind of experience is at least shared by other athletes. It is philosophically interesting as an intersubjective phenomenon.
3 See Strube (1979).
4 Glenn Parsons and Allen Carlson (2008) conducted thorough research on the concept of functional beauty and the history of its corresponding theories in the 18th Century, from George Berkeley to Archibald Alison.
5 Hume's consideration of utility is in fact mainly related to his principles of morals. But for him judgments of both morality and beauty are based on the faculty of taste generating the same type of qualitative sentiment (e.g., pain and uneasiness in either case).
6 Edmund Burke (1764: 191–202) argues against the theory of beauty as utility with his counterexamples of peacock fan and pig snout. With the former he argues that an object's form may be ill-fitted for its end or purpose, but still be beautiful. Burke seems to assume that the purpose of birds or the end of the form of birds is to fly, and peacock tails are not fit for this purpose (as they are too long and too heavy). First of all, peacocks do fly and in this sense we can say that the tail is consistent with and thus fit for its purpose (and is beautiful). Secondly, the purpose of peacock fans is in fact to attract a mate and the fan does serve this purpose (and is beautiful).

The other counterexample of the appearance of animal organs, such as the snout of a swine and the bag under the bill of a pelican, demonstrates contrarily that an object which appears to be fit for its purpose may still displease its observer. However, this example is only against the sufficiency of utility for beauty *in general*, which is not the claim in this chapter.
7 The five levels are physique, movement, performance, framework, and significance.

References

Allen, B. (2013) 'Games of Sport, Works of Art, and the Striking Beauty of Asian Martial Arts', *Journal of the Philosophy of Sport*, 40(2): 241–254.
Burke, E. (1764) *A Philosophical Enquiry into the Origin of Our Ideas of the Sublime and Beautiful: With an Introductory Discourse Concerning Taste, and Several Other Additions* (4th Ed.), London: R. and J. Dodsley.
Cordner, C. D. (1984) 'Grace and Functionality', *British Journal of Aesthetics*, 24(4): 301–313.
Heidegger, M. (1990) *Being and Time*, J. Macquarrie and E. Robinson (trans.), Oxford: Blackwell.
Holt, J. (2020) *Kinetic Beauty: The Philosophical Aesthetics of Sport*, New York: Routledge.
Hume, D. (1988) *Enquiries Concerning Human Understanding and Concerning the Principles of Morals* (3rd Ed.), Oxford: Clarendon Press.

Hume, D. (1960) *Treatise of Human Nature*. Oxford: Clarendon Press.
Mumford, S. (2013) 'Ways of Watching Sport', *Royal Institute of Philosophy Supplements*, 73: 3–15.
Parsons, G. and Carlson, A. (2008) *Functional Beauty*, Oxford: Oxford University Press.
Strube, W. (1979) 'Interesselosigkeit: Zur Geschichte Eines Grundbegriffs Der Ästhetik', *Archiv für Begriffsgeschichte*, 23 (2): 148–174.

7 An aesthetic apology for MMA

Jason Holt

The idea that MMA is a beautiful thing, a suitable object for aesthetic appreciation, would strike many people, critics and fans alike, as absurd. Many critics dismiss the sport as not only morally objectionable but utterly repulsive, a spectacle of extreme and pointless violence – an *ugly* thing. Such critics are closed to the possibility of appreciating MMA as an acquired taste, as are many disgusted by a first exposure to alcohol or tobacco, and perhaps rightly so. Unable to overcome an initial revulsion to, say, beer or wine, one will fail to develop their taste to acquire the sort of aesthetic pleasure that connoisseurs enjoy. MMA could prove suitable for aesthetic appreciation in a similar way, being too off-putting at the outset for everyone to appreciate.[1]

Even fans may likewise deny that their love of this aggressive, hypermasculine sport has anything to do with something so airy-fairy and effete as the *aesthetic*. Quite the opposite. What they claim to take pleasure in, perhaps, is the violence itself, for its own sake or as an expression of dominance and masculine prowess, an affirmation by proxy of their own identity and sense of self-worth. Unquestionably many fans of MMA fit this profile, as do many sports fans generally. Such an attitude toward sport is not the only one possible, however. Take Mumford's distinction between purist and partisan spectatorship (2012: 19): the purist 'is a fan of sports whose interest is mainly in the aesthetic experiences it can provide. The partisan is a fan whose interest mainly is in winning' and who 'prefers a dull victory to an exciting defeat'. Consider also what he calls elsewhere (2014: 183, original emphasis) 'the aesthetic hypothesis: that *aesthetic considerations are essential to the being of sport and continue to shape its development*'. What this means is not only that sports generally and MMA in particular are legitimately framed as sources of aesthetic gratification, but also that aesthetic considerations may underlie sports fandom generally, insofar as such considerations could not only consciously inform purist attitudes but also unconsciously inform many partisan attitudes. In other words, aesthetic considerations might influence fandom far more than many MMA fans would admit. At any rate, my hypothesis is that a significant part of the distinctive appeal of MMA lies in certain features that are aesthetically noteworthy.

My discussion will focus mostly on the aesthetics of MMA from the fan's rather than the fighter's point of view.[2] In considering the fan's perspective here we should distinguish between mere preference (as in '*I find* strikers more pleasing to watch than grapplers') and transpersonal judgment (as in 'Strikers *are* more pleasing to watch than grapplers'). With preferences, there is no room for debate (to each their own), but with transpersonal aesthetic judgment there is room for debate. We need not commit to the untenable view that aesthetic properties are somehow *out there* in the world

DOI: 10.4324/9781003122395-8

independent of our responses, but nor need we commit to the sort of principle advocated by David Hume, among others, that human nature is ultimately uniform such that any apparent differences in taste can be explained in terms of preferers lacking the required expertise (1760/2002: 44). Human nature is probably equivocal on whether everyone should or should not find MMA aesthetically pleasing. But MMA fandom is not entirely arbitrary either. Among the great number of people who find MMA pleasing to watch, several aesthetic features of the sport may be identified as plausibly underlying such responses. As I hope to show, MMA aesthetics is in many ways a matter of preferences that are not just personal but principled.

In exploring the aesthetic appeal of MMA, four distinct features of the sport will come to the fore: (1) *minimalism* vis-à-vis rules, clothing, and equipment; (2) *diversity* of techniques and body types; (3) *violence* as forcing definite outcomes – particularly in cases of knockout – which becomes more compelling in an increasingly uncertain world; (4) what I will call the *empathetic sublime*, in which we identify with a submitted fighter who is overwhelmed by an opponent as if by a force of nature. I will discuss each of these in turn before ending with a sobering discussion of MMA's aesthetic flaws. But first some general remarks are in order about the aesthetic appeal of different types of sports.

Levels of analysis

Although much of the aesthetic appeal of MMA derives from its uniqueness, some of its appeal is shared with other sports by virtue of belonging to the same types. Consider Kupfer's (1988) threefold typology of sport: quantitative/linear (based on measurement), formal/qualitative (based on style), and competitive sports (where one struggles *against* an opponent). Although aesthetic qualities are foregrounded in the scoring required in formal/qualitative sports such as diving and gymnastics, other types have aesthetic advantages of their own. From Kupfer's perspective, 'the complications introduced by human opposition multiply the aesthetic possibilities in competitive sports – dramatic possibilities due to social interaction' (ibid.: 396). Since on this account MMA is clearly a competitive sport (in the relevant sense), with competitors actively struggling against each other, we have some explanation of the sport's dramatic potential. I would propose, further, that in a combat sport like MMA the dramatic potential of contests is distinctively enhanced.

Another important sport type distinction originally proposed by David Best (1974) is that between purposive and aesthetic sports. Purposive sports, which include both quantitative/linear and competitive sports on Kupfer's typology, are distinguished by the fact that their competitive outcomes are *not* determined by judged aesthetic criteria. Aesthetic sports, or in Kupfer's terms qualitative/formal sports, are by contrast those with outcomes determined by judges according to aesthetic criteria, where what matters is not simply *what* an athlete does (e.g., scoring a goal) but *how* they do it (e.g., maintaining good form). It is not that purposive sports lack aesthetic appeal but rather that such appeal is not necessary for scoring and winning. Where MMA outcomes are determined by knockout or submission, they appear to fall into the category of purposive sports; yet where judges' decisions determine these outcomes, because scoring is based on assessments of strike quality, degree of aggression, octagon control, and so forth, counterintuitively we seem to have an aesthetic sport. If so, MMA stands as a purposive/aesthetic hybrid sport.[3]

80 *Jason Holt*

The aesthetic aspects of different types of sport are further distinguishable by a five-level analysis proposed elsewhere (Holt 2019: 6–14).[4] Level 1 is that of the athlete's physique, where particular types of sport practice condition the body to excel in that domain. The physical profile of a mixed martial artist in fighting trim is a prime example. Level 2 is that of the movements of athletes, which may have aesthetic properties like fluidity or aesthetically appreciable properties like power. Think of a well-executed spinning kick or smooth ground reversal. Level 3 is that of performances, which comprise different individual movements and exhibit such properties as an athlete's style, the distinctive, balanced style of a Georges St-Pierre, for instance. Level 4 is that of the framework of the sport or types of sport, including not only the formal framework of rules governing competition (e.g., the unified rules of MMA) but also the physical and internal social frameworks involved (e.g., the cage, the history of MMA). Level 5 is that of further significance including the drama of a bout, the revelation of a fighter's character, and so on. These levels are distinguishable yet related and sometimes overlapping. For instance, the octagon is aesthetically appreciable in terms of both its geometry (Level 4) and as drawing some of its significance from the Chuck Norris film *The Octagon* (1980) (Level 5).[5] Note how the 'UF' in 'UFC' suggests the rank of 'ultimate fighter', an aesthetically powerful aspiration that transcends the sport itself.

Minimalism

The first of four major facets of MMA aesthetics that I will examine is minimalism, which I can characterize somewhat roughly if accessibly as the notion that *less is more*, that in some matters of taste it will be more aesthetically piquant the more one is able to minimize. This applies even on such a mundane level as home décor. Many people have minimalist tendencies in furnishing their living spaces with a sparsity of furniture and highly selective ornamentation. Not everyone has a minimalist aesthetic, of course. (Some people have what may be called a clutter aesthetic!) It is however an aesthetic value prized by many, in art as well as living spaces. Good poetry will often be marked by sparse use of language, as will some styles of visual art by simplicity of line. Such minimalism seems implicit in Best's account (1978: 106) of graceful movement in sport as a matter of economy and efficiency of motion and effort. Take as an example a submission with a subtle, almost indiscernible movement that turns an opponent's struggle into a tap out.

Perhaps the most obvious way MMA rewards minimalists is by offering a fight spectacle where at least superficially it seems that *anything goes*, a kind of rule minimalism. Indeed, at its outset the sport was promoted as a type of 'no holds barred' fighting competition. But the notion that MMA, in any strict sense, is – or was – a no-rules competition is simply false. First, as Suits (2005: 74–5) so persuasively argues, if one imagines an instance of supposedly no-holds-barred mortal combat, in which everything is permitted in trying to kill your opponent, so long as there is an agreed-to start time, that in itself will constitute a constitutive rule and therefore gamify the activity by artificially limiting attempts to achieve the prescribed goal. Even in the earliest, most dangerous days of MMA, there were many more rules than this in effect. Now, of course, under the unified rules of MMA, there are *dozens* of proscriptions – head-butting, eye-gouging, biting, fish-hooking, strikes to the groin or back of the head, for instance – to say nothing of rules about the fighting area, weight classes, number and duration of rounds, and so on (UFC 2018).

Still, MMA does legitimately appeal to minimalist sensibilities. Some sports may do this by specifying conditions and imposing rules that very narrowly circumscribe what may be done or done legally to achieve the object of the game: a sort of task minimalism. In MMA the appeal is realized rather differently, not by closing off but by *opening up* what may legally be done in a structured contest of unarmed fighting. If sports are certain types of physical games, MMA may be construed as *unarmed fighting games permitting techniques derived from a variety of martial arts and combat sports*. Aside from disqualification, one achieves victory in MMA by knockout, technical knockout, submission, or decision, and apart from the basic structure of the contest (no weapons, five-minute rounds, and so on), the only restrictions in place are meant to ensure minimally adequate safety of the fighters. MMA is designed, in other words, to maximize its technical and spectacle potential under minimally decent safety protocols. For this reason, the sport can satisfy minimalists in a way other combat or violent contact sports simply cannot.

Another minimalist feature of MMA pertains to clothing and equipment. With respect to clothing, the fighters' bodies are bare except for the dictates of conventional modesty: shorts for men and shorts and tops for women. This minimization of attire stresses not only the physicality of the contest but also that of the fighters themselves. MMA fans appreciate a fighter's function and form together: action and anatomy. The stereotypical MMA fighter's anatomy, furthermore, reflects the minimalist aesthetic of attire, especially in lower weight classes, where fighters tend to be exceedingly lean. With respect to equipment, likewise, the principle of minimally adequate safety is once more applicable: mouthguard, cup, and fingerless 4-ounce gloves. In contrast with boxing's baggy shorts, ankle boots, and much bigger and heavier mitt-gloves, the accoutrements of MMA are positively elegant.

The draw of diversity

The second major facet of MMA aesthetics on my analysis is diversity, particularly diversity of techniques, styles, backgrounds, and bodies. The idea that diversity is desirable from a moral or political point of view is familiar, and though MMA does exhibit diversity in this sense it is not the primary sense in which the sport has a notable pluralist aesthetic appeal. It cannot of course be denied that the explosion of MMA as a truly global phenomenon, with athletes from different countries, races, classes, genders – and ages[6] – illustrates not only the desirability of diversity as a social ideal but also how such values and aesthetic values can interact. As Mumford (2012: 68) puts the point, 'Factors that are ethically bad can detract from sport's aesthetic value, and factors that are ethically good can improve sport's aesthetic value'.[7] Not everyone champions diversity, of course, social or otherwise. Indeed, many sport subcultures are unfortunately characterized by monolithic, aesthetically biased perspectives.[8]

Part of the reason diversity of technique and style in MMA is aesthetically pleasing is by opening up the possibilities of surprise, as the less sure one is about the possibilities of what will happen next the more psychological tension builds and enhances the fight's drama. We should however distinguish between technique, which is more or less conventional, and fighting style, which lends itself more to individual expression. No doubt the most obvious distinction in technique among MMA fighters is that between grapplers and strikers – take Ronda Rousey vs. Holly Holm in UFC 193. As the sport evolves it becomes more incumbent on fighters not to be *too* disadvantaged in their weaker areas. Conventional techniques and strengths aside, diversity among individual fighters' styles, whether signature moves or creative improvisation, is also dizzyingly complex. Consider your favorite MMA fighters and what makes them unique, why – if you can discern the reason – they rank as your favorites.

Related to but distinct from diversity of techniques and styles in MMA is the diversity of backgrounds, not just geographical and cultural – which adds to the gravitas of premier events – but also, more importantly, fighting backgrounds. Many successful MMA fighters are pedigreed from other combat sports and martial arts: Henry Cejudo came from Olympic freestyle wrestling (gold medal), Lyoto Machida from karate (8th Dan), Kimbo Slice from street fighting, and Kayla Harrison from judo (Olympic gold medal). Sometimes a fighter's background will show through in their MMA style, but sometimes hardly at all. Ronda Rousey's judo techniques can be seen in her MMA style, but one may not suspect from her MMA fighting style as a striker that Amanda Nunes is a black belt in Brazilian Jiu-Jitsu. Whether they show themselves in the octagon or not, however, such credentials are invariably part of a fighter's profile and mentioned alongside their MMA statistics and achievements – a throwback to the early days of MMA where contests were framed as not just between different fighters but between different fighting *styles*.[9] This trend is still evident in MMA, though in a more nuanced form. Nowadays it is more of a duality between fighters' MMA styles and their pre-MMA fighting expertise. This convention may well taper off as the sport continues to evolve and more fighters start out in MMA rather than winding up there after an apprenticeship in other fighting domains.

Above I mentioned the stereotypical MMA fighter's body in fighting trim: lean, compact, forceful. This is oversimplified. In fact, unlike many demanding sports, MMA allows for a rather wide range of body types and attributes to excel: very thin wiry frames, very muscled builds, and stocky, even noticeably fat physiques. To some extent such variety depends on weight class. All else being equal, the heavier weight classes allow for a significantly wider variety of excellence-compatible physiques. Even at lower weight classes, however, one often sees a relatively tall and wiry fighter versus a shorter, stockier one. It is not just body types but physical prowess that also varies in a pluralistically appealing way. Take for instance the unusual flexibility of a B. J. Penn or the power of a Francis Ngannou. Such outstanding physical attributes no doubt guide athletes in choosing their original sports and in the evolution of their MMA fighting styles. Variety here is the spice of the fight as well as life itself.

Violence as definitive

The third significant factor in my analysis of MMA aesthetics is the sport's violence, admittedly a feature that many people find aesthetically *un*appealing. Following Ramsay (2017: 1), we may observe that by the term 'violence', 'we are usually talking about the intentional use of physical force against another person; the level of force is particularly high and it indicates the likelihood of serious physical harm'. Violence and physical harm are not coextensive (as violence need not cause and is often not the cause of physical harm), and it is difficult to distinguish in a principled or morally significant way the violence in combat sports like boxing and MMA and that of non-combat contact sports such as rugby, American or Australian rules football, and hockey (ibid.).[10] Considered aesthetically, the violence in these different types of sport seems to address a certain basic need yet finds in MMA a singular expression.

Violent impulses represent one side of autonomic arousal, the fight-or-flight response to situations of extreme conflict, stress, and uncertainty. At less extreme levels, such conflicts may characterize everyday human psychology, and as I argue elsewhere (Holt 2015: 85–6), the value of aesthetic experience consists partly in the pleasurable resolution of such conflict.[11] The violent impulse arises when conflict and uncertainty reach an unbearable extreme. One just can't take it anymore. The result is a desperate will to force from conflict and uncertainty something definite and resolved. The apotheosis of such an impulse may come at the end of the movie *Beneath the Planet of the Apes* (1970) in the form of Taylor (Charlton Heston), unable to tolerate a dystopian world in which there is no room left for humanity, with his last breath muttering 'You bastards', decisively triggering a device that blows up the world. Whatever deep moral objections we may have to such an action, the impulse is certainly understandable, and one we would hope could be answered in less desperate and devastating ways.

Even in civilized society such impulses need to be acknowledged and managed, and this becomes more important the more one's culture is characterized by conflict and uncertainty, for the greater such psychological needs, the greater the urgency for – and the aesthetic rewards of – appropriately contextualized violence, particularly in art and sport. The popularity of MMA may reflect badly on contemporary culture, but that is precisely the point. It is an important source of badly needed aesthetic pleasure. Among all sports, however violent, MMA is arguably uniquely capable of meeting this psychological need. Its violence is controlled and admittedly artificial to this extent, but also within those limits the most open and plausibly therefore the most authentic violent sport there is.

The violence of MMA is at its most striking in the ground and pound but arguably peaks in the singularity of the definitive knockout: the flying knee, the head kick, the vicious elbow, or the devastating punch that lays a fighter out cold, the sort of strike that elicits from Joe Rogan an unmistakable 'Oh my goodness!'. I maintain that the violence of no other sport is so effective or appropriate for satisfying the will to definitiveness behind violent impulses. There can of course be decisive knockouts in other combat sports such as boxing, kickboxing, and Muay Thai, but in these contexts the violence is less decisive both because of the heavier padding of the gloves and because knockdowns result in counts, a suspension rather than continuation of the action. That a knockdown in MMA will lead to a continuation rather than suspension of the fight makes MMA violence more decisive. Indeed, this ability to change modes is distinctively appealing, in part no doubt because in this respect it more closely resembles real-world fighting.[12] Still, violence in the real world is unruly, destructive, pointless self-assertion, the opposite of violence in the octagon. In this way MMA provides fans with a vicarious, aestheticized venting of the will to *definitivize*, and to this extent is the most beautiful of sports, with the octagon among the noteworthy venues of human expression.

The empathetic sublime

I have argued that the deep-seated desire for definitive outcomes is uniquely satisfied in sport by the violent peaks of MMA, particularly the ground and pound and the decisive knockout. If this view is mistaken, however, we may observe similarly that whatever aesthetic appeal victories by submission have is clearly to be found in certain other combat sports such as Brazilian Jiu-Jitsu. Since submissions are comparatively non-violent, it may turn out after all that the special appeal of MMA violence and submission depends more on the balance between such outcomes than on either individually. One might argue, however, that submissions are more pleasing in MMA, all else being equal, because unlike pure grappling sports, the possibility of finishes by knockout in MMA makes MMA submissions comparatively rare and special. In any case, since a significant part of the aesthetic appeal of MMA depends on the possibility of such climaxes, in this section I turn to considering submissions as providing for a unique kind of aesthetic experience, for which I coin the term 'empathetic sublime', whose meaning will take some unpacking.

The first notion to explicate is that of the sublime. Aesthetic experience is of the sublime rather than the beautiful in that its object is understood as something to *fear*. Natural phenomena may be sublime, specifically what Kant calls the dynamically sublime, when we appreciate their *might*, which is 'an ability that is superior to great obstacles. It is called *dominance* [*Gewalt*] if it is superior to the resistance of something that itself possesses might' (1790/1987: 119). Some of Kant's examples of natural sublimity are overhanging rock formations, gathering thunderclouds, active volcanoes, hurricanes, the ocean 'heaved up', and high waterfalls (ibid.: 120). Relative to these forces of nature, 'our ability to resist becomes an insignificant trifle. Yet the sight of them becomes all the more attractive the more fearful it is, provided we are in a safe place' (ibid.). To experience such sublimity furthermore raises 'the soul's fortitude above its usual middle range', arousing our courage even though 'the irresistibility of nature's might' makes us cognizant of its ultimate dominance over us as natural beings (ibid.).

The next step is to adumbrate an application of Kant's view of the sublime to the martial arts, specifically aikido (Barham 2014). This may seem counterintuitive. Kant focuses on natural rather than human examples, and it is vision that provides the safe distance required for aesthetic appreciation of the sublime.[13] For Barham, in aikido it is rather a superior opponent experienced not visually from the sidelines but kinesthetically – that is, bodily – by a participant that may be sublime (ibid.: 121). This can work in aikido as 'a civil art' because ensuring the safety of one's opponent is deemed no less important than protecting one's own body: 'the techniques of aikido aim to avoid all physical violence (i.e., collisions and tussles) by blending and harmonizing with the movement and energy of one's attacker' (ibid.: 119). The unique nature of the art allows for the safe appreciation of an opponent's fearful dominance.[14]

How on earth could this be transposed to the octagon if, as I argue above, violence is key to the combat sport's aesthetic appeal? Surely I don't claim that MMA fighters can have sublime experiences when submitted by an opponent as if by a force of nature. No, when we see fighters tap out it will not be sublime for them, but it may well be sublime for *us* watching. I propose we designate this the 'empathetic sublime' in the following way. The safe vantagepoint required for sublime experience is provided by seeing the action from outside the octagon. The conception of the object as fearful comes from recognizing the submitter's irresistible dominance (as of a force of nature) and identifying, perhaps subconsciously, with the submitted fighter. (If one identifies rather with the submitter, the experience cannot be sublime and often will not count as aesthetic either.) Such a process might be facilitated by mirror neurons, which are activated when certain activities are either performed or perceived.[15] Thus the submitted fighter can become a tragic yet heroic symbol of humanity itself in the inevitable grip of ultimate defeat.

Aesthetic flaws

My discussion of MMA aesthetics would be incomplete without at least acknowledging, despite its evident aesthetic virtues, that MMA exhibits certain unignorable flaws. I have acknowledged already how the violence of its action and the sometimes hypermasculinity of its subculture may be found off-putting if not downright ugly. My focus, however, is what seem to be two aesthetic flaws in the sport's very design.

Consider first Kretchmar's distinction (2005: 38–9) between T games, which are limited by a prescribed span of time, and E games, which are limited by a prescribed number of untimed events. Soccer, for instance, is a T game normally comprising two 45-minute halves, whereas golf, each round of which comprises 18 holes, is an E game. For Kretchmar (ibid.: 40), T games such as soccer, despite their popularity, are aesthetically flawed because they encourage stalling when one side is ahead, which makes for a duller contest. On this distinction, MMA seems to count as a T game, consisting of three or five 5-min. rounds. Indeed, a fighter ahead on points might well be motivated to stall, thus illustrating Kretchmar's view, although Mumford counters (2012: 24) that the time limits of T games add to their dramatic quality by reflecting human mortality. Such disputes about T games would seem to apply more, however, when MMA bouts go the distance, though a fighter obviously ahead on points in a given round might be motivated to stall however the outcome is eventually determined. When a bout is decided by knockout or submission, MMA seems, despite the round limitations, much more like an E game, and so appears to cut across the T games/E games distinction.

Last, given the appeal of knockout and submission outcomes as discussed above, there is a complementary point to consider about matches decided by scorecard. Such outcomes patently lack the definitive appeal of the knockout or the sublime appeal of the submission. This does not mean, of course, that judges' decisions are arbitrary. Often the judges' decision will cohere with an audience's sense of justice (who *should* win the fight), though when partisanship divides fans one side will inevitably feel denied. This is especially true in especially close fights with pundits admitting that the outcome seems too close to call and judges have the unenviable task of having to call it anyway. To be clear here, beautiful fights are often close, and many close fights go the distance. But although one can find it beautiful, say, that Diaz vs. McGregor 2 went the distance and was so close, we may wistfully observe that a decisive late finish by either would have been better still.[16] Split decisions in particular disappoint aesthetic satisfaction, as do outcomes where judges' decisions controversially frustrate audience and pundit expectations. One can argue that such thwarting of expectations echoes a realistic sense of how nebulous life itself often is, but it nonetheless disappoints a hope that in the octagon things will turn out differently. Such aesthetic flaws are unfortunate but seemingly unavoidable elements in a sport that otherwise often packs a spectacular punch and submits us so delightfully.[17]

Notes

1 I assume that the aesthetics of MMA as a sport will be markedly different from, though related to, that of the traditional martial arts, which stress long-established ritual practices and character development. On the aesthetics of traditional martial arts, see Allen (2015: 112–58). Allen (ibid.: 132) contrasts an aesthetic of real-world efficacy in traditional martial arts with that of a context-limited efficacy of sport skills, which appears to marginalize the useful real-world application of skills developed in certain combat sports.

86 Jason Holt

2 For a philosophically nuanced account of the ecstasies and agonies of MMA spectatorship, see Kerry Howley's semi-fictional memoir *Thrown* (2014).
3 For an analogous perspective on boxing, see Yeomans and Holt (2015).
4 For an application to traditional martial arts, see Burrow and Holt (2019: 76–8).
5 Not all MMA contests occur in an octagonal cage. The Bellator cage, for instance, is closer to a circle, and some bouts take place – as in Pride and almost all in the sport's early days – in boxing rings. See Rossen (2013) on the Chuck Norris film as inspiration for the MMA octagon.
6 Six-time double weight class UFC Champion Randy Couture fought well into his forties, often defeating much younger and heavier opponents.
7 See Holt (2017) for a sympathetic critical analysis of Mumford's view.
8 See Holt (2019: 66–75) for an extended discussion of aesthetic bias in sport. See Holt and Holt (2010) for discussion of aesthetically biased approaches to golf technique and physique.
9 The aesthetic appeal of the duality of pitting different fighters/styles against one another is well captured in the Jean-Claude Van Damme film *Bloodsport* (1988). On a related note, Bruce Lee's Jeet Kune Do fighting style is interpretable as a precursor to MMA insofar as it blends aspects of different fighting traditions.
10 Although compare Torres and Parry (2017: 189): 'Nonetheless, the central failing in boxing cannot be escaped: that, despite the values of honorable combat and courageous resilience, the activity does nothing to prevent or to discourage the intention to inflict injury and harm. Whilst the infliction of harm need not necessarily be a boxer's motivation or intent, the rules fail to rule out such intent. This is what distinguishes boxing (as a combat sport) from other body-contact sports, such as varieties of football, which explicitly rule out violence (the intention to harm).'
11 My term for this is 'resolutive' experience. Think of 'Music hath charms', etc.
12 For more on the semblance of realism and hyperviolence in MMA, see Downey (2014).
13 As Barham observes (2014: 118), although Kant focuses on examples from nature, he does not rule out the possibility of human sublimity. Consider also Kant's mention (1790/1987: 98) of the sublime in art. Although it may seem dehumanizing and un-Kantian to appreciate a submitter in terms of the Kantian sublime, the sublimity here involves recognition of the submitter's agency, which is entirely Kantian in spirit.
14 The scope of Barham's claim might be suitably broadened to the extent that the Asian martial arts as traditionally practiced have generally, in Allen's (2015: 158) terms, 'eliminated the dread of actual violence from the training environment'.
15 See Holt (2019: 35) for a discussion of how mirror neurons may proprioceptively enhance the aesthetic experience of observed body movements.
16 A notable exception is the Mark Hunt vs. António Silva main event (UFC Fight Night 33), an exceptionally close and beautiful fight with many momentum shifts and both fighters giving and taking phenomenal punishment. The fight ended in a draw, which was aesthetically pleasing – in part, I suggest, because of the extraordinary sportsmanship both fighters deservedly showed, not only at the end of the fight, then again after the announcement of the decision, but more so when the final round began with a customary glove touching then a moving embrace. This gesture has since become something of a trope for fighters moved by extraordinary surges of mutual respect when on the verge of concluding what has been an epic fight.
17 Earlier versions of this chapter were presented at the Czech Philosophy of Sport Conference and a colloquium at Dalhousie University, Canada. Thanks to participants at both for feedback.

References

Allen, B. (2015) *Striking Beauty: A Philosophical Look at the Asian Martial Arts*, New York: Columbia University Press.
Barham, R. (2014) 'A Sublime Peace', in G. Priest and D. Young (eds.) *Philosophy and the Martial Arts: Engagement*, New York: Routledge, pp. 117–126.
Best, D. (1974) 'The Aesthetic in Sport', *British Journal of Aesthetics*, 14: 197–213.

Best, D. (1978) *Philosophy and Human Movement*, London: George Allen & Unwin.
Burrow, S. and Holt, J. (2019) 'The Interconnection of Aesthetics and Ethics as Revealed in Martial Arts', *Fair Play*, 14: 73–91.
Downey, G. (2014) '"As Real as It Gets!" Producing Hyperviolence in Mixed Martial Arts', *JOMEC Journal*, 5: 1–28.
Holt, J. (2015) *Meanings of Art: Essays in Aesthetics*, Montreal: Minkowski Institute Press.
Holt, J. (2017) 'Mumford on Aesthetic–Moral Interaction in Sport', *Journal of the Philosophy of Sport*, 44(1): 72–80.
Holt, J. (2019) *Kinetic Beauty: The Philosophical Aesthetics of Sport*, New York: Routledge.
Holt, J. and Holt, L. E. (2010) 'The "Ideal" Swing, the "Ideal" Body: Myths of Optimization', in A. Wible (ed.) *Golf and Philosophy: Lessons from the Links*, Lexington: University Press of Kentucky, pp. 209–220.
Howley, K. (2014) *Thrown*, Louisville: Sarabande Books.
Hume, D. (1760/2002) 'Of the Standard of Taste', in T. E. Wartenberg (ed.) *The Nature of Art: An Anthology*, Orlando: Harcourt, pp. 39–47.
Kant, I. (1790/1987) *Critique of Judgment*, W. S. Pluhar (trans.), Indianapolis: Hackett.
Kretchmar, R. S. (2005) 'Game Flaws', *Journal of the Philosophy of Sport*, 32(1): 36–48.
Kupfer, J. H. (1988) 'Sport – The Body Electric', in W. J. Morgan and K. V. Meier (eds.) *Philosophic Inquiry in Sport* (2nd Ed.), Champaign, IL: Human Kinetics, pp. 390–406.
Mumford, S. (2012) *Watching Sport: Aesthetics, Ethics and Emotion*, New York: Routledge.
Mumford, S. (2014) 'The Aesthetics of Sport', in C. R. Torres (ed.) *The Bloomsbury Companion to the Philosophy of Sport*, London: Bloomsbury, pp. 180–194.
Ramsay, M. (2017) 'Violent Sports', in *International Encyclopedia of Ethics*, Malden: Wiley, pp. 1–5, https://onlinelibrary.wiley.com/doi/abs/10.1002/9781444367072.wbiee841, accessed 11 June 2020.
Rossen, J. (2013) 'Changing the Shape of Fighting', *ESPN*, 22 May, https://www.espn.com/mma/story/_/id/8515933/changing-shape-fighting, accessed 6 June 2020.
Suits, B. (2005) *The Grasshopper: Games, Life and Utopia* (2nd Ed.), Peterborough: Broadview.
Torres, C. R. and Parry, J. (2017) 'Boxing and the Youth Olympic Games', *Diagoras: International Academic Journal on Olympic Studies*, 1: 169–190.
UFC (2018) 'Unified Rules of Mixed Martial Arts', *UFC*, https://www.ufc.com/unified-rules-mixed-martial-arts, accessed 7 June 2020.
Yeomans, M. and Holt, J. (2015) 'Purposive/Aesthetic Sport: A Note on Boxing', *Fair Play*, 3(2): 87–95.

8 The line of permissibility
Gladiators, boxers, and MMA fighters

Marc Ramsay

The first Ali-Frazier fight was a sensational moment in American history. Celebrities such as Woody Allen, Miles Davis, Frank Sinatra, Burt Lancaster, and Norman Mailer lined the ringside seats of a packed Madison Square Garden. 'Patriotic' Americans such as Sinatra had adopted Frazier as their standard bearer against Ali, the brash 'anti-American' who refused the military draft in protest of the Vietnam War. After 15 rounds, Frazier was awarded a unanimous decision victory, but Ali gained grudging respect from many of his critics. Soon after, however, the *New York Times* published an editorial calling for a ban on professional boxing (Editorial 1971). Appalled rather than satisfied by the match's brutality, the author likened Ali and Frazier to gladiators made to fight for the perverse satisfaction of crowds in Rome's Colosseum. The obvious liberal response appeared in a subsequent letter to the editor (Sidhu 1971). Unlike Roman gladiators, Ali and Frazier chose to fight. *Volenti non fit injuria*.

Cue Irving Kristol's famous hypothetical:

> I know of no one, no matter how free in spirit, who argues that we ought to permit gladiatorial contests in Yankee Stadium, similar to those once performed in the Colosseum at Rome – even if only consenting adults were involved.
>
> (Kristol 1971: 24)

Critics of boxing and MMA see a common moral problem running between these sports and Kristol's voluntary gladiatorial contests, a problem that distinguishes them all from other seemingly violent sports. According to former Canadian Medical Association President Anna Reid,

> cage fighting, like boxing, is distinct from many other sports, in that the basic intent of the fighter is to cause harm in order to incapacitate his or her opponent... And an activity in which the overriding goal is to pummel one's opponent into submission does not promote good health.
>
> (CBC 2013)

Consent, so the story goes, has limits – some activities are too dangerous or perhaps just too immoral to be permitted. Some critics claim boxing is a weaker but still condemnable version of the death-match – still too dangerous or immoral. Others, such as the late Senator John McCain, suggested that while boxing remains a civilized endeavor, MMA falls too far down the line. Of course, early UFCs were marketed as

DOI: 10.4324/9781003122395-9

outrageous gladiatorial spectacles, but the UFC 'cleaned up' and the moral campaign against MMA floundered (Greene 2018). But opposition remains. Physicians concerned about chronic traumatic encephalopathy (CTE) still want to ban professional boxing and MMA, and their arguments use moralistic rhetoric.

This chapter provides a cautious defense of MMA against paternalistic and moralistic arguments. My main interlocutor here is Nicholas Dixon – Dixon provides a case for a legal ban on professional boxing and additional moral arguments against MMA (Dixon 2001, 2015). I argue that reflection on MMA sheds new light on the case against boxing as well as more general debates concerning paternalism and legal moralism.

The first section provides a brief overview of Dixon's case against boxing and MMA, as well as major concepts such as paternalism and legal moralism. The second section responds to paternalistic arguments, the appeal to soft paternalism, the argument from economic coercion, and Dixon's pre-emptive paternalism. The third section responds to the moralistic case against boxing and MMA. It covers Dixon's Kantian argument against MMA and the so-called basic intent argument, and it includes some reflections on Kristol's hypothetical.

Concepts

Dixon (2001) makes a cumulative case for a legal ban on professional boxing – more specifically a ban on blows to head (324). His case draws on three elements: soft paternalism, economic coercion, and a restrained version of hard paternalism (pre-emptive paternalism), which focuses on brain damage. Dixon claims that most boxers lack adequate information about long-term risks. He also thinks that most boxers experience their career choice as coercive – they pursue it only because boxing offers the slim hope of escape from poverty. Finally, boxing is an objectionable choice because it undermines basic human capacities through cumulative brain damage.

Clearly, pre-emptive paternalism carries the most weight in Dixon's case against boxing. Thus, he is open to similar legal restrictions on American football, even though he regards it as morally better than boxing (Dixon 2016: 112 n5). Likewise, while he sees MMA as morally worse than boxing or American football, he forgoes judgment on MMA's legality, because he is unsure of its brain damage risks (relative to boxing). He seems to think that pre-emptive paternalism's verdict on American football and MMA cannot be rendered without further study (2015: 366).

Legal moralism provides another method of justifying legal restrictions on MMA. This view calls for bans on 'free-floating' evils – immoral actions that do involve personal wrongs or individual harms – in other words, the law may act against immorality per se. Joel Feinberg is careful to distinguish legal moralism from 'moral conservatism', the view that a society is entitled to enforce its current view of morality (1990: 124–6). The legal moralist accepts that the law should enforce only true morality – principles validated by rigorous critical reflection. Likewise, while legal moralism holds that there is always *some* reason to use law against immorality, it also accepts that factors such as enforcement costs inform *all-things-considered* decisions about legal enforcement (ibid).

Supposedly, voluntary gladiatorial matches would constitute a grave free-floating evil, even if we set paternalistic concerns about fighters' interests aside. It is grossly immoral to participate in such destruction, and the audience's enjoyment of the spectacle makes matters much worse (in fact, Kristol saw the audience's enjoyment of the death spectacle as the primary moral problem). For Dixon, boxing, MMA, and gladiatorial contests have the same basic intent – to create suffering for the enjoyment of an audience (Kristol 1971; Dixon 2001: 339).

However, Dixon eschews direct appeals to legal moralism. The cumulative paternalistic case against boxing is, he thinks, sufficient to justify a legal ban on head-strikes (he notes, with some satisfaction, that this would most likely lead to the sport's overall demise) (Dixon 2001: 343). And while Dixon recognizes the distinction between moral conservatism and legal moralism, he still worries that the latter is subject to abuse (as a practical matter, the current majority still determines the content of 'true' morality) (ibid: 338–40).

Others, including the CMA, seem less concerned with the overreach of legal moralism. Physicians such as Reid seem to think that, even if American football, boxing, and MMA have comparable CTE risks, the case for a legal ban on the latter sports is stronger. Dixon defends the basic intent distinction, but he declines to press it as a reason for legal restrictions (which explains his ambivalence concerning American football and MMA).

Paternalism, slavery, and brain damage

Soft paternalism

In my view, concerns about information access cannot carry much weight in arguments for long-term restrictions on personal liberty. As Dixon seems to acknowledge, the liberal response to lack of information is better information (2001: 325–6). We should, however, accept a moral duty to avoid participation in the spread of disinformation, especially where disinformation leads people to underestimate serious risks. Here, we should be wary the popular folklore concerning MMA's relative safety (Kirk 2020).

> The Simple Theory: Because MMA involves sustained periods of grappling and shorter fights, MMA fighters absorb less punishment than boxers. Even the seeming brutality of permitting fights to continue after knock-downs lessens cumulative damage – a fighter who is finished on the ground in seconds isn't permitted to stand for several minutes of additional blows. So MMA fighters must have a lower risk of cumulative brain damage than boxers (perhaps even lower than American football players).

The Simple Theory, which finds support in some early empirical work on MMA (Ngai et al. 2008), has entrenched itself in the thinking of many MMA supporters, but it must be rejected. The Simple Theory ignores more recent empirical work on MMA, and it ignores other difficulties in the assessment of CTE risk (Kirk 2020). While it is still plausible to think that MMA's CTE risk is somewhat lower than CTE risk in boxing, it is hard to see how this difference makes a moral difference.

Fans who use the Simple Theory to justify their consumption of MMA are deceiving themselves, and their promulgation of the Simple Theory is irresponsible. Fighters who pursue MMA under the influence of the Simple Theory work from a naïve picture of risk.

Economic coercion

According to Dixon, '[i]f boxers are primarily motivated by the intrinsic enjoyment that they gain from the activity, we would expect that they would be evenly distributed throughout all socioeconomic classes' (2001: 328). While some fighters find boxing's machoism, status, skill, and courage attractive, the majority are motivated primarily by profit. In Dixon's words,

> I suspect that the majority of fighters, while they may share some of all of these motives, are more ambivalent toward their occupation. They regard the pain and injuries that they suffer, the damage that they inflict on opponents, and the indignity of performing in public in their underwear before a crowd that wants to see at least one of the two fighters get hurt, as unpleasant necessities to be endured in order to achieve financial and physical security and have a shot at the rich rewards that are available to highly successful boxers.
>
> (Dixon 2001)

Boxing's defenders often valorize it as the sport of the poor, insisting on admiration for fighters' heart and determination (Anderson 2007: 155). But, as Heather Reid (2006) argues, Roman gladiators were also worthy of admiration, genuine athletes who cultivated Stoic dignity in their awful circumstances. Similar points apply to laborers such as coal miners. Our admiration for coal miners and gladiators cannot validate enslavement, appalling working conditions, or the manipulation of economic disadvantage (Anderson 2007: 160).

I admit that the argument from economic coercion gives me pause. I love to watch MMA, but I do not fight (do not share in its risks) and that makes me feel uneasy. For similar reasons, I find the picture of wealthy white men around the ring of Ali-Frazier 1 unsettling. However, because my friends who do fight would probably see my hesitation as silly or offensively paternalistic, I press on.

Dixon's argument involves group soft paternalism, legal restrictions on an entire group to protect a vulnerable subgroup where targeted restrictions are not feasible (Malmqvist 2014). The threshold for justifying such restrictions may be quite low where the liberty lacks significant value. Paid live kidney donation is a good example – while the risks of such donations are low, financial gain is the only plausible reason for them. Boxing and MMA, by contrast, involve serious exercises of purposive capacities – skills or arts that people can dedicate themselves to. Clearly, Dixon places little weight on the liberty interests in question, but this low weighting derives, in part, from his moralistic judgment concerning boxing and MMA.

Of course, we should not ignore professional boxing's demographics. But many aspects of the social institution have no necessary connection to boxing contests themselves. People who find the prospect of fighting attractive may be deterred by boxing's sad history of corruption and poor regulation. Likewise, longstanding moralistic attitudes towards fighting and entrenched socioeconomic class expectations (fighting, like menial service work, is an occupation of the poor) provide further disincentives for would-be fighters. Obviously, similar considerations apply to would-be female fighters. Dixon's demand for an 'even distribution' of fighters among socioeconomic classes ignores these considerations. Fighting sports may always, absent the emergence of a martial aristocratic social class, bias towards the poor. But even if the distribution contrast for fighting sports is starker than that of other professions, no professional sports or dangerous professions are likely to meet an even distribution criterion.

MMA poses additional problems for the economic coercion argument. Dixon has little interest in MMA's particulars, but he seems to regard it as more demeaning than boxing because MMA permits attacks to continue on the ground (2015: 365). All other things being equal then, MMA's demographics should reflect an even greater concentration in poverty. However, the story of MMA's demographics is more complex.

MMA has a healthy supply of anecdotal evidence for disputing the economic coercion argument's demographic expectation. Elite-level MMA gives us examples of fighters from well-to-do backgrounds (e.g., B. J. Penn) and many, many college-educated wrestlers (e.g., Ben Askren, Mark Coleman, Ryan Bader, Daniel Cormier, Brock Lesnar). And it seems likely that National Collegiate Athletic Association (NCAA) wrestling will serve as an important recruiting ground for future MMA fighters in North America (Hockensmith 2019). Wrestlers who opt to pursue an MMA career post-college are unlikely to fit the model of the poverty-stricken boxer. Moreover, since the high end of MMA pay-offs remain far below boxing's greatest financial rewards, Dixon's coercive incentive story has less traction against MMA.

We should, of course, be wary of over generalization. There are plenty of MMA fighters from poor backgrounds, and a full picture of MMA requires us to look beyond elite-level fighters and elite organizations. We should also consider whether the Simple Theory influences MMA fighter choices.[1] But I suspect that thorough analysis of fighter demographics would make more trouble for the economic coercion argument.[2]

Pre-emptive paternalism

Dixon's pre-emptive paternalism is central to his case against boxing. Pre-emptive paternalism requires us to block choices that would seriously compromise people's future autonomy. Here, Dixon sees a clear analogy with J. S. Mill's rejection of slavery contracts – consensual slavery undermines the basis or purpose of liberty, our right to pursue and develop our own authentic conception of the good. Brain damage, according to Dixon, is even worse than slavery, as slavery contracts do not, by themselves, undermine a person's basic capacity to determine her ends (2001: 332–5). Thus, because a majority of professional boxers suffer some degree of brain damage, boxing agreements should be treated as invalid. Pamela Sailors (2015), with contemporary concerns about CTE in mind, extends this same line of argument to American football.

Dixon acknowledges Feinberg's worries concerning excessive paternalism. If the state is entitled to protect my future interests against my own (informed and free) judgment, where do we stop (Feinberg 1986: 77; Dixon 2001: 333)? Should we also ban the consumption of fatty foods? Dixon, however, insists that there must be some room for judgment, especially where the costs of bad choices are grave. He asks us to consider whether we would ban a food product that causes long-term brain damage (Dixon 2001: 334).

There is room for judgment, but the slavery/brain damage analogy is heavy-handed. And it blurs the distinction between different normative considerations. Are we to say that any degree of long-term brain damage is on a par with, or perhaps worse than, chattel slavery? Suppose that a person, *A*, accepts a small level of long-term cognitive loss later in life to maximize their pursuit of a cherished project, a project which involves the development and testing her skills and talents. Assume she has no good reason to think that the later loss of ability will be so bad as to overwhelm the sense of satisfaction obtained by maximizing satisfaction of her current project (Lopez Frias and McNamee 2017: 271–3). Dixon's view implies that pursuit of the current project is comparable to a slavery contract, but this seems wildly implausible. *A* does not sacrifice her basic capacity to set her own ends.

Of course, one might complain that this line of argument parallels Gerald Dworkin's questions about the possible legitimacy of slavery contracts. If a person decides that her overall interests are satisfied by the benefits of a slavery contract, why should we not respect such a contract as an exercise of autonomous choice (Dworkin 1983)? Here I follow Arthur Ripstein's reading of Kant – one aspect of autonomy is relational – autonomy requires us to maintain our basic independence from the choices of other persons (2009: 33–5). If *A* agrees to be a slave, she abandons the idea of herself as a self-directing agent – she becomes her master's chattel. And, as a chattel slave, she gives her master the right to destroy her basic capacities (or what remains of them) if the master so chooses. Dixon's slavery comparison misses this distinctive aspect of slavery. *A* neither fundamentally disables herself nor agrees to be another person's chattel (Lopez Frias and McNamee 2017: 272).

Neither boxers nor MMA fighters give another person the right to cause them long-term brain damage, as this problem is tied to the cumulative effects of a fighting career. Arguably, fighters accept a fairly high risk of some later capacity loss, and a lower but non-trivial risk of more severe capacity losses, for the sake of their profession. How should we assess such risks?

Setting the magical moral line for acceptable risk is difficult, perhaps impossible. But before we consider that problem, let us examine the relevant risks in more detail. Awareness of what we now call CTE emerged in the early 20th century with the study of 'dementia pugilistica' among professional boxers. A random survey of retired UK boxers showed that 17% suffered problems similar to those now associated with CTE, and 40% of the remaining fighters some cognitive or behavioral problems (Bernick and Banks 2013; Clausen et al. 2005) However, in the last decade the explosion of concern with CTE has focused on American football and its seemingly high risk of CTE (Asken and Bauer 2018).

CTE is generally described as a neurodegenerative disease characterized by abnormal aggregation of tau proteins, which generate distinctive patterns of 'neurofibrillary tangles' or lesions in the brain. While much research is being conducted to determine clear biomarkers for CTE, decisive diagnosis must be made post-mortem (Finkel and Bieniek 2019). The disease is associated with repeated head trauma (RTH). However, recent work on CTE holds repeated concussions (head blows that cause familiar concussive symptoms) do not provide a good indicator of CTE risk. Rather, it now appears that CTE is caused by prolonged exposure to sub-concussive (or symptom free) RTH. (Tagge et al. 2018). The clinical manifestation of CTE appears to follow two distinct paths – some cases begin in to the 30–50 years age-range with behavioral/mood problems but modest cognitive impairment. In other cases, initial onset comes much later with more serious cognitive problems and, sometimes, motor control losses (Finkel and Bieniek 2019: 573).

Some authors complain of a media driven panic over CTE, with caution (or skepticism) being pressed on multiple issues, including evidence of causation. (Asken and Bauer 2018). Fans of boxing themselves are entitled to some level of skepticism too. The much-cited study from the UK is seriously dated, with no similar study of retired boxers since. Most contemporary boxers have shorter careers with fewer bouts (Clausen et al. 2005). However, while there is some confounding evidence, RTH remains the single biggest risk factor (in fact the only clear risk factor) that we can identify in CTE causation. Atypical cases and ambiguities concerning CTE's classification do nothing to change this. It is distantly possible, but highly unlikely, that CTE itself will turn out to be artefactual (benign brain lesions are not especially common). Even if CTE did turn out to be artefactual, the powerful correlation between RTH and the relevant symptom cluster would still require explanation (Finkel and Bienek 2019). Causation does not preclude exceptional cases and speculation about unknown genetic factors (if they exist) cannot guide risk mitigation for current athletes. As Finkel and Bienek note, the claim that many (or even most) athletes will escape CTE misunderstands the notion of risk (2019).

Consider their assessment of CTE risk in the NFL. Finkel and Bieniek (ibid.) use the 110 confirmed NFL CTE cases to calculate the absolute lower bound for CTE risk in an NFL career. They assume that the 110 cases confirmed are the only cases in the history of the NFL (cohort 1963–2008), and then calculate total risk with reference to the total number of players in NFL history. Depending on the method of setting the length of an average NFL career, the resulting CTE risk comes in between 6 in 1,000 and 13 in 1,000. According to Finkel and Bieniek, accepted legal safety standards (in areas under the jurisdiction of the US Occupational Safety and Health Administration) would call for workplace modifications for any similar 1 in 1,000 risk. While there is some non-zero risk of CTE for the general population, there is little if any reason to think that adjusting for this general risk would come close to taking the specific NFL risk below 1 in 1,000. Really, we have good reason to think that the distinctive minimum NFL CTE risk must come in at around 1 percent (ibid.: 580–2).

There are no comparable assessments of the minimum CTE risks for boxers and MMA fighters. The Simple Theory, of course, holds that MMA's CTE risk must come in significantly lower than that of boxing. But the Simple Theory is empirically naïve. A recent systematic review (Thomas and Thomas 2018) complains about the quality and consistency of measures in studies of MMA injury rates, but two studies are worth noting. Hutchinson et al. (2014) draw attention to the number of blows that downed fighters receive before a match is called (by TKO); they also find that the concussion rate in the UFC exceeds that of boxing. More recently, a study by Bernick et al. (2020a) conducted an extensive video review of 30 high level MMA matches and 30 high level boxing contests. The authors found a higher concussion rate per minute in the MMA matches. While recent work on CTE emphasizes sub-concussive RTH, these findings should still undermine confidence in the Simple Theory.

There two confirmed CTE cases, and at least five more suspected cases, in MMA fighters (Magraken 2019). Moreover, as Bernick's fighter brain study notes, because the sport is young, we do not have a significant retirement class to study. Reviews of current fighters showed somewhat lower levels of brain volume loss in MMA fighters compared with their boxing peers, but this, by itself, cannot tell us much about long term risks (Bernick et al. 2020b). An accurate assessment of the comparative CTE risks in American football, boxing and MMA would appear to require large long-term epidemiological studies. And keep in mind that firm diagnosis of CTE can only achieved post-mortem (ibid). So, if a refined (or complete) assessment of risk is needed for decisions about whether any of these sports should be legally banned, or radically modified, all three are entitled to a much longer and more thorough test run. Boxing fans can complain that the conditions of their sport have changed in the relevant ways since the mid-20th century (Clausen et al. 2005).

And what if some clear difference in risk did emerge? Suppose for the sake of argument that the NFL's career CTE risk comes in at 7 percent, while boxing and MMA come in at around 12 percent. Dedicated NFL fans might valorize this difference as vindicating their sport – but they could not pretend that the NFL risk, unlike the others, satisfies some more general, and widely accepted, threshold for CTE risk.

If the general idea of workplace (say for factory work) set the standard for acceptable risk, none of these sports would be permissible in their current forms. Imagine a factory work example that parallels Finkel and Bienek's minimum NFL CTE risk. Repeated exposure to this carcinogen carries a 1 in 100 chance of developing of brain lesions powerfully correlated with the clinical conditions associated with CTE. None of the current skepticism concerning CTE could justify a government's refusal to impose workplace modifications.[3] For this reason, I find Dixon's hesitation concerning legal restrictions on MMA and American rules football (given his appeal to food safety standards) puzzling.[4]

For reasons of distributive justice, people should have access to both safe food and satisfying forms of work that do not involve significant risks of physical harm. But people should also be permitted to pursue life plans that involve more serious risks. Here, the simple distinction between soft paternalism and hard paternalism misses important distinctions – both Dixon and Feinberg seem to agree that a ban in trans fats constitutes excessive paternalism. But it is difficult to see how a ban on trans fats interferes with anyone's deeply held religious views or subjectively valued life-plans. On their own terms, virtually everyone would agree that the liberty to consume trans fats is trivial or unimportant to their actual plan of life (a ban may even be beneficial given their personal values) (Conly 2017: 212–7). Likewise, it is hard to see how the internal goods of factory work require one to prove their mettle through long term exposure to a carcinogen.

The internal goods of boxing and MMA appear to require higher levels of risk. Like Anderson, I find it hard to see how boxing could still be boxing if we removed head-strikes (Anderson 2007: 185). For some, the internal goods of MMA are rooted in the chimerical notion of a real fight – MMA shows what would happen in a real fight. Seen through this lens, the development of MMA's rules, along with the addition of features of such as rounds and gloves, compromises its internal goods. Others, such as the legendary brawler Tank Abbott, complain that grappling techniques would be ineffective in the real world because of biting, eye gouging, hard floor surfaces, and the availability of crude weapons (Downey 2014). So even the early UFC's prohibition on biting and gouging, along with its lack of asphalt or concrete surfaces (real fights cannot occur in a meadow it seems), compromised reality and unduly favored grapplers. Real fights are a matter of punching and kicking, spectacular punching and kicking. Thus, rules that incentivize action, or give the referee the discretion to stand up fighters engaged in an apparent grappling stalemate, approximate reality. But, as Greg Downey argues, this sense of realism is influenced by aesthetic expectations of what a real fight should look like, and these expectations are in turn influenced by action films and video games (ibid). Fans should consider whether their desire for exciting fights increases MMA's CTE and brain damage risks, and whether this increased risk is justified. Likewise, those who now grudgingly accept MMA as sufficiently civilized, in comparison with UFC 1, should consider whether the development of MMA's rules uniformly reduces its risks (the question of the effects of gloves and their effects on grappling techniques comes to mind).

I do think that MMA provides a useful testing ground for fighting techniques, and I find Bas Rutten's perspective on reality (Rutten has a more charitable perspective on grappling) more plausible than Tank Abbott's (Interview 2021).[5] But the notion of a real fight must remain problematic and elusive. Better to approach MMA as the combination of striking and grappling arts that can be trained and tested over time. This, I think, helps to explain the exclusion of biting, gouging, and at least some of the moves excluded by contemporary North American MMA rules.

But CTE risk is a cost of MMA, and it seems unrealistic to hope that further scientific research will say otherwise. Since sub-concussive RTH is the main (or the only) risk factor in CTE, capping career fights (fights can serve a rough proxy for the accumulated damage from training) should reduce CTE risk. Refined assessments of accumulated damage (by video survey) might be developed, but I doubt that such measures could be implemented outside elite level organizations. Even a cap on the number of fights requires cooperation between various jurisdictions and regulatory authorities.[6]

Moralism, intent, and violence

Of course, risk reduction strategies will not satisfy critics' deeper moral objections to MMA and boxing. Consider, again, the comparison with voluntary gladiatorial contests. In his paper on boxing, Dixon asserts that:

> [i]f anything is so inherently immoral, regardless of the voluntary participation of both fighters and spectators, as to justify prohibition, such gladiatorial contests are ... If this example allows a foot inside the door for strict legal moralism, may we not use the same principle to justify restricting the brutal business of professional boxing, which differs from gladiatorial combat only in the severity of the injuries inflicted? Granted, the difference in degree is huge – the certainty of death for the losing gladiator v. the probability of brain damage for both boxers if they fight many contests – but the morally troubling feature is the same in both cases: the infliction of pain and injury for the pleasure of onlookers.
>
> (Dixon 2001: 339)

Gladiatorial contests remain gravely immoral, even if we set paternalistic concern for fighters aside. Moreover, the enjoyment of the audience generates an enormous free-floating evil, one that merits a legal ban. A similar case applies to boxing, despite the difference of degree in harm.

But Dixon worries that arguments from legal moralism are subject to abuse. Supposedly, his paternalistic arguments are strong enough to ban head strikes in boxing, but perhaps insufficient for legal restrictions on MMA. Others appear to endorse a sort of combined approach – the basic intent of MMA and boxing makes the case for legal restrictions against these sports stronger than the case against American football (even if brain damage risks turn out to be equal or closely comparable).

Kantian respect

Dixon's MMA paper drops the gladiatorial example, making use of somewhat less dramatic examples. His purpose, I think, is to show that MMA remains immoral even if it should not be subject to a legal ban. We are supposed to see MMA as morally worse, in Kantian terms, than his other examples of legally permissible immoralities. Some consensual activities run afoul of Kant's second formulation of the categorical imperative, which requires us to treat humanity, in ourselves and others, as ends, never solely as means. We must never treat other persons as mere things, nor allow ourselves to be treated as mere things. For Dixon, participants in fighting sports treat each other as things, things to be injured, hurt, or incapacitated (2015: 367).

Kant, of course, insisted that sexual intercourse outside marriage reduces participants to mere things. Dixon waives this aspect of Kant away – he appears to think that Kant's concerns are satisfied if sex occurs within the context of a loving or mutually respectful relationship (ibid.: 371–3). Fighting, however, parallels objectionable practices such as dwarf-tossing and servile sex (where a woman subordinates her own pleasure to that of her husband). The attitudes of aggression that fighters show each other during bouts must, it seems, parallel the attitude of the tosser or self-concerned husband. Indeed, the disrespect in fighting must be worse than that found in male-centered sex, because the former involves intent to injure, not mere indifference to pleasure. Thus, each fighter, in waiving his right against attacks, accepts an even greater indignity than the servile wife or the tossee. The relevant disrespect cannot be made good by any subsequent (post-fight) displays of admiration – treating a person respectfully tomorrow does not change the fact that I disrespected them today. And the moral wrong is made all the worse by the fact it is performed for an audience that comes to enjoy human suffering. That, in a nutshell, is the argument (Dixon 2015).

Danny Rosenberg (this volume) responds to Dixon's Kantian argument at some length, so I will keep my own comments brief. Dixon's demand that fighters show (or perhaps express) their respect for each other's personhood during every moment of their bout is illegitimate. Few service relationships would satisfy this standard – often, it is the understanding that one will be paid afterward that makes things good. And Kant, as I understand him, did not insist that every moment of our interaction with another person express our respect for them. He worried (perhaps implausibly) that mutual respect could be utterly lost in the animalistic use of another's body during sex (Herman 1993). Similar considerations, I suppose, apply to fighting. Yet fighting requires you to be mindful of your opponent's own intentions. More importantly, boxing and MMA fights occur within an understood framework. Each party comes to test their own skills, and the relevant permissions or waivers end where one participant is either unable or unwilling to continue. And, because of the risks of such tests, the rules are enforced by a specially trained third party. Absent such a background the post-fight shows of respect that Dixon deems irrelevant would not be possible.

It is no accident that Dixon's other examples lack any parallel of post-fight respect.[7] Servile behavior does not induce shows of respect. But a fighter struggling to secure a triangle choke from her back is not practicing servility. She does not consent to be used as a passive throwing object or choose to subordinate her own interests (or goals) to those of another. Rather, she is engaged in a difficult and risky test of her own skills – in one way, her striking opponent is thing-like (the blows and ferocious intent are a challenge to be overcome, like a cliff-face or a dangerous obstacle course). In short, because each fighter is engaged in a test of her own skills (and each can see her opponent engaged in their own such test), fighting is, unlike servility, consistent with Kantian respect for persons.[8] By contrast, a person who lives a servile life fails to recognize her own status as a purposive agent – her conduct is immoral even if she never abandons her formal rights. And a person who encourages servility in others, unlike a fight opponent, acts immorally even if he violates no formal rights.

In straining to show MMA in a bad light, Dixon downplays the moral significance of servility, and he places unreasonable limits on the class of morally permissible activities. I've been choked unconscious a few times (three I think) in years of Brazilian Jiu-Jitsu (BJJ) sparring. Perhaps I should have tapped quicker, but comparisons with the tossed little person and the servile wife just do not ring true. For Dixon, any competition where one person wins by the infliction of pain or temporary unconsciousness is an afront to human dignity (2015: 380). But once the pain passes and/or you wake up, how are you different from any other loser? You lost. Isn't that what really hurts?[9]

Basic intent and double effect

The counterargument, I guess, is that the basic intent in boxing and MMA involves lasting harm rather than transitory hurt.[10] Surely, knockouts and TKOs by strikes, if not submissions by chokes or joint locks, are relevantly similar to death by the sword. Thus, real harm, and the enjoyment of it, is the basic intent in both sports. Or so the critics say. In truth, we should be much more careful about concepts such as basic intent – MMA and boxing, like all sports, come together and are sustained by a variety of sometimes overlapping, sometimes conflicting, interests. But, if there is a suitable organizing concept for MMA, it is the one I suggested in the second section, the combining of striking and grappling arts (arts that can be tested and developed through training). Within certain safety parameters and time limits, an MMA contest goes far enough (in terms of violence and risk of injury) to determine a decisive winner – no further. Some fans and some fighters may desire to see or inflict permanent injuries, but that is not sufficient for the categorical moral condemnation that critics such as Dixon claim.

Of course, Dixon mocks the claim that fighters need not intend harm (Dixon 2015: 377). No doubt, a game fighter may hit her opponent with no less force than someone who has the goal of doing as much long-term injury as possible. And, on reflection, fighters must accept that they enter the ring/cage planning to cause (hopefully) transitory but potentially serious injuries (we may want knockouts to function as they do in old Hollywood films, but, sadly, they don't). Many fans and fighters do find the immediate elation of the knockout is followed by a sense of concern for the downed fighter's well-being (Sokol 2004). We want the spectacular. But we want things to be OK afterwards. You can call that contradictory. I see it as cutting things a bit close.

BJJ-focused MMA fans may wish to downplay the importance of knockouts in MMA. For them, the pinnacle of MMA may be submissions wins by fighters such as Demian Maia (wins that need not deliver any real injury at all). But plenty of fans want to see knockouts, and there is no question that knockouts are, like submissions, highly prized forms of victory in MMA. And Maia's submissions are as impressive as they are because they occur in a context where he is at risk of being knocked out by strikes.

A contrast with actual Roman gladiatorial contests is useful here. Those matches were products of careful selection – fighters were usually paired with opponents of comparable skill, size, and experience. While matches had no specific time limit, most did not last beyond ten or 15 minutes. When one fighter suffered a serious (or potentially fatal) wound, the referee would halt the contest – the fighter with the upper hand would back away (failure to comply with that rule might itself prove fatal). Whether the downed fighter would live was left to the editor (or promoter), who usually followed the vocal assessment of the audience. A loser who had failed to provide a satisfactory performance was expected to kneel and accept execution by the victor (Strauss 2010: 13–16). Of course, some match-ending moves were fatal by themselves, and some excused losers succumbed to their wounds. An utterly boring stalemate might end badly for both contestants. But it was also possible for matches to be called a draw and both fighters 'released standing' after a sustained, exciting and closely fought match (Potter 1999: 307). I do not say that Roman audiences lacked bloodthirst – but describing their enjoyment of these contests as simple schadenfreude misses a great deal.

Consider a consensual version of Roman contests. Fighters satisfy whatever standard of informed consent you like, and they have a right to save themselves by surrender. Promoters also have the right to call a released standing – under the influence of an impressed audience. One such contest, a 20-minute dance on the edge of death where neither fighter suffered more than a scratch is widely regarded as the match of the century (again, Maia's submission wins provide something of a parallel for BJJ-loving MMA fans). We should, I suppose, see these gladiatorial contests as both morally and legally impermissible, but they are harder to dismiss than the picture of two unskilled fools vying for a million-dollar prize in a one-must-die contest (Fagan 2014: 470). Ripstein answers Kristol's challenge by arguing that voluntary gladiatorial contests must be, unlike boxing contests, construed as slavery agreements. Each fighter affords the other a master's right over life and death (2009: 140–3). Elsewhere, I argue that my modified gladiatorial contests are not slavery agreements. The killings that occur, while they are in some sense intentional, are not comparable to masters disposing of their slaves (Ramsay 2017a).

The best explanation of the impermissibility of my modified gladiatorial contests still shows a firm contrast with boxing and MMA. In the former, the highest most decisive victory just is the destruction of one's opponent, and this victory is special because it is obtained by facing death by another's hand. Similarly, the audience's appreciation of the sport, however sophisticated, requires a background of death. The match of the century is what it is because the threat of death is real, a reality grounded in deaths that have come before. Death is close and that is exciting. It makes the fighters' performances more impressive (as Maia's submission wins are made more impressive by the background threat of being knocked out). My gladiatorial matches do more than risk human destruction – they require human destruction for their appreciation.

By contrast, brain damage is not required for the appreciation of boxing or MMA. Far from it. You can see death on the sand of the arena, but you cannot observe the CTE that *may* manifest years later. Do we think that fight fans crying for action (or blood, if you like) are also bringing up mental images of aged fighters' later cognitive impairments? If you are wondering why that question is relevant, think back to legal moralism. What magnifies the free-floating evil of the death-matches is the audience's enjoyment of death – treating death as a public entertainment. Dixon's moralistic comparison between boxing and gladiatorial matches has the probability of long-term brain damage paralleling death in the arena, but this parallel doesn't make sense in an (audience focused) moralistic argument.[11] In fact, many MMA fans seek comfort in the Simple Theory because the prospect of long-term brain damage threatens to disrupt their enjoyment of fights. Similar considerations apply to the CTE skepticism of boxing fans and American football fans.

You may still insist that fight fans enjoy suffering, but this a bit simplistic. Think of the thrills and cheers sometimes generated by the 'bad boxing' in MMA. This is a label that refined boxing fans might place on Griffin-Bonnar 1, a slugfest filled with primitive reciprocity. In schadenfreude, we savor the suffering of another person – sometimes bare knowledge of their misfortune is enough. But where is the time for that in Griffin-Bonnar 1? And what thrills is not the brief look at the pain on Bonnar's fighter's face; what thrills is that even as his head is snapped back Bonnar wails back on Griffin, and vice versa. It seems like they aren't feeling the pain that must be there or are just waiving it off with furious contempt. Perhaps I am projecting too much of myself on the rest of the audience, but I don't think so. When there are pauses, moments to be savored, what gets cheers? The scene of a pained face in a submission hold? Sure. But what about the fighter who smiles and laughs off (as convincingly as possible) what seemed like a finishing strike? There cheers are there too. Patient and clearly painful extended periods of grappling (perhaps regrettably) don't always generate the same interest (Bowman n.d.). And one-sided violence becomes boring. I still remember sitting in a bar in Waterloo, Ontario watching Velasquez-Silva, booing along with the rest of crowd, wanting a stoppage when Silva was clearly beaten.

Critics may still insist that MMA and boxing differ, in terms of basic intent, from sports such as American football. According to Dixon,

> In football, tackles and hits are aimed at stopping opponents from advancing the ball. Any pain and injury is incidental to this goal. When a hit no longer achieves the goal of stopping the opponent, such as a late hit on a quarterback who has already released the ball, we condemn it, since it becomes gratuitous violence. In contrast, causing pain and injury is inseparable from achieving victory in MMA. The claim that a punch, kick, elbow, or choke hold was intended to achieve victory, but not to cause pain or injury, would be risible. This moral distinction between MMA and football would remain even if our increased awareness of the risk of CTE in football revealed the sport to be even more dangerous than MMA. The crucial difference would be that causing pain and injury is a side effect of football whereas it is the explicit goal of MMA.
>
> (Dixon 2015: 377)

As I understand it, this line of argument appeals to the doctrine of double effect, the idea that we may sometimes cause otherwise wrongful consequences for the sake of morally important objectives. The relevant consequences must be merely foreseen, not desired for their own sake or used as means to one's ends (McIntyre 2019).

As noted earlier, I lack the intuition that pain or temporary loss of consciousness are, in the context of a consensual contest, wrongful (a gap in my moral knowledge helpful to my enjoyment of BJJ). Moreover, strikes delivered after the bell, or after the referee has called a match, are as illegal in boxing and MMA as they are in other sports. While play is on, it seems wildly implausible to think that pain is not used (routinely) as a means of securing the ball or impeding opposing players' performance in other sports. (Ramsay 2017b; Sailors 2015: 275). You might say that other injuries, including long term brain damage, are merely a foreseeable risk of football, but that is a lame response.

Perhaps you can, in a just war, legitimate bombing a military target knowing that some civilian casualties are inevitable – the stakes are high and you never wanted to face such circumstances of choice. Sport is different – we choose (in a collective sense) to make and sustain sports – their character is within our control. The NFL could become a touch football league, though like Dixon's professional boxing without headstrikes, it probably would not last very long. You can appeal to double-effect in difficult circumstances, but you cannot use it to justify creating (or perpetuating) those difficult circumstances. Double effect doesn't permit you to set up a world in which crucial military targets are always close to civilian populations. 'Not a fair comparison!', you might say. Someone who did that would want to see civilians killed – football fans don't want to players to suffer long term injuries or CTE. Fair enough, but they probably do want to see the game played in a way not much different from the way it is played now, and many of them enjoy the visual thrill of the game's more spectacular collisions (Fagan 2014: 466). So fans must say that the goods secured by the game, *as is*, are worth their costs in terms of brain damage and long-term injuries (or argue that these costs are radically overestimated by the sport's critics). That is not much different from what boxing and MMA fans must (or can) say about their sports (Sokol 2004).

Conclusion

I have attempted a qualified defense of MMA, and by extension boxing, against paternalistic and moralistic criticisms. But I admit to some continuing reservations about both sports. The Romans seemed to regard their gladiators with a mixture of admiration and contempt. Fighting in the arena was an ordeal, one in which fighters could win redemption. Romans could feel comfortable watching fighters face such an ordeal in part because they saw these fighters as inferior or condemned. Boxers and MMA fighters face something similar, and this informs my discomfort with our fight of the century, Ali-Frazier 1. It feels as if those rich celebrities, absent some claim to superiority, did not deserve to watch Ali-Frazier 1. I am not interested in hero worship of fighters, but I sometimes feel I do not deserve to watch the fights that I enjoy.[12]

Notes

1 Since Dixon thinks that most boxers are unaware of brain-damage risks, it is hard to see how this risk can feature in his appeal to economic coercion. Boxers cannot experience this risk as coercive if they are unaware of it.
2 Of course, some will insist that the appeal of MMA is tied to a story about the rise of hypermasculinity in late capitalism, or something like that. I must leave my thoughts on such stories for another day.
3 In fact, according to Finkel and Bieniek, for jobs that fall within the jurisdiction of the US Occupational Health and Safety Administration, a distinctive 1 in a 1,000 risk of a CTE-like condition would justify governmental intervention (2019), But they make no specific claims concerning appropriate risk reduction policies for the NFL.

4 To be fair, Dixon's hesitant approach to legal restrictions on MMA precedes a good deal of the CTE and MMA risk literature that I cite here, though he does take note of the Hutchinson et al. (2014) assessment of head injuries in MMA (Dixon 2015. 382n6). Why not call for a ban on blows to the head in MMA? If MMA ends up with an acceptable level of risk because it limits total head trauma through grappling and shorter fights, why shouldn't we allow boxing to pursue a similar risk reduction strategy? His confident assessment of boxing's excessive risk is based on empirical claims from the 1980s, Morrison (1986) for example (Dixon 2001: 323). Should Dixon be confident that contemporary boxing is still too risky, if he is unsure about MMA?
5 See Kesting (2018).
6 And the question of where to set a cap on fights brings us back to the more basic question of acceptable risk. Even if we had a much firmer grasp on MMA's CTE risk (a strong sense of how each fight or career year increases CTE risk), we would still have to ask ourselves where the line of acceptable career risk lies. Perhaps we could tie this to some notion of plausible peak performance, a point where fighters have been given sufficient opportunity to demonstrate how good or effective they can be.
7 But, as I once told Dixon, if dwarf-tossing was routinely followed by tearful or emotional embraces between tosser and tossee, I would feel obliged to further evaluate the practice before rendering moral judgment.
8 'Mighty' Mike Murga maintains that being tossed properly requires training. But Murga, in my opinion, overstates the importance of weightlifting to his 'ability' to be thrown across a room. Of course, one might become 'skilled' in taking directions or satisfying the desires of other persons. The relevant skills might be interesting in their own right, but if they are deployed only to satisfy the particular whims or goals of others, one remains servile. See Nover (2019).
9 But see Tremblay (this volume) for a fighter's perspective on loss in MMA.
10 Borrowing terms from Parry (1998).
11 It's no accident that Kristol himself had no intention of criticizing boxing. To my knowledge, he articulated no views about MMA, though it is easy to imagine him objecting to it, for homophobic reasons.
12 I thank the ARPA 2020 audience for their comments on my presentation of an early version of this chapter. I also thank Charlotte Peak for her comments on a subsequent draft of the chapter. And I thank Theodore Giesen, Patrick Gouthro and Ryan Whiston for discussion of this chapter's themes during my 2020 philosophical topics seminar.

References

Anderson, J. (2007) *The Legality of Boxing: A Punch Drunk Love?* New York: Routledge.
Asken, B. and Bauer, R.M. (2018) 'Chronic Traumatic Encephalopathy: The Horse Is Still Chasing the Cart', *Journal of Orthopaedic and Sports Physical Therapy*, 48(9): 672–675.
Bernick, C. and Banks, S. (2013) 'What Boxing Tells Us About Repetitive Head Trauma and the Brain', *Alzheimer's Research & Therapy*, 5(3): 23.
Bernick, C., Hansen, T., Ng, W., Williams, V., Goodman, M., Nalepa, B., Shan, G., and Seifert, T. (2020a) 'Concussion Occurrence and Recognition in Professional Boxing and MMA Matches: Toward a Concussion Protocol in Combat Sports', *The Physician and Sportsmedicine*, https://www.tandfonline.com/doi/abs/10.1080/00913847.2020.1856631?journalCode=ipsm2, accessed 15 January 2021.
Bernick, C., Shan, G., Zetterberg, H., Banks, S., Mishra, V. R., Bekris, L., Leverenz, J. B. and Blennow, K. (2020b) 'Longitudinal Change in Regional Brain Volumes with Exposure to Repetitive Head Impacts', *Neurology*, 94(3): 232–240.
Bowman, P. (n.d.) 'On Ground Fighting', https://www.academia.edu/13745553/On_Ground_Fighting, accessed 23 January 2021.
CBC (2013) 'Medical Advice to MPs: Don't Legalize Mixed Martial Arts', *CBC*, 16 April, https://www.cbc.ca/news/politics/medical-advice-to-mps-don-t-legalize-mixed-martial-arts-1.1313826, accessed 15 January 2021.

Clausen, H., McCrory, P. and Anderson, V. (2005) 'The Risk of Chronic Traumatic Brain Injury in Professional Boxing: Change in Exposure Variables over the Past Century', *British Journal of Sports Medicine*, 39: 661–664.

Conly, S. (2017) 'Paternalism, Coercion and the Unimportance of (Some) Liberties', *Behavioral Public Policy*, 1(2): 207–218.

Dixon, N. (2001) 'Boxing, Paternalism, and Legal Moralism', *Social Theory and Practice*, 27(2): 323–344.

Dixon, N. (2015) 'A Moral Critique of Mixed Martial Arts', *Public Affairs Quarterly*, 29(4): 365–384.

Dixon, N. (2016) 'Internalism and External Moral Evaluation of Violent Sport', *Journal of Philosophy of Sport*, 43(1): 101–113.

Downey, G. (2014) '"As Real as It Gets!" Producing Hyperviolence in Mixed Martial Arts', *JOMEC Journal*, 5: 1–28.

Dworkin G. (1983) 'Paternalism: Some Second Thoughts', in R. E. Sartorius (ed.) *Paternalism*, Minneapolis: University of Minnesota Press, pp. 105–112.

Editorial (1971) 'The Fight', *New York Times*, March 10, https://www.nytimes.com/1971/03/10/archives/the-fight.html, accessed 15 January 2021.

Fagan, G, (2014) 'Gladiatorial Combat as Alluring Spectacle', in P. Christesen and D. G. Kyle (eds.) *A Companion to Sport and Spectacle in Greek and Roman Antiquity*, West Sussex: Wiley-Blackwell, pp. 465–477.

Feinberg, J. (1986) *Harm to Self: The Moral Limits of the Criminal Law (Volume 3)*, Oxford: Oxford University Press.

Feinberg, J. (1990) *Harmless Wrongdoing: The Moral Limits of the Criminal Law (Volume 4)*, Oxford: Oxford University Press.

Finkel A. M. and Bieniek, K. F. (2019) 'A Quantitative Risk Assessment for Chronic Traumatic Encephalopathy (CTE) in Football: How Public Health Science Evaluates Evidence', *Human and Ecological Risk Assessment: An International Journal*, 29(3): 564–589.

Greene, N. (2018) 'How John McCain Grew to Tolerate MMA, the Sport He Likened to "Human Cockfighting"', *Slate*, 26 August, https://slate.com/culture/2018/08/john-mccain-ufc-how-he-grew-to-tolerate-mma-the-sport-he-considered-human-cockfighting.html, accessed 15 January 2021.

Herman, B. (1993) 'Could It Be Worth Thinking about Kant on Sex and Marriage?', in L. Antony and C. Witt (eds.), *A Mind of One's Own: Feminist Essays on Reason and Objectivity*, Boulder: Westview Press, pp. 49–68.

Hockensmith, R, (2019) 'From NCAA to MMA: More College Wrestlers Are Fighting On', *ESPN*, 2 April, https://www.espn.com/mma/story/_/id/26424694/more-college-wrestlers-fighting-on, accessed 15 January 2021.

Hutchison, M. G., Lawrence, D. W., Cusimano, M. D., and Schweizer T. A. (2014) 'Head Trauma in Mixed Martial Arts', *American Journal of Sports Medicine*, 42(6): 1352–1358.

Interview (2021) 'Bas Rutten on Brazilian Jiu-Jitsu's Effectiveness for Self Defense', *Eastern Europe BJJ*, 22 January, https://www.bjjee.com/articles/bas-rutten-on-brazilian-jiu-jitsu-self-defense/, accessed 15 January 2021.

Kesting, S. (2018) 'Do Dirty Fighting Moves Work in Grappling?', *Grapplearts.com*, 16 October, https://www.grapplearts.com/dirty-fighting-in-grappling/, accessed 21 January 2021.

Kirk, C. (2020) 'Opinion: We Cannot Downplay CTE in MMA', *Sherdog*, 4 July, https://www.sherdog.com/news/articles/Opinion-We-Cannot-Downplay-CTE-in-MMA-173782, accessed 15 January 2021.

Kristol, I. (1971) 'Pornography, Obscenity, and the Case for Censorship', *New York Times*, 28 March, Section SM: 24, https://www.nytimes.com/1971/03/28/archives/pornography-obscenity-and-the-case-for-censorship-pornography.html, accessed 15 January 2021.

Lopez Frias, F. J. and McNamee, M. (2017) 'Ethics, Brain Injuries, and Sports: Prohibition, Reform, and Prudence', *Sport, Ethics and Philosophy*, 11(3): 264–280.

Magraken, E, (2019) 'Documenting CTE in Mixed Martial Arts', *Combat Sports Law*, 14 June, https://combatsportslaw.com/2019/06/14/documenting-cte-in-mixed-martial-arts/, accessed 21 January 2021.

Malmqvist, E. (2014) 'Are Bans on Kidney Sales Unjustifiably Paternalistic? ', *Bioethics*, 28(3): 110–118.

McIntyre, A. (2019) 'Doctrine of Double Effect', in *The Stanford Encyclopedia of Philosophy* (Spring 2019 Edition), https://plato.stanford.edu/archives/spr2019/entries/double-effect/, accessed 23 January 2021.

Morrison, R. G. (1986) 'Medical and Public Health Aspects of Boxing', *Journal of the American Medical Association*, 255(18): 2475–2480.

Ngai, K. M., Levy, F., and Hsu, E. B. (2008) 'Injury Trends in Sanctioned Mixed Martial Arts Competition: A 5-Year Review from 2002 to 2007', *British Journal of Sports Medicine*, 42(8): 686–689.

Nover, S. (2019) 'How a Trump Judicial Nominee Reignited the Debate over Dwarf Tossing', *Washington Post*, 22 January, https://www.washingtonpost.com/lifestyle/magazine/how-a-trump-judicial-nominee-reignited-the-debate-over-dwarf-tossing/2019/01/22/65fd885a-0d21-11e9-8938-5898adc28fa2_story.html, accessed 15 January 2021.

Parry, J. (1998) 'Violence and Aggression in Contemporary Sport', in M. McNamee and J. Parry (eds.) *Ethics and Sport*, New York: Routledge, pp. 205–224.

Potter, D. S. (1999) 'Entertainers in the Roman Empire', in D. S. Potter and D. J. Mattingly (eds.) *Life, Death, and Entertainment in the Roman Empire*, Ann Arbor: University of Michigan Press pp. 256–325.

Ramsay, M. (2017a) 'Slaves, Gladiators, and Death: Kantian Liberalism and the Moral Limits of Consent', *Legal Theory*, 23(2): 96–131.

Ramsay, M. (2017b) 'Violent Sports', in *International Encyclopedia of Ethics*, Malden: Wiley, pp. 1–5, https://onlinelibrary.wiley.com/doi/abs/10.1002/9781444367072.wbiee841, accessed 15 January 2021.

Reid, H. (2006) 'Was the Roman Gladiator and Athlete?', *Journal of the Philosophy of Sport*, 33(1): 37–49.

Ripstein, A. (2009) *Force and Freedom: Kant's Legal and Political Philosophy*, Cambridge: Harvard University Press.

Sailors, P. (2015) 'Personal Foul: An Evaluation of the Moral Status of Football', *Journal of the Philosophy of Sport*, 42(2): 269–286.

Sidhu, G. S. (1971) 'Letter to the Editor', *New York Times*, 18 March, https://www.nytimes.com/1971/03/18/archives/letter-to-the-editor-2-no-title.html, accessed 15 January 2021.

Sokol, D. K. (2004) 'The Not-So-Sweet Science: The Role of the Medical Profession in Boxing', *The Journal of Medical Ethics*, 30: 513–514.

Strauss, B. (2010) *The Spartacus War*, New York: Simon & Schuster.

Tagge, C. A., Fisher, A. M., Minaeva, O. V., Gaudreau-Balderrama, A., Moncaster, J. A., Zhang, X.-L., Wojnarowicz, M. W., Casey, N., Lu, H., Kokiko-Cochran, O. N., et al. (2018) 'Concussion, Microvascular Injury, and Early Tauopathy in Young Athletes After Impact Head Injury and an Impact Concussion Mouse Model', *Brain*, 141(2): 422–458.

Thomas, R. E. and Thomas, B. C. (2018) 'Systematic Review of Injuries in Mixed Martial Arts', *The Physician and Sportsmedicine*, 46(2): 155–167.

9 Friendship as a moral defense of mixed martial arts

Danny Rosenberg

Mixed martial arts (MMA) may be the most vicious and violent form of sport competition in society today and exhibits a spectacle like no other (Spencer 2012b). Fighters incorporate Eastern and Western martial arts skills from a variety of disciplines and compete within the confines of a ring or cage (Mayeda and Ching 2008). While there are similarities between boxing and MMA – both are defined as violent activities, there are also significant differences between their respective rules, officiating protocols, and injury outcomes – overall MMA appears to be a more brutal and often gruesome-looking sport. Many medical associations recommend boxing and MMA be banned (Sokol 2004, 2011). While a substantial body of literature exists that examines the ethics of boxing (McCormick 1979; Davis 1993; Burke 1998; Schneider and Butcher 2001; Jones 2001a; Dixon 2001; Herrera 2002; Simon 2004), only recently has the moral status of MMA come under serious scrutiny (Dixon 2015; Watson and Brock 2015; Weimer 2017; Kershnar and Kelly 2020).

This chapter will present a moral defense of MMA based on the concept of friendship between MMA fighters. It is in part an extension of Dixon (2015) who argues MMA is intrinsically immoral because mutual consent is insufficient to ethically justify the pain and injury MMA competitors intentionally inflict upon each other, and of the way opponents are objectified and degraded. However, according to Dixon there is an exception to the infliction of pain between partners that is morally permissible, namely, between lovers who engage in bondage, domination, sadism, and masochism (BDSM) as part of their consensual sexual activities. Based on the preceding context, this chapter will describe and examine friendship between MMA sparring partners and opponents to show the sport is morally defensible.

To develop my thesis, I will begin by outlining Dixon's argument and the critiques of Weimer (2017) and Kershnar and Kelly (2020) who refute the assertion MMA is intrinsically immoral. In the next section, auto ethnographic and ethnographic evidence will be presented that describes how MMA opponents experience and negotiate pain and injury in environments where friendships can be and are forged. The chapter will conclude by stating friendship is a worthy value in MMA and its presence is quite prevalent; however, close friendship is unnecessary to dispel the claim it is intrinsically immoral.

Dixon and his critics

Dixon believes MMA is the archetypal violent sport 'because its explicit goal is to hurt and incapacitate opponents' (2015: 365). He begins his essay by comparing

DOI: 10.4324/9781003122395-10

boxing with MMA and demonstrates there may be good paternalistic reasons for eliminating blows to the head in boxing due to the incidence, severity, and long-term effects of brain damage. As a relatively new sport, there is less empirical evidence about physical injuries in and other potential harmful outcomes related to MMA to justify paternalistically motivated reforms in the sport. However, Dixon steers clear of a utilitarian-based critique and examines the morality of MMA from a non-consequentialist perspective, namely a Kantian one.

The viciousness displayed by and objectification of MMA fighters in bouts call into question whether they adhere to Kant's (1785/1959) categorical imperative: 'Act so that you treat humanity, whether in your own person or in that of another, always as an end and never as a means only' (47). Without going into detail, Kant is stressing the intrinsic worth of human beings and the primacy of respecting the selfhood, autonomy, and self-determination of others. The idea of treating others 'always as an end' carries implications like not exploiting or harming others, respecting their rights, enhancing their wellbeing and trying to further their ends. For Kant, slavery, torture, political oppression, sexual assault, and other forms of degradation are immoral because they totally objectify victims and violate their basic value as human beings. Still, we do have encounters with others on an instrumental level, like a server in a restaurant or a parent who helps a young adult child complete a tax return, but we should never treat others 'as a means *only*' (ibid: 47, emphasis added). Even when engaged in these exchange-based interactions dignity must always be respected, and people must be treated as autonomous, independent human beings.

Given this brief overview, Dixon asserts, 'Mixed martial arts is a prolonged mutual assault' and further, it is a 'prime instance of treating opponents as worthless objects rather than as intrinsically valuable ends in themselves' (2015: 369). Before elaborating on this main point, he addresses the issue of consent. Defenders of MMA argue mutual consent 'overrides the *prima facie* wrongness of hurting and injuring others' (370). However, critics of this view state that consent cannot override inalienable rights like waiving one's freedom to willingly become a slave. Regarding MMA, Dixon writes, 'cage fighting violates inalienable rights to dignity and against being treated as an object of damage' (2015: 371). Other problems with consent refer to whether it can be given in a fully voluntary and autonomous way, if for example, one lacks adequate education, is coerced and/or is relatively poor. Dixon (2015) provides three cases to show the limits of consent. First, is a hypothetical society where only male sexual gratification with consenting females is the norm. The second is a hypothetical TV game show where paid contestants yell racist, sexist, and homophobic slurs at each other. And last, is dwarf tossing that was popular in American bars and office parties in the 1980s. In these instances, the objectification and demeaning behavior toward women, minority groups and little people cannot be justified even if these individuals consent to be treated in such ways.

Explanations of the first two examples from a Kantian perspective might show that men could be indifferent to the integrity and interests of women rather than objectify them, and the game contestants might be motivated by money and do not mean what they say (Dixon 2015). As for dwarf-tossing, it is comparable to MMA where, 'Mere consent does not provide a sufficiently respectful context to override the malicious attitude that MMA fighters [dwarf-throwers] display toward opponents [dwarfs] for the duration of the contest [while tossing], treating them [dwarfs] as mere objects to be damaged [demeaned]' (ibid.: 372). In this and in another article, Dixon goes further by arguing, 'In the case of actions that are inherently degrading [i.e., dwarf-tossing and MMA bouts], we are not morally free to consent to let others treat us this way, nor does our consent release others from the duty to refrain from treating us this way' (2016: 110).

At this point in his original paper, Dixon (2015) raises the example of sexual activities that involve bondage, domination, sadism, and masochism (BDSM) between adult lovers who mutually consent to inflict pain either one to the other or to each other. Such practices may also include demeaning behavior. But BDSM is morally unproblematic because it occurs in the context of a loving relationship, is part of sex play, and usually expresses respect and encourages mutual trust. In contrast, MMA contestants exchange blows and holds that 'represent nothing beyond the participants' desire to win by hurting and injuring their opponent' (ibid.: 373). However, if MMA adversaries 'are romantic partners, family members, or close friends' the moral indictment of the sport would presumably not apply (ibid.). However, two qualifications are raised to explain this exception.

First, sparring sessions are significantly different from actual MMA contests. The former involve more cooperative elements, and if pain and injury occur when sparring, they are not associated with the primary goal of seeking a victory by inflicting pain as in real MMA bouts. In this sense, 'It seems safe to assume that the vast majority of MMA fights are very different from sparring and involve participants who are not loved ones or close friends' (ibid.: 374). This chapter will dispute the preceding point. The second qualification refers to BDSM partners 'who actually *enjoy* being subjected to pain and humiliation... in order to meet their idiosyncratic emotional needs... compatible with respecting them as ends in themselves' (ibid.). Dixon maintains most MMA fighters do not seek pain for its own sake and would rather win their matches without getting hurt. A morally permissible MMA bout would require both opponents be family members or close friends who know the other enjoys BDSM-like sport activities and compete to fulfill each other's BDSM-like sport desires. In relation to pain inducing BDSM acts, this chapter will provide evidence that MMA participants find the experience of pain meaningful and see injury as inevitable and not entirely unwanted, and these factors can be shared as the foundation of friendships. Finally, Dixon (2015) notes while a loving relationship may be the optimal context for morally permissible BDSM practices, it may also be morally permissible for BDSM activities to occur during casual sex. In the final analysis, even if MMA is intrinsically immoral, this claim does not imply BDSM is morally wrong as an intimate relationship, and there may be grounds to justify BDSM during casual erotic encounters.

This ends Dixon's argument about the intrinsic immorality of MMA regarding cage fighters, and he is not without his critics. Two extensive critiques challenge the veracity of Dixon's claim and it is beyond the scope of this chapter to examine them at great length. However, an outline of their criticisms will be presented. The first by Weimer (2017) zeroes in on the discussion of BDSM and begins by showing a lack of clarity regarding two points. One is a distinction between two kinds of desires, desiring pain for its own sake and desiring pain to meet one's emotional needs. The other point relates to what is meant by 'idiosyncratic' emotional needs. Does 'idiosyncratic' refer to something deemed unusual or unacceptable once an emotional need is met, or does it carry some sort of moral weight itself? Weimer rejects the latter sense and raises empirical ethnographic evidence to show some BDSM recipients meet alternative emotional needs without pain and humiliation being sought for their own sake or to fulfill some idiosyncratic emotional need. Armed with this distinction Weimer refines Dixon's argument to include pain and suffering being satisfied for their own sake and/or to realize one or more emotional needs. He also makes clear he will focus on BDSM and MMA cases where it is assumed autonomous mutual consent is granted. However, given the improved version of Dixon's argument, BDSM *and* MMA behavior appear less dissimilar as *prima facie* morally permissible practices. Weimer explains, 'For while Dixon is surely correct to say that the vast majority of fighters do not intrinsically desire to be hurt, it is plausible to think that many do desire such treatment as a way to meet certain emotional needs' (2017: 264). Thus, BDSM and MMA participants may fulfill emotional needs to 'temporarily escape from reality, test one's limits, and overcome challenges' (ibid.: 265).

Weimer's critique does not stop here. Perhaps there are other needs beyond emotional ones, like physical and social needs? At one point, he mentions 'belonging and companionship' as relevant human needs (ibid.). Once again, Weimer refines Dixon's morally permissible conditions for BDSM and MMA actions such that pain and suffering may be sought for themselves and/or to fulfill one or more needs. With this further fine-tuning he suggests amateur MMA fighters participate and want to mutually satisfy any number of acceptable needs. Professional cage fighters may be motivated in the same way, but even those who primarily have a mercenary attitude toward MMA may indirectly satisfy different needs with their prize money. In the end, even if professional MMA fighters do not conform to the second improved formulation of Dixon's argument, amateur MMA participants 'more often *will* exhibit the necessary mutual concern, and [there is] certainly no reason to deem the sport as a whole *intrinsically* immoral' (ibid.: 267).

At this point Weimer considers a possible objection to his critique in reference to Dixon's (2015) suggestion that if there are certain values to be appropriated in MMA like courage, discipline and perseverance to fulfill needs, these should be pursued in activities less morally objectionable. In a lengthy examination of this line of thought, Weimer proposes another formulation of Dixon's argument whereby there are 'other *recognized* and *not overly-demanding* harmless ways in which those needs could be met' (2017: 268). This third approach may lead to a differentiation between BDSM practices where there is no other way to satisfy needs other than to inflict pain and humiliation, and MMA needs that can be satisfied in other activities where the exchange of painful blows and holds are not paramount. But Weimer shows this account is misleading and he rejects it for two reasons. One is the inconsistent application of autonomous consent between BDSM and MMA contexts, and two, BDSM partners *choose* to engage in such activities to fulfill needs rather than participate because they must, and this pertains to MMA fighters as well.

Weimer concludes by comparing his first and second revised formulations of Dixon's argument. He believes the second version demonstrates better that when mutual autonomous consent is given amateur MMA fighting is *prima facie* morally permissible, and this applies to some professional MMA bouts. As such, 'despite its [MMA's] violent nature, the sport is not intrinsically immoral' (ibid.: 272).

The next critique of Dixon's claim MMA is intrinsically immoral focuses on the issues of rights and consent. Kershnar and Kelly (2020) assert MMA 'is not wrong for participants' and begin by presenting their supportive argument for their position before responding to Dixon's argument. Again, the following will be a brief overview, however, the full text of the main argument must be quoted (ibid.: 106):

(P1) If an act does not infringe on anyone's moral right or violate another side-constraint, then it is morally permissible.
(P2) MMA-violence does not infringe on anyone's moral rights or violate another side-constraint.
(C1) Hence, MMA violence is morally permissible. [(P1), (P2)]

In explanation of the first premise, the authors clarify that if a person commits a wrong act then she wrongs someone. This is to exclude free-floating wrongs that do not wrong anyone. The second clarification is that if a person wrongs another person, the first encroaches on a second's right and 'fails to satisfy a duty he owes a second' (ibid.). Given this right-duty relationship the authors do not agree that MMA fighters engage in wrong-making behavior, self-harm is always impermissible, and harm is inevitable, though probable, in MMA bouts. They then criticize Kant's dictum of treating others 'always as an end'. In brief, they show that MMA fighters do not necessarily exploit each other when viewed from a transactional perspective. As far as cage adversaries assuming an objectionable attitude toward each other, this may refer to the wrongness of their thoughts not their acts, and some fighters do not possess this attitude. Kershnar and Kelly (ibid.) provide evidence of 'camaraderie after fighting' and 'respect between MMA fighters' and this 'serves to maintain relationships perceived as valuable, such as friendship and membership in a social group' (ibid.: 108–9). A third point is that 'badly motivated acts in MMA fighting are [not] intrinsically wrong' (ibid.: 109). Even if MMA combatants hold degrading attitudes, and of course attitudes may change in the course of a bout, they are still in control of their acts for the most part.

Kershnar and Kelly continue their critique by examining what constitutes valid consent. Briefly, 'any act that has been validly consented is permissible in the sense that it does not wrong the consenter' (ibid.). Should one validly consent to a degrading or exploitative act, for instance, its wrongness would 'have to be explained in terms of a failure to satisfy a duty owed to the person acted upon' (ibid.: 110). Here, the consenter would surely understand the meaning and possible outcomes of such acts, but this expressive view is not wrong in itself. And even if degradation-producing wrongness is a significant factor it does not trump the valid consent, right-demanding posture of the consenter. At this point, Kershnar and Kelly address the foregoing of inalienable rights.

For the most part, the authors maintain no inalienable rights are relinquished by the acts of MMA fighters and they do not treat themselves as merely means when fighting because they have good reasons for fighting as part of their life plan. Moreover, the concept of rights rests on autonomy, moral autonomy, and the application of autonomy to itself, which means one has the autonomy to end being autonomous (e.g., consenting to doctor-assisted death). Not only does autonomy justify rights, but without it one would be constrained to creatively control one's life, and this would hold true even if curtailing autonomy would bring about more pleasure, wealth, good and happiness. After a lengthy summary, Kershnar and Kelly turn to analyze Dixon's argument.

Without repeating the account of Dixon given above, the authors present two useful and clear tables illustrating the deductive logic of Dixon's argument as well as the Kantian argument. After stating five strengths of Dixon's argument Kershnar and Kelly (ibid.) show how it fails by criticizing the premises of his deductive reasoning. The first premise speaks to the wrongness of treating people as merely means. For the authors the only way to interpret Kant's categorical imperative is within a system of rights that 'justifies and explains boundaries of non-interference and consequences' related to the bodies and property of people (ibid.: 115). Otherwise there would be no clear way to apply and determine the Kantian principle of treating others 'as a means only'. And as stated above, Kershnar and Kelly contend MMA fighters do not violate the inalienable rights of others and themselves through their acts.

The second premise refers to the wrongness of treating others as incorrectly objectified. However, there may be two senses of such objectification. One may refer to treating others with an attitude of objectification, but this may not be directly linked to wrongful acts and violate the rights of others. If objectification refers to acts, it is unclear where the objectification lies unless an act is tied to 'an improper intention or motive' (ibid.: 116). Or suppose a person thought of someone 'as neither rational nor self-governing' (ibid.). In both these cases, the authors state the oddity of one person having a right to deny a second not have certain intentions or demand a second not think about one in certain ways. For the authors, objectification is either irrelevant or a right related issue when held up against Kant's categorical imperative.

The third premise states that MMA fighters incorrectly objectify one another. Once again, wrongful objectification is associated with the infringement of rights, but Kershnar and Kelly (ibid.) argued earlier MMA fighters do not violate the rights of each other. Moreover, they state, 'a person is treated in a dignified manner if and only if his rights are respected' and this holds true of cage fighters (ibid.). A second issue with this premise is its failure to recognize the equal value of people. Many MMA combatants have a respectful attitude toward one another knowing that pain will be inflicted and experienced in a bout and mutual consent has been given to follow the rules. Finally, if MMA requires the objectification of opponents by expressing a vicious attitude, then it suggests they have a 'love of evil or hatred of the good' (ibid.: 117). Most MMA fighters do not intrinsically love seeing their adversaries in pain, or they see 'the other's pain is aesthetically pleasing or personally satisfying, but not good' (ibid.). This ends the criticisms of Kershnar and Kelly against Dixon's argument in support of their position that 'MMA fighting in a competition is not necessarily wrong and is often, as we can tell, permissible' (ibid.: 118).

The nature of friendship and friendship in sport

Whether needs-based or consent/rights-based arguments conclusively refute Dixon's claim that MMA is intrinsically immoral, they were discussed in part because camaraderie and friendship were mentioned as possibilities in MMA. Dixon as well states that close friendship would justify MMA as *prima facie* morally permissible much like BDSM lovers who consent to the infliction of pain and demeaning behavior with each other. In this section, I will describe and explain the general features of friendship followed by a characterization of friendship in sport.

The meaning and value of friendship has a long history in Western philosophical thought and the body of work on the subject is far too extensive to review here. Instead, I will refer to Telfer's (1970/71) informative essay on the topic because it addresses the central of elements of friendship, its moral dimension and why friendship is important. These issues should suffice for the purposes of this chapter.

In explaining the nature of friendship Telfer begins with the necessary, but not sufficient, condition that friends must be jointly engaged in some type of shared activity like work and leisure pursuits. However, actions while participating in cooperative activities must be 'performed for specific reasons – out of friendship, as we say, rather than out of duty or pity or indeed self-interest' (ibid.: 224). Such reasons are tied to desires, or passions of friendship, that motivate and explain performing actions out of friendship. The first of these is affection 'as a desire for another's welfare and happiness *as a particular individual*' (ibid.).

A second passion of friendship 'is a desire on the part of the friend for each other's company, as distinct from a desire for company as such' (ibid.: 225). In friendship friends assume two attitudes to explain their desire to be in each other's company. One is the attitude of liking the other person, although the reasons for liking someone are limited and difficult to pin down. The second attitude is a sense of bond or something we have in common with someone else. This is different than liking because we can like another person but provide a reason for not being their friend like 'we just don't click' or 'we don't understand each other'.

At this point, Telfer rejects the idea assumed by Plato and Aristotle that friends must be good people. As she says, 'there seems no *necessary* incompatibility between fondness, liking, and a sense of a bond, on the one hand, and disapproval of some qualities in a person, on the other' (ibid.: 227). Still, some moral defects in someone may not lead to liking, and the strongest of bonds with another person may be due to similar moral outlooks and admiration rather than the virtues of being a good person.

An objection to Telfer's account of friendship so far is its silence on choosing friends based on one's feelings and how these feelings give rise to reasons we have for our choice of and commitment to friends, and those for breaking off friendships. In reply to this objection, Telfer recalls that the passions of friendship may not obtain (i.e., one instead acts out of pity or duty), but behaviors persist toward others. Choice therefore is necessary to friendship in the way right passions are manifest in actions directed toward a specific individual. In sum, Telfer has shown three necessary conditions for friendship: shared activities, passions of friendship, and with the fulfillment of the first two conditions acknowledgement and consent to the relationship.

In the final portion of her essay, Telfer addresses the value of friendship because friendship is a voluntary relationship and it is not inevitable. She recounts Aristotle's well-known explanation why friendship is important and valued.

One reason for friendship refers to the usefulness of friends to help us when we are in need and to receive their generosity, which only they can provide in specific ways. Second, friendship is pleasant in relation to the enjoyment we experience when in a friend's company and sharing activities with her. However, Telfer (ibid.) indicates that in reference to pleasure is the potential for pain and in many instances a balance must be sought between the two. But in friendship there are pleasures with no corresponding pains like 'playing games, playing music, conversation, philosophy – in which case the presence of the friend enhances the pleasure' (ibid.: 239). Clearly Telfer did not have MMA in mind when making the preceding statement. Finally, Aristotle holds friendship enhances life in various ways. It heightens our emotions and makes us feel more and 'more alive'. Friendship intensifies our absorption in and the quality of our activities and increases our pleasure and emotional attachment to them and those whom we share such activities. It also expands our knowledge about human needs and experiences through our charitable identification with friends, things that might elude us on our own. In this sense, there is empathy between friends.

Turning now to the nature of friendship in sport, I will discuss two articles that examine the topic extensively, one from a Socratic viewpoint and the other from an

Aristotelian perspective. The first by Hyland (1978) begins by identifying two common experiences in competitive sport, alienation and friendship. He also observes there is a tendency to associate competition with alienation rather than friendship, and his task will be to elucidate upon the latter which is less prevalent and less well understood. An often-asked question is, are human beings naturally competitive or is our natural disposition open to friendship? And further, are individuals basically monadic, that is, autonomous and self-reliant, or are we relational beings? After providing support for each side within these questions, Hyland concludes,

> the conception of the individual as monadic typically and most easily develops an understanding of human being in which competition is present and tends toward alienation; whereas the relational view more easily develops a version of natural friendship, either as original or as a goal.
>
> (Hyland 1978: 30)

However, rather than posit an either-or dichotomy here, we often perceive ourselves as monadic and relational. Hyland then shows how these opposites may be reconciled by appealing to Socrates' thought in Plato's *Symposium*.

For Socrates the human soul (spirit) is fundamentally imbued with eros or love, and eros has three basic features as part of human character: incompleteness or partiality, recognition of this incompleteness, and the drive to overcome incompleteness and seek wholeness. These three facets of our erotic nature are played out in all our activities and reflect our monadic and relational selves. If we are incomplete, we are not autonomous, and in my relations with others I try to overcome my incompleteness and acquire wholeness. Also, 'our eros *individualizes* us – makes us each the unique individuals that we are – but it individualizes us *as* relational beings' (ibid.: 32). If the monadic and relational aspects of human beings are compatible, what implications are there for comprehending the relationship between competition and alienation, and competition and friendship in sport?

Before answering this question, Hyland recounts earlier writings of his on the nature of play where he introduces two relevant themes. The first he calls the stance of 'responsive openness' whereby in all our play activities we are open to new possibilities about ourselves, others and the environment and must actively react to these dimensions in all sorts of ways. In fact, this stance naturally reflects eros and is basic to our nature as human beings. The second theme, also an aspect of eros, refers to 'the Socratic conception of philosophy as a stance of questioning, or as Socrates regularly put it, of aporia' (ibid.: 33). This stance is the philosophical equivalent of the first one whereby questioning involves responsive openness.

Armed with this account and its distinctions, Hyland describes the etymology of competition and contest to show the meaning of these terms tend to refer to friendship as a striving together rather than as sites of alienation. However, beyond this, he points to 'existential evidence' that friendships arise as 'demand relationships' and deepen in competitive activities. He also describes the 'ontological framework' of competition rooted in eros where intimate and dynamic affiliations with others often lead to recognizing our deficiencies and overcoming these with the assistance of others. Hyland cautions there is no causal relationship to these modes of being, but he explains the connection of competition and friendship from a teleological perspective such that the 'highest version of competition is as friendship' (ibid.: 35). He also submits this is the most natural circumstance that implies 'an ethical injunction: we ought to strive at all times to let our competitive play be a mode of friendship' (ibid.).

Although Hyland does not extensively examine the meaning, moral, and relevance features of friendship, Jones does from an Aristotelian viewpoint. He begins by asserting friendship is one of the top motives for participating in sport and 'ranks as one of the highest human values' (Jones 2001b: 131). Three reasons are given for sport being open to friendship. The first refers to 'a measure of pain, risk, and physical danger…intrinsic to many sports…. [and] this shared pain and danger bring their own special kind of intimacy and dispose us to friendship' (ibid.: 131–2). The second reason refers to the experiences of defeat that are often followed by humiliation. Opponents become aware of their own vulnerabilities and those of others, recognize they share a common frailty, and feel an emotional attachment to one another. Third, sport violates norms of privacy. Nudity in the locker room, spitting, vomiting, flinging snot, smelling bad, looking dirty and sweaty, and 'letting it all hang out' are examples of relinquishing privacy in sport. However, the point of this reason and the others is to show that while there is no necessary connection between sport and friendship, sport is a prime site for friendship.

Given these introductory remarks, Jones quotes Aristotle and describes the nature of friendship as a 'non-utility (non-sexual, non-kinship) relationship between two or more people, one that takes time to develop and is characterised by mutual goodwill' (ibid.: 133). Friendship is distinct from romantic love because sexual relations demand different kinds of intensities and passions, and one may have a few sexual partners but a single love whereas one may have several friends. Also, family relationships are involuntary and goodwill between family members need not obtain, while friends are chosen and reciprocate goodwill.

He next asks the question, what are friends for? Answer: 'Friendship is not *for* anything' (ibid. 134). Friendship is sought for its own sake, and to think of friends as a means threatens friendship. We simply enjoy being and doing things with friends not as a means toward happiness because friendship itself is happiness. Therefore, a life without friends is an unhappy one. And since sport is open to friendship, failing to make friends in our athletic pursuits is a missed opportunity to enhance our lives and attain 'one of life's highest goods' (ibid.: 135).

Although friends are always to be treated as ends, there are consequential advantages once having made friends. For example, friends help each other even to the point of undermining their own interests. In sports friends depends on the depth of friendship in relation to concern, time, convenience, and cost that are expended. Pleasure is a foundational feature of sport and many pleasures among friends are experienced before, during, and after competition. A third advantage of friendship is trust. To expand this idea Jones states, 'a friend would no more deliberately harm me than I would myself' (ibid.: 137). Of course, this statement is not quite accurate in relation to MMA. The point Jones wants to make is that there are different levels of trust in sport.

Another positive consequence of friendship refers specifically to team sports where friendship encourages team spirit and strong player bonds which can lead to greater success. A final benefit of friendship in sport is the way it influences competitive behavior in two principal ways. According to Jones, 'it is going to be much harder to feel hostility to fellow competitors if one has friends in sport than if one has no friends since some of your fellow competitors may well be friends' (ibid.: 138). This advantage of friendship in MMA would have to be qualified. The second point is that 'a person with friends in sport is more likely to "play fair" and not cheat than a person without friends' (ibid.). Jones contends athletes who have no friends and cheat in sport have little or no sense of betraying others who agree to play fairly and by the rules. This ends the general characterization of friendship and friendship in sport.

The nature of friendship in MMA

Before describing friendship in MMA, I want to address some ambiguity in Dixon's (2015) qualification that MMA would be morally permissible if professional fighters in a bout were close friends and his thesis that MMA is intrinsically immoral. The issue also involves the type of BDSM he describes and its intrinsically moral status. In several ways, according to Dixon the two contexts are significantly different, but he does not fully explain why this is so.

For example, Dixon quotes Paul Davis who describes the face of a boxer possessing 'an attitude of unbridled ferocity toward the opponent...[and] as vicious'; Dixon comments: 'This description is all the more applicable to MMA, which is far more akin to a street fight, albeit between highly trained and skilled athletes' (ibid.: 367). Also, as quoted earlier, Dixon states, 'defenders of MMA [must] show why the practice is not a prime instance of treating opponents as worthless objects rather than as intrinsically valuable ends in themselves' (ibid.: 369). Now it is unlikely but possible BDSM partners in a loving relationship might express a vicious attitude toward each other while engaged in demeaning behavior or treating one another as 'worthless objects' and not as ends in themselves. These same allowances would presumably apply when two professional MMA competitors and close friends fight each other. But what is it about close friendship that makes MMA bouts morally permissible? Must MMA fighters who are good friends and fight each other necessarily not assume a vicious attitude, not treat one another as 'worthless objects' and rather as ends in themselves? Dixon does not answer or elaborate on these questions.

I maintain close MMA friends (and most MMA opponents) who fight each other, treat one another instrumentally *and* as ends, and accept and withstand any temporary viciousness and extreme objectification between them. This in fact may be a test of the closeness of their friendship and the respect for the dignity they have for each other. Further, Dixon argues for the moral permissibility of BDSM between partners and their sexual activities exclusively in loving relationships and leaves room for a possible justification of casual BDSM sexual encounters. However, he provides no details of the latter justification or BDSM circumstances and conditions that would make the practice intrinsically immoral. In sum, I find Dixon vague about these issues.

A few additional points can also be raised. First, as Telfer (1970/1971) observes, friendship can still occur even when a friend detests a certain trait or two in her friend. However, this does not mean that if two professional MMA fighters are not friends, they *must* adopt the attitude and treatment Dixon ascribes to them. In the MMA community, conventional wisdom has typically shunned the thought of teammates (those from the same gym) and friends fighting each other. However, there are those who argue respect and honor between opponents can and should override this sentiment (ArmChairMMA 2011). Second, Kershnar and Kelly (2020) indicate a wrongful attitude does not necessarily make one's actions wrong. They also state attitudes may change during a bout, and when fighting each other MMA opponents do not necessarily display a vicious attitude in the give and take of pain infliction as though they had a love of evil. Third, if BDSM is not intrinsically immoral during a casual erotic rendezvous with paid professionals let's say (i.e., a non-loving relationship), perhaps this is a permissible situation comparable to professional MMA bouts where basic respect, but no close friendship, need obtain. Finally, while less common, romantic partners are a possibility among MMA athletes who fight each other given that there are gay, lesbian, and bi-sexual MMA fighters (Channon and Matthews 2015). Also, an Internet search shows there are professional MMA fighters who are siblings. As far as I know no professional sibling MMA fighters have fought each other but this is mainly due to each being in a different weight category. The last point shows the other two exceptions Dixon identifies, besides close friends, are possibilities. In all these ways, BDSM and MMA may conceivably be less dissimilar. But let's continue the search for relevant differences between the two practices.

Perhaps MMA bouts are distinct from BDSM sexual activities because professional MMA opponents seek victory and follow formal prescribed rules with a referee in the octagon, and officials, judges, and medical personnel at cage-side. In this sense, a professional MMA bout is not a street fight as Dixon suggests, and by following rules there is cooperation between competitors. MMA is now a highly regulated sport and even the medical protocols to engage in official professional bouts are some of the most rigorous in sport. From what I understand, there are informal rules and signals (safe words) when engaged in BDSM practices to ensure no severe pain and injury occurs to partners. This objective may be similar to what takes place in the cage although far more public oversight occurs in professional MMA fights given the presence of referees, officials, judges, and physicians. Dixon may respond to this by saying such supervision is needed to curtail the brutality and ferociousness in MMA. However, tapping out to end an MMA fight shows some self-imposed mutual regard for the safety of the fighter who taps out. As an aside, deaths are rare but do occur in both practices; however, the number of BDSM linked deaths is difficult to ascertain. Related to victory in sport, perhaps a certain degree of BDSM sexual gratification or pleasure and reaching climax are experienced like sport victories, though not in the mutually exclusive way as in sport that produces winners and losers. Once again there are parallels between BDSM and MMA behaviors regarding the infliction of pain that perhaps make these contexts not significantly unalike.

The final point that might show BDSM is distinguishable from MMA in important ways is found in the following conditions. Dixon states,

> Even in the case of a pair of MMA fighters who both also enjoy BDSM [for its own sake], this argument would provide a possible justification of the their cage fights only when each one is aware of the opponent's predilection for BDSM and is motivated by the desire to meet that opponent's needs.
>
> (Dixon 2015: 374)

These conditions must be coupled with another assertion: 'we may safely assume that the vast majority of cage fighters do not desire to be hurt' (ibid.). Both statements need clarification.

The second sentence depends on what is meant by 'hurt', how much hurt one anticipates and can tolerate, and how well one defends himself from getting hurt. In a trivial sense, almost all sport competitors, and especially those in high risk sports, wish to avoid getting hurt. But can MMA fighters really prepare for and expect no harm, pain, and injury will be experienced in MMA bouts? Even though MMA fighters may want to win with a single knockout blow in just seconds and avoid getting hurt, this occurrence is rare and not a realistic goal and expectation. This is like saying bowlers desire scoring 300 every time they bowl, which is likely true. And while a perfect score can and does occasionally occur, it does not accurately reflect the expectations, experiences, and common results of bowling practice. Moreover, one does not stop bowling after the first missed strike or call off an MMA bout the first instance a fighter is hurt by a non-bout-ending blow. MMA fighters rigorously prepare to endure pain and being wounded to some degree, what one researcher calls 'body callusing', and assume they will get hurt (Spencer 2009). They also meticulously train to defend themselves from getting severely injured. Their drills in practice sessions and actions in the cage involve numerous defensive moves to protect themselves when attacked with blows, hits, punches, kicks, kneeing, throws and grappling holds and grips. The latter set of actions and defensive moves are almost entirely ignored by Dixon (2015). In fact, MMA bouts where there is mostly grappling may produce relatively less pain and injury, even when a chokehold is applied.

As for the first statement above, knowing and fulfilling each other's desire to inflict and feel pain for its own sake, I have two replies. Dixon only describes and couches BDSM in its milder, benign version within a loving relationship, part of sex play, pretend objectification and humiliation that may 'be an expression of mutual trust and other respectful attitudes' (ibid.: 373). To me, this is easily comparable to MMA sparring and amateur bouts 'in sharp contrast with actual MMA fights' which are Dixon's focus when he argues MMA is intrinsically immoral (ibid.: 374). However, loving BDSM partners also engage in more serious and potentially dangerous BDSM contexts and activities, of the rough sex variety, privately and in BDSM sex clubs and professional BDSM establishments, that may be more akin to professional MMA fights. If Dixon examined this qualitatively different level of BDSM he would likely find more similarities between the two practices where the infliction of pain for its own sake and the treatment of others as means *and* ends exist in both contexts. He may also better explain why and how loving relationships and casual sexual encounters in extreme forms of BDSM make these contexts morally permissible.

The second reply refers to the stipulation of mutual awareness of specific attitudes, motives, and knowledge of the needs of and what BDSM partners and MMA fighters want. Here I agree with Weimer (2017) who develops a compelling argument to show several significant emotional and social needs are fulfilled by BDSM and MMA participants that are not relevantly unique to either practice. Moreover, Dixon suggests awareness of these mutual factors are evident, readily aligned and understood more clearly in BDSM situations rather than MMA ones. However, this is so because he 'only justifies BDSM in the context of loving relationships' (Dixon 2015: 374). Perhaps other BDSM contexts are intrinsically immoral as he submits MMA is, but Dixon does not discuss these BDSM settings and what would make them so. He therefore erroneously, I think, forecloses to professional MMA opponents when fighting the desire to treat one another as means *and* ends and to experience the give and take of pain for its own sake, unless for some inexplicable reason they are close friends. I will now address the preceding topic and assume whether in amateur or professional MMA training sessions and bouts, the sport is disposed to friendship that makes MMA not intrinsically immoral.

Unsurprisingly, there is scholarly literature that examines elements of friendship and the nature of MMA in amateur and professional contexts, and an internet search reveals fights between close friends in professional MMA have occurred. In one such study on the violence and pain experiences of MMA fighters, Andreasson and Johansson describe the MMA gym as a second home and state, 'The athletes spend a lot of time together, and over time sometimes friendships develop.... This creates a sense of social community, where fighters take care of, and cherish, each other' (2019: 1193). They also observe, 'There is a sharp discrepancy between the spectacle, when the fighters clash and try to beat each other unconscious, and the friendships, support and comraderies that develop during the long preparations for the fights' (ibid.). In speaking about the experiences of one MMA fighter, Andreasson and Johansson state, 'Like many others he [the fighter] talks about club members (and opponents) with great respect and dignity'. And they quote another fighter who says, '"Most decent people [MMA combatants] don't look upon their opponent as an enemy or an idiot"' (ibid.: 1194). The authors conclude by claiming MMA fighters do not label themselves as 'violent and uncivilized', but instead, they focus on 'the formation of the MMA community and the social and positive aspects of the sport. Solidarity, friendship and brotherhood and sisterhood are very much in focus...' (ibid.: 1195).

In another account of MMA experiences, Green includes a section called 'Choking your way to friendship: community through pain' where MMA promotes a certain kind of intimate community. He notes, 'Fighting, in its rawest form, is a shared encountering of one's temporality through giving and taking pain' (2011: ibid.: 390). He quotes from an MMA fighter who reflects, 'it is kind of cool, the bond that develops so quickly between fighters, you know... when you are fighting someone, for a second it's like your souls clash; you understand each other like no else does' (ibid,). Green also writes, 'The seduction of violence remains within the body... existing as a drive to transform and discover the self through pain and pleasure, blood and sweat, self and other.... We build intimacy through shared vulnerability and toughness, the two extremes' (ibid.). An instructor of the author states, 'when you train hard you build friendships that are different than any others' (ibid.: 391). Green draws several noteworthy conclusions: 'pain helps build confidence... leads to an inward movement... a discovery of self'; MMA fighters 'are seeking a type of contact and intimacy that is not present in their lives and is seen as worth pursuing'; and 'painful exchanges of newfound knowledge speak to the increase of communities oriented around experiences that test the limits of the body' (ibid.).

Massey, Meyer, and Naylor investigate self-regulation in MMA and the social supports in the sport. They observe, 'Athletes involved in MMA exist in a violent world where it is imperative to harm one another in practice and competition, yet.... the depth of the relationship among MMA training partners appears to differ qualitatively from other athletes and their training partners' (2013: 17). In this same study, MMA participants 'welcomed physical pain and psychological distress', to prepare 'for the demands of competition, support efficacy beliefs upon entering competition, and entrust fighters that they can successfully inflict pain on their opponents during competition' (ibid.).

In his examination of MMA fighter habitus, reflexive body techniques and body callusing, Spencer notes, 'professional MMA fighters' bodies are subject to immense levels of pain and must inflict a level of pain almost unrivalled in sport' (2009: 127). He also mentions, 'All fighters in this study stated that some of the toughest, most successful fighters in the world are the nicest, most humble guys outside the ring' (ibid.: 138). In another study where the experiences of pain and injury among MMA fighters are investigated, Spencer asserts, 'withstanding pain and injury is interpreted as elemental to participation in MMA' (2012: 120). In relation to one's attitude toward opponents, 'research subjects were generally reluctant to say that a "mean streak" is necessary to participate in MMA, most thought that in order to succeed, a fighter must destroy his or her opponent if necessary' (ibid.: 125). Regarding an injured MMA fighter, Spencer describes the consequences of his injury as removing 'an activity from his life that brings a considerable level of joy' (ibid.: 130). One of his conclusions is that 'pain reveals the potentialities of bodies and not merely reduces bodies to meaninglessness' (ibid.: 132).

Exploring the cultural meanings of MMA, Stenius states, 'While the goal of the sport is not to deliberately cause injury, MMA fighting is about bodies and the intentional use of massive force to succeed in breaking down one's opponent' (2015: 85). Regarding safety in MMA, one fighter he quotes says, 'There is mutual consent between my combatant in the ring and me. We are just like any sportsmen. We don't try to injure each other, that's not what MMA is about.... We control our bodies and we know how to exercise self-restraint' (ibid.: 86). As for violence expressed by MMA fighters, Stenius concludes, 'individuals engage in violence for the sake of violence – as an end in itself.... The effect of this more pleasurable aspect of pain and violence indicates that means and ends become fluid, inseparable concepts' (ibid.: 88). In a later comment, he says, 'giving and receiving physical pain is intrinsic to the art of [MMA] competition' (ibid.).

In another MMA study, Stenius and Dziwenka address

> the intersubjective experience of feeling the pain and pleasure running through one's hurt and stained body.... [and the] fighters' willing embrace of and submission to the pain and rigors of the sport, which are absorbed "together" corporeally.
>
> (Stenius and Dziwenka 2015: 7)

On the nature of violence in MMA, the authors write, 'Through the prepared pre-game plan at the gym, violence is rehearsed, scripted and organized in advance.... Thus, disorder and anarchy are avoided [in the cage]' (ibid.: 8). Stenius reflects on his own experiences as an MMA fighter: 'I felt the strikes and I could handle the pain, as I was also filled with pleasure while getting hit.... My experience in pain and pleasure, and my getting "turned on"... [helped me] transform the pain so that the violence doesn't become hurtful' (ibid.: 10). The researchers also describe the emotional highs and lows of MMA training and fighting and state, 'Amidst the fighting, pain constantly shifts what violence means and says about their [fighters'] bodily experience' (ibid.: 18). In one of their conclusions about MMA they assert, 'we have come to understand that fighting another human being in a controlled and defined safe setting involves a process of overcoming the "delight and disgust" feeling of hurting someone, and also involves shifting bodily self-awareness' (ibid.: 20).

Conclusion

The observations, interpretations, and quotes in the preceding section demonstrate how amateur and professional MMA training sessions and bouts are disposed to friendship and provide insight into how MMA fighters perceive their sport, themselves and opponents. As mentioned earlier, friendship is not necessary in sport, but as Hyland (1978) and Jones (2001b) argue, to not have friends in sport is incredibly unfortunate, results in less meaningful experiences, and falls short of leading an enriched, happy life.

If we consider Telfer's (1970/1971) necessary conditions for friendship, namely shared activities, passions of friendship, and acknowledgement and consent to a superior relationship with someone, all three are or may be present in the discussion in the previous section. MMA fighters engage in a joint activity, can and do show affection (or at least respect) for each other, desire to be in each other's company, feel a mutual bond with one another, and express commitment and certain worthy duties to other combatants. Following Aristotle, some friendships in MMA are utility-based, others defined as pleasurable, and close friendships are life-enhancing in relation to heightened emotions, the intensification of absorption in and the quality of shared activities, and the enlargement of knowledge of ourselves, others, and the culture of MMA. What may be missing in MMA bouts, though more evident in training sessions, is Telfer's insistence friendships are directed to specific individuals for their uniqueness that attracts one to the other.

Turning to Hyland's account of competition and friendship, MMA fighters discussed in the previous section conform to his description of human beings as naturally friendly, autonomous, and relational, and expressing the three components of Socrates' notion of eros. They also assume the stance of play as responsive openness and the philosophical stance of questioning. Hyland also explains sport competition invokes a demand relationship and an intimate association between opponents due to our erotic nature. MMA athletes above described incompleteness or shortcomings in training sessions and bouts, becoming aware of their corporeal and emotional limits, and striving to overcome these inadequacies. As well, Hyland addresses risks in competition from physical and emotional ones to the non-natural risk of alienation, and when the latter occurs, he calls this 'a "deficient mode" of play'. For him, 'competition, as a striving or questioning together towards excellence, *in so far as it most adequately fulfills its possibilities*, does so as a mode of friendship' (Hyland 1978: 35). The research on MMA above often referred to strong social bonds and support between fighters with reference to the importance of friendship and camaraderie in the sport.

If one recalls Jones (2001b), he begins his essay by explaining why sport is conducive to friendship. His first reason refers to pain, risk, and danger as intrinsic to sport. As described in the previous section, MMA exemplifies this truism most explicitly and in the extreme. MMA fighters not only seek pain for its own sake, it is shared and negotiated in a give and take manner, can be and is a pleasurable experience, and leads to intimate relations with others. One also gets a sense from the above research an acute awareness of the vulnerability of MMA athletes and the high level of discipline and self-control they must exert. Vulnerability was the second reason Jones provides for sport encouraging friendship, while the third was the violation of privacy which was addressed earlier.

As far as the meaning of friendship in sport, Jones (ibid.) speaks about mutual goodwill between sports friends. In a few quotes, MMA fighters insist their intention and the goal of MMA is not to injure their opponents, despite the bruises and wounds that result from fighting. In posing the question, what are friends for, Jones answers, *for* nothing, and that friends are to be treated as ends. I would answer perhaps more accurately and say when MMA friends compete against each other they treat one another as means *and* ends. This is reflected in some of the quotes above where in some instances MMA fighters assume a 'mean streak' and opponents are viewed as objects that should be crushed. However, these attitudes and behaviors are temporary and can alter in the course of a bout. MMA fighters rarely hold the view opponents should not be accorded dignity and esteem as human beings, even if they are not friends. While the sport is brutal and gruesome, there is a basic mutual respect between most amateur and professional MMA fighters in training sessions and bouts.

Even though friends should be treated as ends and friendship itself is happiness, there are benefits to having friends in sport. For example, Jones (ibid.) notes friends help each other and sometimes undermine their own interests, and this depends on the depth of friendship. Friends enhance our enthusiasm for sport and make sport more pleasant, promote a different kind of trust than the one has for coaches and experts, and encourage team and club spirit. Finally, having sports friends may temper hostility between competitors and reduce cheating in sport due to the meaning of betrayal. The research on MMA presented in the previous section refers to some of these benefits of friendship, though perhaps not explicitly. Clearly MMA fighters cannot learn, improve, and test their mettle without sparring partners and opponents, whether they are friends or not. But the social dynamics of MMA gyms, the creation of an intimate community, self-restraint and control, and friendships in MMA are dominant ways the sport is described and experienced. As far as tempering hostility, I would say unbridled or reckless hostility is rare in MMA because of the discipline and rigorous training of MMA fighters and the stringent oversight and supervision of MMA bouts.

To conclude, I echo Hyland (1978) and Jones (2001b) who state friendship is not necessary in sport, but to have no sports friends is to have a diminished, less meaningful experience in one of life's most rewarding and joyous (and sometimes alienating) activities. Friendship can and does exist in MMA where violence, pain, and injury are exemplified, shared, and publicly celebrated. MMA fighters mutually consent to engage in the practice, they often inflict and receive pain for its own sake and experience pleasure in doing so, are well trained and exhibit self-control, and almost always hold no malice toward opponents but instead fundamentally respect one another as human beings at all levels of and contexts in the sport. These features alone ethically justify MMA. I have shown MMA is conducive to friendship, which is a worthy and noble value, to demonstrate the sport is not intrinsically immoral. However, unlike Dixon (2015), I think close friendship is too ambitious and an unnecessary requirement for MMA to be morally permissible.

References

Andreasson, J. and Johansson, T. (2019) 'Negotiating Violence: Mixed Martial Arts as a Spectacle and Sport', *Sport in Society*, 22(7): 1183–1197.

ArmChairMMA (2011) 'Why Can't We Be Friends? Teammates Fighting Teammates in MMA', *ArmChairMMA*, 14 April, https://www.mmamania.com/2011/4/13/2083454/from-the-armchair-teammates-facing-teammates-in-mma, accessed 5 August 2020.

Burke, M. (1998) 'Is Boxing Violent? Let's Ask Some Boxers', in D. Hemphill (ed.) *All Part of the Game: Violence and Australian Sport*, Melbourne: Walla Walla Press, pp. 111–132.

Channon, A. and Matthews, C. R. (2015) '"It Is What It Is": Masculinity, Homosexuality, and Inclusive Discourse in Mixed Martial Arts', *Journal of Homosexuality*, 62(7), 936–956.

Davis, P. (1993) 'Ethical Issues in Boxing', *Journal of the Philosophy of Sport*, 20(1): 48–63.
Dixon, N. (2001) 'Boxing, Paternalism, and Legal Moralism', *Social Theory and Practice*, 27: 323–345.
Dixon, N. (2015) 'A Moral Critique of Mixed Martial Arts', *Public Affairs Quarterly*, 29(4): 365–384.
Dixon, N. (2016) 'Internalism and External Moral Evaluation of Violent Sport', *Journal of the Philosophy of Sport*, 43(1): 101–113.
Green, K. (2011) 'It Hurts So It Is Real: Sensing the Seduction of Mixed Martial Arts', *Social & Cultural Geography*, 12(4), 377–396.
Herrera, D. C. (2002) 'The Moral Controversy Over Boxing Reform', *Journal of the Philosophy of Sport*, 29(2): 163–173.
Hyland, D. (1978) 'Competition and Friendship', *Journal of the Philosophy of Sport*, 5(1): 27–37.
Jones, K. (2001a) 'A Key Moral Issue: Should Boxing Be Banned?' *Culture, Sport, Society*, 4(1): 63–74.
Jones, K. (2001b) 'Sport and Friendship', *Journal of Philosophy of Education*, 35(1): 131–140.
Kant, I. (1785/1959) *Foundations of the Metaphysics of Morals*, L. W. Beck (ed. and trans.), Indianapolis, IN: Bobbs-Merrill.
Kershnar, S. and Kelly, R. (2020) 'Rights and Consent in Mixed Martial Arts', *Journal of the Philosophy of Sport*, 47(1): 105–120.
Kretchmar, S. (2019) 'The Nature of Competition: In Defense of Descriptive Accuracy', *Sport, Ethics and Philosophy*, 13(2): 237–246.
Massey, W. V., Meyer, B. B. and Naylor, A. H. (2013) 'Toward a Grounded Theory of Self-Regulation in Mixed Martial Arts', *Psychology of Sport and Exercise*, 14: 12–20.
Mayeda, T. D. and Ching, E. D. (2008) *Fighting for Acceptance: Mixed Martial Artists and Violence in American Society*, Lincoln, NE: iUniverse.
McCormick, R. A. (1979) 'Is Professional Boxing Immoral?', in E. W. Gerber and W. J. Morgan (eds.) *Sport and the Body: A Philosophical Symposium* (2nd Ed.), Philadelphia: Lea & Febiger, pp. 258–263.
Schneider, A. J. and Butcher, R. (2001) 'Ethics, Sport and Boxing', in W. J. Morgan, K. V. Meier and A. J. Schneider (eds.) *Ethics in Sport*, Champaign, IL: Human Kinetics, pp. 357–369.
Simon, R. L. (2004) *Fair Play: The Ethics of Sport* (2nd Ed.), Boulder, CO: Westview Press.
Sokol, D. K. (2004) 'The Not-So-Sweet Science: The Role of the Medical Profession in Boxing', *Journal of Medical Ethics*, 30: 513–514.
Sokol, D. K. (2011) 'Boxing, Mixed Martial Arts, and Other Risky Sports: Is the BMA Confused?', *British Medical Journal*, 343, doi:10.1136/bmj.d6937.
Spencer, D. (2009) 'Habit(us), Body Techniques and Body Callusing: An Ethnography of Mixed Martial Arts', *Body & Society*, 15(4): 119–143.
Spencer, D. (2012a) 'Narratives of Despair and Loss: Pain, Injury and Masculinity in the Sport of Mixed Martial Arts', *Qualitative Research in Sport, Exercise and Health*, 4(1): 117–137.
Spencer, D. (2012b) *Ultimate Fighting and Embodiment: Violence, Gender, and Mixed Martial Arts*, New York: Routledge.
Spencer, D. (2014) '"Eating Clean" for a Violent Body: Mixed Martial Arts, Diet and Masculinities', *Women's Studies International Forum*, 44: 247–254.
Stenius, M. (2015) 'Attacking the Body in Mixed Martial Arts: Perspectives, Opinions and Perceptions of the Full Contact Combat Sport of Ultimate Fighting', *Journal of Arts & Humanities*, 4(2), 77–91.
Stenius, M. and Dziwenka, R. (2015) ' "Just Be Natural with Your Body": An Autoethnography of Violence and Pain in Mixed Martial Arts', *International Journal of Martial Arts*, 1: 1–24.
Telfer, E. (1970/1971) 'Friendship', *Proceedings of the Aristotelian Society*, 71, 223–241.
Watson, N. J. and Brock, B. (2015) 'Christianity, Boxing and Mixed Martial Arts: Reflections on Morality, Vocation and Well-Being', *Journal of Religion and Society*, 17: 1–22.
Weimer, S. (2017) 'On the Alleged Intrinsic Immorality of Mixed Martial Arts', *Journal of the Philosophy of Sport*, 44(2): 258–275.

10 MMA as a path to stoic virtue

Michael Tremblay

There is a cultural association between martial arts and moral philosophy. Martial arts are typically seen as a vehicle to transform character. If you imagine the ideal martial artist, it will probably look something like this: they are tough, but gentle. They know how to fight but would never use this knowledge unless provoked. They are disciplined, confident, and fight for what is right. There is, in this way, a kind morality built into our understanding of martial arts. A great martial artist is not just the best at their sport, but they are also a great person, or at least strive to be one.

Opposed to the idea of the martial artist is that of the 'brawler' in the worst sense of the term. They are physically capable and skilled, but they do not think this ability comes with additional responsibility. They might use their skills for selfish means, or even to harm, intimidate, or bully others. They practice the same physical techniques as the martial artist, but they see no connection between these techniques and their character.

In traditional martial arts, this distinction is captured by the concepts of *jutsu* and *do*. *Jutsu*, which means technique, refers to the physical skills applied in combat. *Do*, which means 'the way', refers to the cultivation of character which occurs by practicing martial arts.

A classic example of the divide between *jutsu* and *do* is seen in *The Karate Kid*. Cobra Kai teaches karate, but they are still the villains of *The Karate Kid* because their approach to training teaches only *jutsu*, or technique. Their goal is to win, even if it means having to 'sweep the leg' and do something dishonorable. They have the technique but do not care about the *do*. Compare this to Mr. Miyagi's teaching of Daniel. Miyagi emphasizes both technique and character. Both Mr. Miyagi and Cobra Kai teach *jutsu*, but only Mr. Miyagi teaches *do*.

With this distinction between *jutsu* and *do* in mind, it is worth asking: does mixed martial arts (MMA) have a *do*? Does it have a unique philosophy which promotes the development of character? Or is it just *jutsu*, a set of techniques? 'Martial arts' is part of the name, but it has also established a reputation for being a brutalist sport, which glorifies violence and rewards aggression. Someone might claim that MMA has no *do* and is thus not a proper martial art. They might say that it has no link to philosophy or character and is solely about learning how to fight.

This chapter argues against such claims. It holds that MMA, if trained with the correct intention, is a valuable means of transforming one's character for the better. More specifically, it will argue that those who train MMA are well positioned to learn the lessons of Stoicism, an ancient Greek philosophy.[1] In this way, while philosophy may not be as explicit a part of MMA as other martial arts, training in MMA can still

DOI: 10.4324/9781003122395-11

provide a philosophical education which improves the character of those who practice it.

What follows is divided into three sections. The first section provides an overview of Stoic philosophy and situates Stoicism in relationship to combat sports. The second section describes three unique parts of MMA, and three Stoic lessons that accompany them. These are

1 Chaos teaches the dichotomy of control
2 Antagonism teaches us to reimagine obstacles as benefits
3 Difficulty teaches us how to gain freedom from external coercion

The third and final section provides a caveat. While MMA provides an opportunity to learn Stoic lessons, it must be trained with the intention of bettering one's character. Otherwise it really is just learning how to fight.

What is Stoicism?

Stoicism is an ancient Greek philosophy which was founded by Zeno of Citium in the early 3rd century BCE in Athens. While Stoicism originated in Greece, it went on to gain popularity throughout the Roman Empire. The most famous Stoics lived during this later period, and included Seneca, Epictetus, and Roman emperor Marcus Aurelius.

Stoicism is a robust philosophical system, which developed innovations in physics, logic, and ethics.[2] Like most Hellenistic philosophies, Stoicism took the question of how one ought to live to be one of central questions philosophy must answer.[3] Following Aristotle, Stoicism thought the greatest good humans could achieve is a happy life or *eudaimonia*. But by 'happiness', these ancient thinkers did not mean a transient good feeling. They meant an excellent life, where one achieves the kinds of things which are good for a human to have.

All major Hellenistic schools of philosophy, including the Epicureans, the Cynics, and the Stoics, were fascinated by this question of what a happy life entailed. They all agreed that the greatest good for a human is happiness, but they disagreed about what a happy life consisted of. For the Epicureans, a happy life consisted of pleasure and the absence of pain. For the Peripatetics, it was a mix of possessing good things and being virtuous. The Stoics were unique in that they considered virtue necessary and sufficient for a happy life.[4] For the Stoics, to be virtuous means to be happy, regardless of other physical, social, or financial circumstances. To demonstrate this point, they went so far as to make the famous claim that the virtuous man would be happy even on the torture rack.[5]

While most would agree that it is better to be virtuous than vicious, the claim that virtue is the only true good, and enough for a happy life, was controversial even at the time. What about wealth, safety, and fame? The Stoic Seneca argues that we all recognize that these things are not enough to make a life good, if they are not accompanied by virtue:

> If someone should be found who has all other advantages – health, riches, a fine family tree, an entry hall crowded with visitors – but it is agreed that he is a bad person, you will criticize him. Conversely, if someone has none of those things I

listed – neither money, nor throngs of clients, nor noble birth, nor a long line of ancestors – but it is agreed that he is a good person, you will approve of him. Hence [virtue] is indeed the sole good of the human, since one who has it is to be praised even if he is lacking in other advantages, while one who does not have it is condemned and rejected even if he is well supplied with other advantages.

(Seneca 2015: 76.12)

Seneca's point was that we already recognize the supremacy of virtue when we praise and admire *good* people, regardless of the circumstances of their life. As for what virtue consists of, it was thought to be the perfection of reason, culminating in the attainment of wisdom.[6] This was because humans were considered by the Stoics to be, essentially, rational beings. A perfect human then is one who reasons perfectly and has a secure knowledge of what is good and bad, and their place within the world.

However, one might argue that virtue, understood as perfected reason, is still not enough to be happy. Perhaps the virtuous person is admirable in a certain sense, but surely a good life involves a degree of pleasure, or freedom from suffering. And that is something which wealth and power can secure, but virtue cannot.

In response to these kinds of criticisms, the Stoics would argue that virtue is the only way to secure peace of mind, and freedom from fear, distress, and unwanted emotions. This is because our worst suffering is self-inflicted, through the poor application of reason. We suffer when we misjudge the world around us.

The argument goes as follows. Virtue is the sole good, and since it is understood as perfect reason, it is up to us whether or not we achieve it. Being happy does not depend on any external circumstance, only on the proper use of our reason. But we mistakenly judge things which are not up to us to be bad. Things such as poverty, social criticism, physical danger, even death, are not bad things, since the only truly good and bad things are virtue and vice. But we ignorantly judge them to be bad, and we suffer for it. As Epictetus puts it,

It isn't the things themselves that disturb people, but the judgements that they form about them. Death, for instance, is nothing terrible… no, it is in the judgement that death is terrible that the terror lies. So accordingly, whenever we're impeded, disturbed, or distressed, we should never blame anyone else, but only ourselves, that is to say, our judgements.

(Epictetus 2014b: 5)

For the Stoics, our mental suffering is self-inflicted. It is caused by fearing or desiring things besides virtue and vice. When we desire or fear things which are not up to us, we suffer from anxiety and distress because we think whether or not our life turns out well is not entirely up to us.

At this point, it is worth questioning the connection between MMA and Stoicism. On one hand, it seems that there is no essential link between MMA and Stoicism. Nothing about MMA commits those who practice it to the Stoic theory that virtue and vice are the only good.

However, Stoicism is not just a theory about the nature of the good. It is also a practically oriented transformative practice. It contains a number of lessons and exercises designed to help students reduce harmful emotions, become more mindful of their values, and reimagine the world around them in a way that is beneficial to their mental health. This applied aspect of Stoicism is transferrable to people of almost any value system. It is this aspect of Stoicism which has been applied in both contemporary military training,[7] and in modern psychology in the form of cognitive behavioral therapy.[8] The remainder of this chapter argues that MMA is well suited for training the individual in this applied aspect of Stoicism.

At the risk of this connection between MMA and Stoicism seeming arbitrary, it is worth noting two parallels between Stoicism and MMA.[9] First, it was commonly understood in Ancient Greek philosophy that sport played a beneficial role in the cultivation of virtue. Long before Stoicism was created, Plato and Aristotle were discussing the benefits sport could have for one's character.[10]

Second, the Stoics thought of themselves as being analogous to fighters. The Stoic Epictetus compares philosophers in training to wrestlers, who should seek out worthy opponents to test themselves against (2014a:1.24.1–2, 1.29.33–35). In his book, *Meditations*, Roman emperor and Stoic Marcus Aurelius reminds himself that he is 'not a dancer, but a wrestler: waiting, posed and dug in, for sudden assaults' (2002: 7.61). Aurelius elaborates later that the student of Stoicism should be thought of as a boxer, and not a fencer. For 'the fencer's weapon is picked up and put down again. The boxer's is part of him. All he has to do is clench his fist' (ibid. 12.9). The Stoics even compared Stoicism to pankration, the ancient Olympic sport which resembled modern MMA, and allowed striking, grappling, and submission holds. The Stoic Panaetius said our mind should be like a pankrationist in a fighting-stance: poised and ready to act.[11]

Overcoming ignorance, removing harmful emotions, and achieving happiness was conceived of as a fight. The student must always be prepared for battle, and their weapon of choice is that which is always with them, their power of reason. So, given that the connection between fighting and virtue was already identified by ancient Stoics, we will examine what stoic lessons can be gleaned from training in MMA.

Three Stoic lessons

The chaos of MMA and the dichotomy of control

Outside of studying philosophy, my greatest passion has always been training and competing in martial arts. I have competed at hundreds of Brazilian Jiu-Jitsu events and wrestled in University. But none of these matches fully prepared me for my MMA fights. There is something unique about the experience of MMA compared to other combat sports. It is these differences which make it particularly well suited to teach Stoic philosophy.

The first thing special about MMA is the degree to which it is chaotic in nature. First, there is an amount of uncertainty and lack of control that comes with any opponent-based sport. Unlike individual sports, like running or swimming, a team or individual competing against an opponent must be responsive to the behavior and choices of that opponent, and this produces a certain degree of uncertainty. We can make a game plan, but we can never fully anticipate our opponent's decisions.

This uncertainty is further compounded in combat sports that have a method of instant victory: wrestling's pin, judo's ippon, boxing's knockout. In soccer or hockey, you can be confident of victory if you are leading 5–0. However, in combat sports, a single movement can cause you to win or lose, regardless of what occurred in the rest of the match.

MMA takes the uncertainty of a sport with split-second wins and losses, and adds more techniques, attacks, and ways to win (or lose) than any other combat sport. Modern MMA combines what is permitted in the least restrictive striking art, Muay Thai, with what is allowed in the least restrictive grappling art, Submission Grappling, and then adds ground-and-pound, something which exists in no other popular combat sport. An MMA fighter has to problem solve while considering more variables than any other modern combat athlete, while facing major consequences for making a mistake. All of this together is what makes an MMA fight so exciting. No matter how much you train or prepare, there is just so much going on that even the best fighters are bound to make mistakes, get hit, and be thrown off their game plan.

Above and beyond this chaos, which is unique to MMA, there is the lack of control which comes with any sport. There are a number of things which are not up to the athlete at all, yet have a major impact on the result of a fight: The skill of your opponent, the quality of the opponent's training camp, who you were selected to fight, whether the crowd cheers for or against you, if you get sick or suffer a fluke injury, your physical talent, etc. Furthermore, there are those things which the fighter influences but does not fully determine: the difficulty of their weight cut, the success of their training camp, the decision of the judges, and ultimately, the result of the fight.

The Stoic solution to navigating chaos is what is called the dichotomy of control (DOC). The DOC refers to the simple but profound idea that some things are within our power and some things are not. Given that fact, Stoicism reminds us that we will be happier if we focus our energy and efforts on making the best of what is in our power. The Stoic Epictetus describes the DOC as follows:

> Some things are within our power, while others are not. Within our power are opinion, motivation, desire, aversion, and, in a word, whatever is of our own doing; not within our power are our body, our property, reputation, office, and, in a word, whatever is not of our own doing… Remember then, that if you regard that which is… not your own as being your own, you'll have cause to lament, you'll have a troubled mind, and you'll find fault with both gods and human beings…
>
> (Epictetus 2014b: 1)

For the Stoics, the only thing which is in our power is how we choose to make use of our 'impressions', or representations of the world. In other words, we are only in control of how we respond to stimuli. The way the world is, and the impressions we receive from it, are not up to us. But, as rational creatures, we have the capacity to reflect upon the world and decide how we will respond. This capacity to reflect and make choices with the information we have is the only thing really up to us. Everything else, including what happens to our body, our reputation, and our property, is not in our power. We may influence it, but it is not fully in our power, because it is also dependent upon luck, the actions of other people, and a variety of circumstances outside of our control.

Most psychological suffering, the Stoics argue, comes from ignorance about this distinction. We attempt to control and determine that which is not within our power. And when things fail to go the way we want them to, as they inevitably will since we cannot control these kinds of things, we become upset and blame others. A crucial step to happiness then is to remember this distinction and apply it when we feel ourselves becoming emotionally invested in something. If it turns out this thing is outside of our power and is not a direct result of our choice, then we are to avoid becoming too emotionally invested in the outcome.

The lesson of the DOC, to focus our attention on the things in our power, is a common ethos in sport, but is especially relevant to MMA. By its very nature, MMA puts the fighter in a situation that is essentially chaotic and unpredictable.

If an athlete is going to succeed in a context with so much outside of their control, they must learn to focus on what is in their control: their effort and how they respond to their circumstances. Following the DOC means that you would still be aware of things outside of your control. The movements of your opponent, or whether or not you won the first round, are out of your control but still matter to the athlete. But, if we adopt a Stoic mindset, they only matter because they give the athlete information about how the athlete should make use of the things they *do* control.

In 2019 I had the opportunity to interview Georges St-Pierre, one of the greatest MMA fighters of all time, about how he remained psychologically focused and ready to perform during fights (Hayabusa 2020). He told me that he developed a system where he learned to have a narrow scope of focus when competing. Inside the scope were the things he could control, like his movements, his decisions, and his responses to the opponent. Outside of that scope were things he could not control, like the energy of the crowd, other people's opinions, whether he feels sick, etc. Georges had adopted for his own use, knowingly or not, the Stoic DOC, and clearly it works well for him.

A common concern about the DOC is that focusing on only that which is up to you will inhibit the motivation of the athlete. For example, winning is not strictly up to the athlete. It depends on a number of circumstances beyond their choice and control. So, if we do not value what is not up to us, why should we care about winning? And if we do not care about winning, why should we fight at all?[12]

The Stoic solution to this problem is to emphasize a shift in focus from the result to the process. The Stoic still strives towards goals outside of their control and works hard to achieve them. But these goals are opportunities to cultivate what is in our control: virtue or good character. To explain this, the Stoics used the metaphor of an archer.[13] The Stoic archer aims at a target, but whether or not they hit that target is outside of their control. A sudden unpredictable wind can knock even the best aimed arrow off course. But the Stoic archer is not discouraged by this, because their true goal is to do everything they can to aim well. Being a good archer is not about doing what is outside of the archer's control (hitting the target) but perfecting what is in the archer's control (aiming well).

Like the archer, a Stoic would argue that an MMA fighter is better off if they shift their primary goal from an external result (winning, fame, money), to something up to them (fighting well, or developing character). In fact, internal and external goals are often opposed to one another. Take two examples of this in the modern UFC. For example, it seems that when Conor McGregor threw a trolley at a UFC bus, and injured innocent fighters, this was an instance of McGregor trying to hype up a potential match with Khabib Nurmagomedov at the expense of his character. He did an immoral thing, that hurt other non-consenting people, in the pursuit of fame and money.

But the opposite can be true. You can hamper your external success in the pursuit of internal development. When Holly Holm had just defeated Ronda Rousey, she was on the precipice of becoming one of the largest sports stars in the world. She had just shocked the world and dismantled Rousey in dominant fashion, and until that match Rousey had looked unbeatable. There was a lot of potential money and hype behind a rematch. People wanted to see if Holm was just that good, or if it was a fluke and Rousey could recover her title.

However, when picking her next fight Holm did not make the financially motivated decision. She did not wait for Rousey to recover and propose a rematch. Holm wanted to fight, so she asked for the next best fighter in the division, Miesha Tate. Holm lost, and the potential for a championship rematch with Rousey was lost. UFC owner Dana White would go on to publicly criticize the decision and note how much potential money Holm lost (Okamoto 2016). But Holm seemed to be motivated by something internal. She was a fighter and she wanted to challenge herself and fight the best. Even though she lost, I gained a lot of respect for Holly Holm as a fighter. In choosing to challenge herself, she was demonstrating a focus on process over result, and an incorporation of the DOC into her own life.

The antagonism of MMA and reimagining obstacles

The first Stoic lesson discussed is that we will do better and be happier if we focus on what is up to us, instead of what is outside of our control. The second lesson follows from this one. It is the lesson to reconceptualize obstacles as opportunities to improve or learn.

We have already learned that according to Stoicism, we are to focus on the things which are up to us, while still aiming at achieving external goals. Like an archer aiming at the target, these external goals give us opportunities to test ourselves and improve what really matters: perfecting the things which are up to us. In the case of Stoicism, the most important thing that is up to us is our moral character, which is a reflection of how we respond to the world around us. Given that this is the case, how is the Stoic to conceive of obstacles to their external goals? How should the archer think of a windy day, or a damaged bow, which impedes their ability to hit the target?

According to the Roman Stoics, we are to view these obstacles as opportunities to learn about ourselves and test our abilities. Difficulties reveal to us the deficiencies in our current progress. Epictetus uses a metaphor involving wrestling to explain this point. Wrestlers train against difficult opponents for the purpose of learning from them what they have to improve on. We are to treat difficulties in life the same way:

> Difficulties are the things that show what men are. Henceforth, when some difficulty befalls you, remembers that god, like a wrestling-master, has matched you with a rough young man. For what end? That you may become an Olympic victor and that cannot be done without sweat. No man, in my opinion, has a more advantageous difficulty on his hands than you have, if only you will but use it as an athlete uses the young man he is wrestling against.
>
> (Epictetus 1995: 1.24.1–2)

Because the true goal of the Stoic is an internal one, the achievement of virtue, it cannot be impeded or prevented by external circumstances. Rather these external circumstances serve as opportunities to teach us about where we still have more to learn.

In this way, what seems like an obstacle to a non-Stoic, is conceived of as a beneficial asset to the Stoic. As Marcus Aurelius puts it:

> Our actions may be impeded by [others], but there can be no impeding our intentions or our dispositions. Because we can accommodate and adapt. The mind adapts and converts to its own purposes the obstacle to our acting. The impediment to action advances action. What stands in the way becomes the way.
> (Aurelius 2002: 5.20)

By shifting the emphasis from what is outside of our control to what is inside our control, what were previously thought of as obstacles (outside of our control) become opportunities to learn and improve our character (inside of our control). Obstacles then are actually beneficial and can help the individual.

MMA is uniquely positioned to teach this lesson. There is a reason Epictetus uses wrestling to make this point. As fighting sports, both MMA and wrestling are inherently antagonistic. You are always put against an opponent who is trying both to win and physically harm you in the process. If the athlete views obstacles and difficult situations as things to be avoided, then they would never even make it into the training room. In order to survive training, the combat athlete must reconceptualize their training partners and the physical difficulty of training from obstacles to be avoided into opportunities to learn and improve.

When this mentality is extended to other aspects of one's life, it has powerful beneficial effects. Someone who spends their time avoiding obstacles and difficulties has to be afraid of chance, change, or chaos. These all indicate a lack of control, and someone vulnerable and averse to difficulties needs control over their environment. But if we adopt the habit of using obstacles for our own benefit, then we learn to also benefit from randomness and change. We not only improve, but we also do not have to be anxious about controlling and determining the world around us.

In fact, Epictetus takes this so far as to say that the proper Stoic would gladly welcome difficulties as a benefit to them:

> When we are called to meet some difficulty, we should know that the time has come to show whether we have been well educated. For a young man who goes from his studies to confront such a difficulty is like a person who has practised the analysis of syllogisms, and if somebody proposes an easy one, says, 'Give me, rather, a fine intricate one, that I may get some exercise'. So also are wrestlers displeased when matched with lightweight young men. 'He cannot lift me', one says, 'now there is a fine young man'.
> (Epictetus 2014a: 1.29.33–5)

Like a wrestler, or MMA fighter, who would be disappointed if none of their training partners could beat them, Epictetus thinks we too should be displeased if our lives are too easy. If they are, we lack the ability to test what we have learned, and so perhaps to learn more. Difficult situations can bring out the best in people, and if we understand this, we can view difficulties as opportunities to improve. This kind of mentality is necessary to succeed in MMA. It might even be necessary to train in MMA in the first place. Regardless, it would be difficult to find an MMA fighter who did not share the Stoic mindset of reimagining obstacles as lessons.

The difficulty of MMA and gaining freedom

The Stoic Epictetus had a unique definition of freedom.[14] For him, freedom was not determined by external circumstances, as one might suspect. You were not free by being released from slavery, or by becoming rich enough to buy anything you wanted. For Epictetus 'that person is free who lives as he wishes, who can neither be constrained, nor hindered, nor compelled...' (2014a: 4.1.1). A free person is one who lives as they wish, which means that what they cannot be forced to act a certain way by other people. It is impossible to be compelled only when you do not desire or fear anything another person can provide or do to you. This is achieved by wanting only what is up to you, i.e. to be a good person.

If you desire something that is not in your control and depends on other people, then other people will always be able to control your behavior by bribing you with what you want. As such, Epictetus says that 'you've delivered yourself into slavery... if you attach value to anything that isn't your own, if you conceive a desire for anything that is subject to anyone else and is perishable' (ibid.: 4.1.77). Likewise, if you fear things that are not up you, then other people will be able to control you by threatening you with them. For example, if you want wealth, or fear physical harm, an unjust dictator can control your behavior by either threatening to throw you in jail, or offering you money. If someone else can control your behavior, then you are not free. So the only way to become free, in Epictetus's view, is to only desire and fear what is up you, namely acting well or poorly.

The idea that we must only desire and fear virtue and vice will not appeal to anyone who does not share the Stoic view that virtue and vice are the only truly good and bad things. Nonetheless, there is a lesson to glean from Epictetus's teachings on freedom which can be applied by those who are not pure Stoics. Often we think of freedom as something determined by changing the world outside of ourselves. But Epictetus points out that we can become free by changing our character and taking accountability for our fears and desires. The fewer things we think we need to have to be happy, the less other people will be able to intimidate or coerce us.

Mastering desire and fear, in this Stoic sense, is to reduce the desire and fear you feel for things outside of your control. This is how you achieve freedom. With this Stoic notion of freedom in mind, MMA is well suited to increase the freedom of those who practice it, because MMA trains our desire and fears. MMA teaches us that many things we were afraid of are not as bad as we suspected, and that many things we thought we must have to be happy we can actually survive without.

First, MMA reduces the amount of fear you experience in two ways. First, like other fighting styles, it empowers those who train in it by making them better fighters. You become less afraid of confrontation or assault, because you become better suited to handle confrontation and assault safely. It is easy to feel less intimidated by others when you know that they have less physical power over you and could not easily hurt you if they wanted to. MMA teaches you how to fight and knowing how to fight makes the possibility of fighting, at least in one sense, less scary. As the most realistic fighting style commonly practiced, MMA is well suited to provide this kind of active empowerment.

But MMA also reduces your fear in another way. MMA is incredibly difficult and forces those who practice it to experience a lot of things most people go out of their way to avoid. If you practice MMA, you will be punched in the face, you will be made extremely uncomfortable, you will experience what it is like to have someone intentionally try to hurt you, and you will make public mistakes with serious implications. These are the kinds of things that most people pursuing happy lives try to avoid. But after undergoing all of this, you will also realize that you are still okay. Training in MMA teaches you that these things are not as bad as most people expect them to be, and that one can still be happy in spite of them. The knowledge that we can survive in situations we previously thought to be terrible makes the individual more confident and secure.[15]

Finally, MMA also helps to regulate our desires. To succeed in MMA, you must manage your desire to be physically comfortable. You must stick to a training regimen. You must diet, abstain from treats, smoking, and alcohol. In some cases, you must abstain from water and food altogether in order to cut weight. In this process, MMA teaches those who train how to put aside their desires in service of greater, long term goals. Someone who is pulled around by whatever they want in the moment will not be able to succeed in MMA, which requires the subjugation of desire in service of training.

By teaching those who practice it to fear and desire less, MMA empowers us to be freer, in the Stoic sense. This type of freedom is important for the Stoics, because often we fail to live up to our moral potential when we are coerced or intimidated. Take a variety of examples: someone is being bullied, but we are afraid to intervene because the bully might direct their aggression towards us. We know we should call out someone's behavior as being inappropriate, but we do not because we are afraid the room will not agree with us and we will be socially ostracized. Our boss is acting in an inappropriate manner, but we refuse to address it because we desire money, or a career, or are afraid of being without a job.

These are all circumstances in which desire and fear for something beyond our control conflicts with our moral intuitions. We are not free to do what we view as right, because we are coerced by our fears and desires. By gaining mastery over fear and desire, we thus gain the freedom to act solely based on what we think is right. And MMA is an excellent means of gaining this Stoic freedom.

A warning

In the previous section, I argued that practicing MMA can improve one's character by teaching three Stoic lessons. However, a caveat is required. The caveat is that MMA *can* be a helpful way of learning Stoic values, but it is not necessarily morally beneficial. Not all MMA fighters are good people, or embody Stoic principles. This is because, in order to be morally beneficial, MMA must be trained with the intention of developing one's character. Otherwise, it might be a harm rather than a benefit.

According to Epictetus, the difference between a sport harming or benefiting the individual is a matter of intent (2014a: 3.12.16). Those who train in order to become better people will incorporate the lessons described in the previous section. But those who train just to impress others, become rich, or achieve fame, will not necessarily experience these benefits, even if they are working hard at training.

How then do we make sure we are training with the right intent and do not fall into the trap of pursuing external rewards? Epictetus recommends modesty: 'If you want to train for your own sake, take a little cold water into your mouth when you're thirsty in hot weather and then spit it out again, without telling a soul' (ibid.: 3.12.16).

Do not brag to others about how good you are, or how hard you train, because you are training for yourself, not for them.

As such, while MMA can serve as an excellent means for a philosophical and moral education, it cannot be recommended unconditionally. But there is no martial art which can be recommended unconditionally. Anything, from karate, to taekwondo, to tai chi, can be practiced in the wrong way and for the wrong reasons. According to the Stoics any sport must be trained with the right intention if it is to be beneficial: the intention to improve yourself as a person. But if this intention is in place, then it seems that MMA is an excellent means to learn some of the most important lessons of Stoicism. As such, it deserves to be thought of as a proper martial art, and a viable practice for moral improvement.

Notes

1 While this chapter focuses on MMA, Fuller (2010) provides a discussion of the connection between Stoicism and traditional martial arts. Fuller argues that both traditional martial arts and Stoicism provide a means to freedom from desires and compulsions through self-discipline.
2 For a selection of primary Stoic sources divided by topic, see Long and Sedley (1987).
3 See Annas (1995) for a discussion of the similarities and differences between different Hellenistic philosophies, in terms of how they viewed the form and content of happiness. See also Cooper (2012), who explores ancient philosophy as a way of life, from Socrates to Plotinus.
4 See Laertius (2018: 7.89)
5 See Cicero (2006: 3.13).
6 See Seneca (2015: 76.15–6)
7 See Sherman (2007).
8 In his 2010 book *The Philosophy of Cognitive Behavioral Therapy*, Donald Robertson explains the influence Stoicism has had on contemporary practices of psychotherapy.
9 There is a concern raised by Holowchak (2010: 344–5) that the Stoics do not think sport is a very good means for cultivating virtue. His argument is based upon the lack of primary Stoic sources which make an explicit connection between Stoicism and sport. I try to address these concerns in the third part of this chapter.
10 Reid (2012) develops the connection between sport and the cultivation of virtue, beginning with Socrates, through Aristotle. For an excellent collection of primary sources on sport in ancient Greek culture, some relating to virtue and some not, see Miller (2004).
11 See Gellius (1927: 13.28).
12 This problem is discussed in the 2004 paper 'The Ideal of the Stoic Sportsman' by Stephens and Feezell. Their solution is to incorporate a moderate form of Stoicism, in which we allow some attachment to external goods and results, but moderate this attachment so that losing is not too painful. This is a reasonable solution, especially for the average individual who does not wish to dedicate themselves fully to Stoicism, although I argue here that it is possible to still be a great fighter without being motivated by winning.
13 See Cicero (2006: 3.6).
14 See Epictetus (2014a: 4.1) for his discussion of the nature of freedom.
15 This is similar to an exercise recommended by Seneca (2015: 18.5) where he recommends that his friend Lucilius intentionally go into poverty for a time. After that, Lucilius will no longer be afraid of losing money because he will understand that poverty is not as terrible as he suspected it to be.

References

Annas, J. (1995) *The Morality of Happiness*, New York: Oxford University Press.
Aristotle (2014). *Nicomachean Ethics*, C. D. C. Reeve (trans.) Indianapolis: Hackett.

Aurelius, M. (2002). *Meditations*, G. Hays (trans.), New York: Modern Library.
Cicero, M. T. (2006) *On Ends*, H. Rackham (trans.), Cambridge: Harvard University Press.
Cooper, J. M. (2012) *Pursuits of Wisdom: Six Ways of Life in Ancient Philosophy from Socrates to Plotinus*, Princeton: Princeton University Press.
Epictetus (1995) *The Discourses of Epictetus*, R. Hard (trans.), London: Everyman Library.
Epictetus (2014a) 'Discourses', R. Hard (trans), in *Discourses, Fragments, Handbook*, Oxford: Oxford University Press.
Epictetus (2014b) 'Handbook,' R. Hard (trans), in *Discourses, Fragments, Handbook*, Oxford: Oxford University Press.
Fuller, J. (2010) 'An Enemy Lying in Ambush', in G. Priest and D. Young (eds.) *Martial Arts and Philosophy: Beating and Nothingness*, Chicago, IL: Open Court, pp. 59–70.
Gellius, A. (1927) *The Attic Nights of Aulus Gellius*, J. C. Rolfe (trans.), Cambridge: Harvard University Press.
Hayabusa (2020) 'Georges St-Pierre Full Interview', *The Gentle Art*, 24 February, https://www.youtube.com/watch?v=lkF9iI20DtY, accessed 31 July 2020.
Holowchak, M. A. (2010) 'A Closer Look at "Sophisticated Stoicism": Reply to Stephens and Feezell', *Sport, Ethics and Philosophy*, 4(3): 341–354.
Laertius, D. (2018) *Lives of the Eminent Philosophers*, P. Mensch (trans.) Oxford: Oxford University Press.
Long, A. A. and Sedley, D. N. (1987) *The Hellenistic Philosophers*, Cambridge: Cambridge University Press.
Miller, S. G. (ed.) (2004) *Arete: Greek Sports from Ancient Sources*, Berkeley: University of California Press.
Okamoto, B. (2016) 'UFC's Dana White: "I Don't Know If Holly Really Knows What She Lost"', *ESPN*, 8 March, https://www.espn.com/mma/story/_/id/14931728/ufc-president-dana-white-feel-bad-holly-holm, accessed 31 July 2020.
Reid, H. L. (2010) 'Seneca's Gladiators', *Sport, Ethics and Philosophy*, 4(2): 204–212.
Reid, H. L. (ed.) (2012) *Athletics and Philosophy in the Ancient World: Contests of Virtue*, London: Routledge.
Robertson, D. (2010) *The Philosophy of Cognitive-Behavioural Therapy (CBT): Stoic Philosophy as Rational and Cognitive Psychotherapy* (2nd Ed.), New York: Routledge.
Seneca, L. A. (2015) 'Letters on Ethics: To Lucilius', in M. Graver and A. A. Long (trans.) *The Complete Works of Lucius Annaeus Seneca*, Chicago, IL: The University of Chicago Press.
Sherman, N. (2007) *Stoic Warriors: The Ancient Philosophy Behind the Military Mind*, Oxford: Oxford University Press.
Stephens, W. O., and Feezell, R. (2004) 'The Ideal of the Stoic Sportsman', *Journal of the Philosophy of Sport*, 31(2): 196–211.

11 Ethics of mixed martial arts

Walter Veit and Heather Browning

Mixed martial arts (MMA), as a combat sport, is frequently criticized both within the academic literature and society more generally; dismissed as barbaric and inhumane. This stands in stark contrast with the booming popularity of the sport, not only among men but also increasingly women (see Weaving 2014). MMA is not new, however, with roots that stretch back far into Ancient Greece and China (see Stenius 2013; Acevedo and Cheung 2010). Indeed, Plato himself is said to have practiced martial arts in his youth, which is what earned him the name *Plato*, meaning 'broad-shouldered'.[1] He, along with Socrates and other Greek philosophers, repeatedly emphasized the need for physical education, even for those who should eventually occupy the role of philosophers within society.[2] Despite this, however, MMA has received almost no contemporary philosophical attention; a glaring omission in the literature that is being remedied in this volume. What little has been written typically depicts MMA as an activity that is inherently wrong (Dixon 2015) or at least problematic (Weimer 2017; Kershnar and Kelly 2020). Contrary to these foregoing analyses, we argue that MMA is not only permissible, but an intrinsically praiseworthy and virtuous endeavor, one that is required to fully develop one's moral character. We thus argue for a return to the Hellenic recognition of an intimate connection between body and mind that is closer to the first school of thought that MacDonald (2012) so elegantly described:

> There exist two competing schools of thought in defining mixed martial arts: there are those who feel that it is about honour and respect, while others think that it is about punching people in the head until they fall over.

This chapter is structured as follows: we begin by analyzing and responding to Nicholas Dixon's arguments against MMA – both his empirical criticism of MMA, and his subsequent depiction of MMA as an intrinsically immoral sport. We then offer a contrary analysis that depicts MMA as an inherently praiseworthy activity – one that fosters our natural moral inclination to treat not only ourselves, but also our opponents, and ultimately humanity itself, as ends in themselves.

Moral critiques of MMA

Though MMA is now one of the most popular sports in the US, it has only recently come to gain popularity and dethrone boxing as the most popular combat sport. As the first 'M' in the name indicates, MMA is a *mixed* sport – not in the sense of Olympic events such as decathlon in which different disciplines are alternated, but in

DOI: 10.4324/9781003122395-12

combining multiple fighting styles such as Muay Thai (Thai boxing), Brazilian Jiu-Jitsu, wrestling, and boxing within a single bout. These fighting styles represent the most popular subdisciplines participants train in to form the most well-rounded fighter. The largest organization in MMA is the UFC, responsible for popularizing the sport and organizing fights across the globe. In their early days, bouts were promoted as the search for 'Which martial art is the *strongest*?', pitting combatants of different martial arts against one another. It was the search for *The Ultimate Fighter*, which is still reflected in the reality TV show of the same name that helped MMA to reach popularity in the public.[2] In the beginning there existed few rules and fights were hyped as a bloody and 'anything goes' free-for-all. This has led to much criticism of the sport, critics deeming it barbaric and inhumane – at worst as a breeding ground for violence and crime (Brent and Kraska 2013) – a picture that was only aided by the octagon-shaped cage the fights take place in.

The sport has evolved, however – now with a more detailed rule-set than most other combat sports, undermining the barbaric picture prevalent within the public conception. Fights usually consist of several rounds, though unlike boxing where the audience can see up to 12 rounds, MMA fights are often limited to three (or at most, five) rounds. Because moves from wrestling and Jiu-Jitsu are allowed, people can throw each other and engage in locking someone's joints – for instance in a so-called 'armbar' – or by choking them. If the fighter then sees no way out of the position, then in order to avoid injury they can end the fight by tapping on their opponent, signaling the referee to step in and call it over. Fights can also traditionally end in a knockout or technical knockout (fighter declared unable to continue) or by an opponent losing consciousness through a chokehold. Fights will continue on the ground and on the cage that separates the fighters from the crowd, both of which are relatively soft. Unlike boxing, there is no ten-second countdown. If one of the fighters falls, the fight continues, thus leading many in the public to utter disapproval. These dissenting voices, however, have become increasingly submerged as MMA events have gained widespread popularity and moved onto prime-time television. Nevertheless, some still persist – including within the philosophical community. Here, we use this opportunity to offer a response to those who try to reinstate the status of MMA as an immoral activity to be condemned and prohibited (Dixon 2015).

The first philosophical treatment of mixed martial arts has been offered only recently.[3] In his 2015 paper 'A Moral Critique of Mixed Martial Arts' the philosopher Nicholas Dixon sets out to depict MMA as an inherently problematic sport. Dixon goes so far as to argue that 'no amount of consent can erase its inherently problematic nature' (ibid.: 381). It is hard to read his paper without feeling the vivid disgust Dixon seems to feel towards the activity. Indeed, he states the thesis of his paper in the assertion 'the initial revulsion that many viewers of MMA experience is based on sound moral arguments' (ibid.: 365), and Dixon's own revulsion is clear throughout. But is the revulsion people feel towards other people's activities really always based in moral arguments – let alone sound ones? This seems to be an unjustifiably strong assertion.

This, of course, need not imply that intuition has to be wrong in all of these cases. There is a justified moral reason, for instance, to feel revulsion against an armed robber killing an innocent customer in a store, a baby being drowned, or an animal tortured, but care must be taken to keep a degree of objectivity in one's assessment of initial moral revulsion. We may be disgusted – almost morally repulsed – by observing people eating pineapple pizza, yet we know that there is no real moral reason to condemn this.[4] A sound reason is required to translate this emotional response into a moral judgement, one which we argue that Dixon fails to provide.

Dixon begins by drawing on one of his earlier articles (2001), in which he likewise criticizes boxing. In it, Dixon argues that blows to the head should be prohibited since research has shown conclusive evidence regarding the negative effects of head blows to the long-term health of boxers. A substantial percentage of boxers suffer from brain damage which drastically impairs their ability to live fulfilled lives.

> On the basis of the evidence of the danger of significant mental impairment, I argued on two paternalistic grounds for reforming boxing to prohibit blows to the head. First, because of the vast rewards that the most successful professional boxers can earn, and because the vast majority of boxers come from lower socio-economic backgrounds, doubts exist about the autonomy of their decision to enter the ring. Second, even if the initial decision to join the profession is fully autonomous, brain damage diminishes fighters' *future* autonomy, and I can use what I call 'preemptive paternalism' to justify restricting their current freedom to protect their future ability to think rationally.
>
> (Dixon 2015: 366)

As Dixon points out, many boxers have a drastically reduced quality of life, since the brain is involved in 'rational, autonomous decision making' (ibid.: 366) and the rate of chronic traumatic encephalopathy (CTE) is high.

The argument that the vulnerable in society might be disproportionately led to become boxers and take injuries because they could not otherwise survive seems to us somewhat weak (though it has a strong cousin in the case of poverty leading to prostitution; see Monroe 2005). Unless they become famous, fighters typically earn very little.[5] They are thus more likely to be injured through their participation in frequent matches, as opposed to professional fighters who can lay off for months before their next fight. However, even if some fighters are drawn to risk themselves for money alone, this should simply lead to a call for stronger regulations – such as fighters with pre-existing injuries being barred from the ring – rather than a ban on the practice entirely.

Dixon's argument also relies on the paternalistic idea that due to brain injury, boxers will over time lose their capacity for autonomous decision-making and thus may enter into fights they would not otherwise have done if they had full autonomy at the time. This argument is more plausible as fighters are known to get 'punch-drunk' and yet continue their careers. However again, this seems more like a call for the strengthening of existing health guidelines and medical checks for fighters than for a wholesale ban on the activity. We are thus in agreement with Dixon, that *if* MMA leads to diminished capabilities in making informed decisions, we may ban anyone showing signs of punch-drunkenness from entering again. But such an exclusion would not prevent healthy individuals from entering fights since it takes many fights to develop the condition. If anything, it would be a call for a limit on the number of fights a fighter could have in their career. This is something we are not opposed to, but it is far from the more radical conclusions Dixon endorses.

Ultimately, Dixon doesn't rely on these arguments to make the case against MMA, as the evidence is still too sparse and currently suggests that the danger of head injuries is lower in MMA than in boxing.[6] Indeed, the rate of injury more generally within MMA does not suggest itself to be significantly higher than in any other combat sport.[7] Neither does he rely on the argument that MMA leads to violence outside the ring (either by the fighters themselves or by spurring violence in the audience). There is almost no data on these matters, so we should be careful not to draw any hasty conclusions, an attitude which Dixon himself adopts.[8] His paternalistic argument is thus little more than a set-up to make us buy into his otherwise exceedingly strong thesis of the intrinsic immorality of MMA.

'The intrinsic immorality of MMA'

In arguing for what he terms the 'intrinsic immorality of MMA', Dixon (2015: 367) draws on an argument Paul Davis made about boxing:

> The face of at least one boxer will suggest an attitude of unbridled ferocity toward the opponent. A snapshot of the face of a fighter on the offensive is liable to reveal an attitude toward the opponent that, in any other context, might be fairly described as vicious.
>
> (Davis 1993: 52 in Dixon 2015)

Dixon believes the viciousness expressed in MMA is all the more pronounced as it resembles an actual street fight in which both parties could end up on the floor, using also their knees and elbows. Dixon thinks that the viciousness inherent in this type of fighting violates the Kantian respect for humans as 'ends in themselves'. We think that Dixon is mistaken here, but shall sketch out the rest of his argument before detailing our response.

According to Kant's categorical imperative, we should never treat another human as a mere means but, Dixon argues, mixed martial artists do just that. They 'treat each other as objects to be hurt and injured and not as ends in themselves' (ibid.: 367). We are all familiar with problematic cases of objectification, and Dixon mentions several:

> A man treats a woman as a sex object if he regards her merely as a source of sexual gratification, without regard for her own desires or interests. Muggers treat their victims solely as objects from which to obtain money. Sycophants treat their rich acquaintances in the same way, albeit in a slightly more subtle manner. Ruthless politicians treat rivals and colleagues alike merely as stepping stones – objects to be manipulated – to their own accumulation of power. I can objectify people in one way but not in others: muggers, for instance, typically do not treat their victims as sex objects, but mugging remains a clear instance of treating people solely as means.
>
> (Dixon 2015: 368)

What matters for Kant is whether we treat people *exclusively* as means. Dixon cites Martha Nussbaum (1995), who has argued as an example that there is nothing problematic in using a partner's stomach as a pillow, since the context is a loving relationship. The context is important, a point we will later return to in order to defend MMA fights. Dixon (2015), nevertheless, recognizes that even if one applies Kant's principles, we are not necessarily equipped with a 'mechanical formula that produces a definitive verdict when I supply the factual details of whatever situation is under moral scrutiny', rather, we are supplied with a 'framework that gives us guidance regarding the questions we should ask, and using this framework in particular cases requires analysis and argument' (ibid.: 368). Even cases that initially appear to be clear-cut can be discussed within the framework; consider for instance the death penalty.

Dixon, however, does not believe that MMA is comparable to the death penalty in this regard, and thinks it much closer to paradigm cases of objectification such as '[m]urder, rape, and robbery' (ibid.: 369). Indeed, he seems to suggest that MMA is intrinsically worse than physical assault in the context of a robbery, since here the intention to injure and hurt another person is the very goal and not just an instrumental means towards robbing the other person.[9] Finally, Dixon argues that unlike our previous stomach-pillow example, there is 'no broader context of respect for the victim that would ["]cleanse["] it' (ibid.: 369). We think Dixon is mistaken in these assertions. This leaves us with two possibilities to restore the moral praiseworthiness of MMA: (i) show that mixed martial artists do not treat each other solely as means, and (ii) show that there is a broader context of respect that does indeed 'cleanse' the violence; to which we will now turn.

The intrinsic praiseworthiness of MMA

It is perhaps not a surprising event that both philosophical treatments of MMA to have come after Dixon (2015) are replies to him. Both Weimer (2017) and Kershnar and Kelly (2020) argue that MMA is not intrinsically wrong and can be a permissible activity. In this section, we will use some of their arguments to support a stronger conclusion: the intrinsic praiseworthiness of MMA. Let us therefore now address what Dixon (2015) dismisses as the possible avenues through which MMA could be found to be morally permissible after all.

Since both (i) and (ii) above rely on respect, the argument against Dixon (2015) will largely be a unified one. Both Weimer (2017) and Kershnar and Kelly (2020) recognize that mutual respect and consensual matches are possible and MMA fights should thus not be seen as intrinsically wrong. Kershnar and Kelly make this more explicit than Weimer, arguing that one can observe 'respect and warm feelings [MMA fighters] have for opponents before and after a fight', that they 'often "pull back" a punch or kick they have thrown, or release a submission hold, when they become aware that their opponent has been sufficiently subdued, sometimes before the referee declares the fight over' (ibid.: 108).[10] Dixon seemingly responds to this possibility that there could be such respect in MMA, raising the point as a possible objection to his view:

> Although the suggestion that the attempt to hurt and injure opponents in the cage is 'cleansed' by fighters' respectful attitude toward each other outside the cage is appealing, it cannot rescue MMA from this paper's critique. First, Nussbaum's defense of objectification in a loving relationship works because the couple's actions, including using the partner's stomach as pillow, and sex itself, are transformed by their love into acts of tenderness. Professional respect among cage fighters, in contrast, cannot transform violent acts into anything more than attempts to hurt and injure. Second, this attempt to justify MMA falls foul of Kant's injunction that we should treat other people as ends in themselves *at the same time* that we treat them as means.
>
> (Dixon 2015: 376)

Upon closer inspection of this paragraph, however, we must realize that Dixon (2015) doesn't actually provide an argument refuting the objection. He merely *asserts* that (a) respect among fighters cannot transform these actions, and (b) the respect occurs after the fight, not during it. The act of injuring an opponent, Dixon thinks, is thus a paradigm case of treating someone merely as a means. Since Dixon does little to support these assertions, we are supposed to take them as given, but this is surprising considering his strong conclusion that MMA is intrinsically bad. In moral philosophy there are very few acts (if any) that are considered intrinsically bad, for it suggests that there cannot ever be any context in which the practice is morally permissible, and that the intentions of the actors could not make a difference – an incredibly bold assertion.

Perhaps MMA would appear to the uninitiated as just such a paradigm case. Imagine someone who has never heard of the sport – be it a woman or a man – walking down the streets of downtown Chicago. They hear a ruckus: people screaming, cheering, and music playing. Wanting to investigate, they enter an old run-down former industrial building, in which they see a cage with two bloody humans hitting each other, while one lies on the ground. We have no doubt that the initial response to this would be shock. The person might very well think: 'What is going on here?' or 'This cannot be legal!'. But as discussed earlier, we should be careful not to use such 'instinctive' moral revulsion as guidance. People used to hold similar emotional reactions to homosexuality, BDSM, interracial marriage (some unfortunately still do). We should be careful not to give in to the temptation of seeing acts and practices we are unfamiliar with – and that may even appear strange to us – as something that must be morally bad. Consider the quote from James MacDonald (2012) in the epigraph:

> There exist two competing schools of thought in defining mixed martial arts: there are those who feel that it is about honour and respect, while others think that it is about punching people in the head until they fall over.
>
> (MacDonald 2012)

We should now try to overcome this strict black and white dichotomy in the debate. Both Weimer (2017) and Kershnar and Kelly (2020) ultimately argue that it is the consent among the participants in MMA matches that renders them permissible. We agree with this line of thought, though will not pursue that line here. Instead, we will argue that the respect found in MMA suggests not merely that MMA is not intrinsically bad, but rather the stronger claim that it makes MMA *intrinsically good*. Let us therefore further examine the respect present within MMA.

Respect, means, and ends in MMA

Respect is an integral part of MMA, a message that every MMA organization is trying hard to convey to the general public. While the UFC is the biggest MMA organization in the world, there exist numerous smaller ones, such as the German RFC, which is short for: Respect Fighting Championship. Fighters frequently pay tribute to their opponents after a fight, praising them and acknowledging their feats. Even fighters that bad-mouthed each other and were seemingly out to kill each other in the ring are often seen hugging each other after a fight. To Dixon, this is not important since despite mutual consent the fighters still violate each others' bodies in fighting, and thus he argues they treat each other merely as means. This, we think, gets Kant backwards. It is instead those that do not engage in MMA fights that treat *themselves* as mere means. Let us elaborate.

Kerstein, in her article titled 'Treating Oneself Merely as a Means', argues that Kant recognizes six duties to oneself: the duty not to kill oneself, a duty not to lie, a duty not to treat oneself as a mere means for lust (e.g., masturbation), a duty not to become a destroyer of the beautiful, a duty not to be cruel to animals, and a duty to 'recognize all our duties as divine commands' (2008: 201). Kant's list is an odd one, and Kant scholars have done much to make his account more coherent. Kerstein (ibid.), for instance, points to an apparent oddity that our duty to treat other animals without cruelty is a *perfect duty to ourselves*, while our obligations to other humans are duties to them. Kant argues that poor treatment of animals 'dulls [man's] shared feeling of their suffering and so weakens and gradually uproots a natural predisposition that is very serviceable to morality in one's relationship with other people' (Kant 1996: 443).

This concept – of *perfect duties to ourselves* – provides the lens through which to see the intrinsic praiseworthiness of MMA. While Kant argued for an imperfect duty to develop our talents, this is not the line of argument we will pursue to defend MMA, though it is of course applicable. We take a stronger line – that fighting in mixed martial arts bouts is itself an instance of a perfect duty to oneself. To omit this kind of engagement inherent to perfect duties would as Kerstein argues, involve 'a failure to give humanity, namely one's own, the respect it demands' – a failure to treat oneself as a rational agent (2008: 207). It is one that must be followed and allows no degree of flexibility, since it gradually strengthens our natural inclination to see our own bodies as ends in themselves, something that (like positive treatment of animals) is serviceable to morality in one's relationship to oneself and other people. To respond to an inevitable criticism of this position, we are not arguing that every human is required to become a professional MMA fighter – no less as our perfect duty to other animals requires everyone to become a professional animal rights activist or animal welfare researcher (though these are undeniably virtuous activities). The activity may be *praiseworthy* without being *obligatory*. Rather, the key here is the development of one's moral character.

A similar but distinct objection would be to hold that while there is something special, perhaps even intrinsically so, about this form of *fighting*, there are numerous other intrinsic goods that require time and effort and would have to be sacrificed for MMA. But here the same reply applies – unless it is necessary to practice MMA daily to develop one's moral character (which we do not hold) it is less clear how it would stand in the way of other goods. It is true that there is a plurality of moral goods, but as with Aristotle we may simply recognize that we have to accept that there will be some trade-offs and the trick will be to find the 'golden middle' so to speak.

Importantly, this position is not any bolder than Dixon's argument that MMA is somehow *intrinsically* immoral, since it merely involves a special development, a special 'coming to terms with' what it means to be a human. We recognize that this is nevertheless a strong position to hold, but it will become more plausible once it is recognized that there is no self, no personal identity, without a physical body. It is frequently acknowledged in the literature that Kant has failed to recognize our embodied nature (Svare 2006): that our identity is physical rather than merely mental. Even our minds are part of this embodied nature of selves, something that was commonly understood in Ancient Greek but lost in the modern world that embraced a mind-body dualism (Reid 2010).

When, as Green points out, MMA fighters report to seek out the sport in order to feel alive – to feel their body – it is a recognition that there is more to MMA than other sports.[11] It is a bodily experience that goes beyond what has been described as the experience of 'flow' or 'being in the zone' (Green 2011: 392). Unlike most sports, fighting involves a special sort of pain that is directly inflicted on oneself by others. Green suggests, that pain 'not only helps build confidence that something "real" is happening, but that pain also leads to an inward movement that cuts through pre-occupations leading to what participants describe as the discovery' (ibid.: 391) of identity or *selfhood*. Unlike other sports where the individual 'dissolves' and becomes one with the environment (e.g., rock climbing or parkour) or a team (e.g. soccer), in fighting this phenomenon is reversed. There is a sort of reverse pull towards oneself. It is a felt motion that Green argues that one is 'left alone, a united, feeling organism' (ibid.: 388). MMA uniquely connects one to their own body, causing a unique awareness of a body's capabilities and vulnerabilities.

This feeling is unparalleled in other sports, but may be approximated in other 'blood sports' and real street fights. However, as we will examine further at the end of the chapter, street fights often lack something that MMA possesses: a sense of *greatness*. In a different paper, Dixon recognizes that the 'concept of athletic superiority... includes not only physical prowess but also mental attributes' (1999: 24). There is no sport in which one could show more superior physical *and* mental prowess than in MMA. In an anime series about mixed martial arts this is made explicit: 'If one is born as a male, at least once in his life, he'll dream of becoming the strongest man alive'.[12] Reinforcing this, fighters in the UFC frequently state that they participate because they want to be the *best*.

Ancient philosophers praised the physical as an integral part of education, some even recommending or practicing the ancient Greek sport of pankration, a sport that closely resembles modern MMA but was less restrictive.[13] Those who do not engage in MMA can never gain the full understanding and respect for their own corporal existence. They treat their body purely as a means to other ends, while MMA fighters engage in the pursuit of mental and physical prowess and greatness for its own sake.[14] True martial art is about respecting one's body as an end in itself – it is a learned recognition for seeing the self as identical to one's body. Training and fighting gradually strengthens our natural inclination to see our bodies as ends in themselves, something that is ultimately serviceable to morality in one's relationship to oneself and other people. Indeed, the very activity is a duty towards one's own corporeality:

> Martial arts... ultimately, no matter what type it is, the objective is how to efficiently destroy your opponents. After that, it just depends on the heart of the fighter. If it is used for your selfish gains, then it becomes 'violence'. But if you use it to help yourself, to protect someone in need, then even a killing technique can ascend into true martial arts.
>
> (Furinji 2014)

It is thus no problem that MMA *necessarily* includes violence as Dixon would have it. The respect in MMA has two targets. On the one hand, it is one's opponent that is treated with respect. When two fighters spend months to prepare their minds and bodies to be in their best possible shape, it would be disrespectful not to go all out against one another – indeed, it would defeat the very purpose of the activity. Some fighters may need to scream and insult their opponent in order to give 100% in the ring, but rather than a sign of disrespect, this is a part of giving respect by engaging entirely.

One possible objection to our argument here is that Dixon emphasizes that professional fighters are not in it for the pain, rather, they aim to minimize the damage they receive and maximize the damage they deal, and thus get paid. This is dissimilar to those engaged in BDSM where pain becomes in a sense transformed through an intrinsic appreciation for the sensation.[15] Those active in the practice do not seek violence for its own sake. It doesn't share the apparent barbaric spirit of MMA because it is merely part of a larger appreciative and consensual act. But as we have argued throughout this section, there is no reason to think that the violence in MMA cannot be similarly transformed. Whereas Dixon places MMA at the extreme of a continuum of increasingly problematic practices such as unequal sexual relations and dwarf tossing, we shall argue that MMA is a deeply equalizing practice. Indeed, by drawing on feminist scholarship we shall show that such a transformation is one of the core features of MMA.

Masculinity, gender-norms, and feminism

The argument thus far may evoke some traditional and misogynistic stereotypes about males. Think of statements such as: 'A true man needs to be able to fight and protect his loved ones' or 'If you're too scared to fight – you're no man'. However, this is far from how we intend our argument be interpreted; rather it applies across the gender spectrum. MMA is importantly not an exclusively male sport and more and more women have joined the sport over the years, challenging traditional gender-norms surrounding fighting. In a small study, Velija et al. (2013) report that female MMA fighters feel empowered by engaging in 'blood sports' that are traditionally considered male. Yet, Velija et al. also report a sense of biological de-powerment in the sense that female MMA fighters realize their power differential to males – even at their peak, female fighters are typically out-performed by males. Nevertheless, women who practice MMA are able to reach their peak levels of both physical and mental resilience, traits that have often been thought of only as male. Indeed, former UFC champion Ronda Rousey[16] argues that female fights are even more impressive in this regard, as they 'have something to prove. They're not in there to win matches. They're in there to make a point. The point is that they deserve to be in there' (2013: 50). Nancy Hogshead-Makar, the Senior Director of Advocacy at the Women's Sport Foundation, similarly argues that the 'participation in combat sports in particular helps break down stereotypes that hold women back' (ibid.: 48).

Within only a few years, UFC president Dana White changed his mind from never expecting women to fight in the UFC to now – largely thanks to Ronda Rousey – allowing multiple weight classes for women (see Gregory 2013). When female fighters clash, the percentage of females in the viewing audience can reach more than one third of total views, a result that is perhaps surprising since the sport is often depicted as *the* man's sport (Weaving 2014). Unlike the female competitions within many other sports, female fighters are thriving surprisingly well, drawing both male and female audiences. Indeed, we think for these reasons that MMA is an intrinsically feminist competition.

Two statements of female MMA fighters recorded by Velija et al. stand out in particular:[17]

> When asked how it felt the first time she hit someone, Emma (Kick Boxing and Thai Boxing) expressed that, 'it was brilliant, you don't realise your own strength till you do it, it's quite a good feeling you feel quite alive'. Similarly, Louise, also explains her first experience of hitting someone, 'it made me feel powerful, because you are exerting a force over someone, it's your force on them' (Louise, Kick Boxing).
>
> (Velija et al. 2013: 530)

Again, we see the notion that MMA makes one feel *alive*. It is not, as Green (2011) seems to suggest, a phenomenon that applies exclusively to (rich and white) males. It is a natural inclination that is a duty to oneself. This might seem strong, but it is perhaps best illustrated as the inverse to Kant's duty to oneself in not committing suicide. An MMA fighter doesn't seek to injure his body for its own sake or to seek death. Quite the opposite: it's a phenomenological – indeed transformative – experience that leads fighters to gain an appreciation of their own embodied nature and that of others. Here, a phenomenological viewpoint in the tradition of Merleau-Ponty (1962, 1983) is a useful one. For Merleau-Ponty, it is the body and our sensory experience that anchors one's conscious experience, as a fundamentally embodied experience. Female MMA fighters undergo a transformative experience that in a sense 'masculinizes' their bodies and minds since fighting has been traditionally associated with manliness and masculinity. It helps to dissemble traditional gender categorizations. The phenomenological experience of hitting a taller, more muscular, and scary looking man in the face is something that empowers women. Again, unlike most other sports, MMA is special in that it enables women to experience equality to men. It is a transformative experience that cannot be gained by, say, outrunning or outlifting a male athlete.

Female fighters challenge traditional gender-norms and thus contribute to a more feminist society in which people are seen as equals. Women are no longer merely objects on which men can exert force and their will; here they become equals, as subjects able to exert force themselves. Weaving (2014), for instance, argues that MMA enables female fighters to overcome the gendered view of the female body as a mere body-object, and instead to become a body-subject, like males. It moreover challenges men to see women as subjects – individuals that pursue greatness and show strength of will – rather than mere objects subject to be dominated by the 'will of men'. Pain is the universal trait that can bring humans together and develop a shared sense of 'brotherhood' or, as we can see in female MMA, collegiality in a more general sense. Physical violence is thus transformed through the context of a fight between two equals (in the Kantian sense of a subject and end in itself) into an act of respect. The blood that flows is no longer an act of mere violence, but a true sign of our equal status as human beings. As Sun-Ken Rock says in the Japanese martial arts manga of the same name, 'In this world, the only thing we truly own is the body we shape every day' (Boichi 2012). Shaping our bodies, using them, and bringing them into contact with others is not treating ourselves or others as instrumental, but treating them as ends.

MMA is the ultimate form of competition. Consider the following statement by Forrest Griffin, former UFC Light Heavyweight Champion, and one of the few athletes to make it into the UFC Hall of Fame:

> A lot of people ask me why I fight, and the answer is pretty simple: I see mixed martial arts as the ultimate form of competition. If you're a hockey or football buff, you might disagree with me. After all, both sports are competitive and oftentimes violent. But what do the players from either sport do when they can't settle a dispute on the field? They don't challenge the person they have a problem with to a race or a goal-shooting contest. No, they rip off their gear and throw down. Why? Because fighting is the ultimate form of competition. If you get beat in Ping-Pong or darts or basketball, you can always save face by saying, 'Well, I could still kick his ass'. If you lose in fighting, you simply got beat. Never once will you hear a fighter say, 'He might have beat me in the cage, but I would slaughter him in shuffleboard'.
>
> (Griffin 2009: 93–4)

Competition is often seen as something male – indeed, often negatively so. But it need not be. By competing, women can likewise strengthen their natural inclination to see our bodies as ends in themselves, as equal to the male body, something that is ultimately serviceable to morality in one's relationship to oneself and other people. The apparent lack of rules, the closeness to a 'real fight' is what makes the subjective experience of MMA unique and thus different from other blood sports such as boxing.

This line of argument invites a possible objection, however, that Dixon might raise: if MMA is morally superior to all other blood sports, due to its closeness to real fights, then why not go a step further and engage in actual street fights? Our response to this objection will occupy us for the rest of this chapter.

Objection: why not street fights?

> If you take four street corners, and on one they are playing baseball, on another they are playing basketball and on the other, street hockey. On the fourth corner, a fight breaks out. Where does the crowd go? They all go to the fight.
> (Max Kellerman, boxing analyst, as quoted by Dana White in Kantowski 2007)

If our argument succeeds, it gives rise to a natural objection – why not go further? Why is fighting within the confines of the rules of MMA the best way of experiencing this unique inhabiting of our own body? Shouldn't we instead loosen the rules of MMA to allow for bites, eye-gouging, and other techniques that are currently forbidden if they would make MMA matches even more realistic? Or, better yet, simply engage in no-holds-barred street fighting? Though we recognize this as a legitimate challenge to the argument we present here, we take it to be ultimately unsuccessful. Our response to this objection is threefold.

Firstly, there is the issue of consent. Many (if not most) fights outside a ring or octagon lack consent, or if there is consent it is often a diminished consent that we would not wish to describe as informed consent. Take, for instance, the common occurrence of two drunk guys in a bar that decide to settle a dispute by fighting it out. We may very well recognize that this is not an informed choice, and indeed here one may disrespect both one's own sober desires and the will of the other. Kant's Categorical Imperative can be interpreted as the requirement not to follow a *maxim* (i.e., a universalized rule) that others could not consent to (O'Neill 1989). Thus if one were to engage in a drunk bar fight, one might need to formalize a general maxim that all such fights are permissible, which it seems is not a rule we can universally consent to. Even if some form of consent has been given, it may not be the consent we are interested in (i.e., the informed consent of rational agents). Even in cases of complete sobriety, too many street fights are either undertaken without the will of one of the participants, or without full understanding of the potential range of actions and results. MMA fights, on the other hand, are undertaken within a controlled context in which there can be full understanding of the intentions and outcomes and thus true consent.

Secondly, it is clear that most of these street fights are not fought in a context of mutual respect. Indeed, it is plausible to think that a large majority of such fights start with mutual disrespect, such as by an insult, be it an actual or merely perceived one. These fights rarely if ever occur under a specified set of rules that both agreed to.[18] Indeed, what starts as a fist-fight can often turn into an unfair fight in which one of the combatants uses a weapon such as a knife, chair, or worse a gun. In any case where a fight is decided through such means, it cannot be thought of as an embodied experience. Instead, both fighters would experience what Green (2011) may describe, as a pull outside of one's body. Rather than fostering one's natural inclinations, the use of weapons – such as the press of a button in order to kill people via a drone strike – seems to actively damage one's inclination to treat oneself and others as ends in themselves. MMA fights, on the other hand, as both Weimer (2017) and Kershnar and Kelly (2020) argue, take place in a context of respect that can transform the activity Dixon characterizes as intrinsically immoral.

Third, as we discussed earlier, MMA possesses a sense of *greatness* that street fights lack. In fact, here we are reversing the argument that the 'naturalness' of street fights is somehow purer and thus superior to MMA fights, a feature that for instance led the Spartans to avoid Olympic pankration matches.[19] True martial arts is about mental and physical prowess and greatness. This feature is lost in a so-called 'true' street fight, that rarely occurs between combatants in either peak physical or mental condition. But more importantly, unlike MMA fights that occur in an octagon with a more or less softened ground, street fights occur in an extraordinary variety of external conditions. These can include hard concrete floors, weapons, and other environmental conditions that can put the fighters at a disadvantage that has nothing to do with their mental and physical prowess. Think of the plot of the movie *Million Dollar Baby* in which the protagonist, a female boxer, dominates her opponent, who eventually cheats in return and gives her a sucker-punch to the back of her head. She falls and lands on a misplaced chair, breaking her neck and becoming a quadriplegic. Here, we can see two failures of the supposed purity of street fights. On the one hand, one fighter uses dirty techniques as a result of their own mental and physical inferiority, something that is akin to bringing a knife to a fist-fight, while on the other hand, an environmental condition fatally injures the greater fighter.

The intrinsic praiseworthiness of MMA comes from its ability to foster our natural inclination to see our bodies as ends in themselves, something that we become painfully aware of in the context of an institutional MMA match. True martial art is about respecting and experiencing human bodies as ends in themselves. It tells us something about what Greg Downey (2014) describes as the very 'nature of human life' though he has doubts that MMA is as realistic as many would like it to be (ibid.: 25). Most street fights, after all, directly undermine the conditions we have determined to be important for the moral praiseworthiness of MMA since they diminish rather than foster our natural inclination to develop our moral sense. Underground fight clubs fail for similar reasons when their sole purpose is to receive money.

Nevertheless, the rules of MMA are not fixed. The rules have changed over the years to make it safer and more appealing to general audiences. If consent and respect can be ensured within an institutional setting, we may very well recognize that a loosening of some rules is in order. Indeed, and this we will have to grant: if say two professional MMA fighters meet in a bar and both decide to engage in a fair street fight than we see no reason to morally condemn this.[20] There might very well be other reasons to prohibit this practice as it will likely lead to a lot of fights that are, in fact, not fought under such conditions (whether fair conditions obtained would be difficult to assess after the fact). But this doesn't imply that the fight itself is morally wrong – this is an instrumental, rather than an intrinsic problem with the practice. It could equally lead to the strengthening of our natural inclination to see our bodies as ends in themselves, something that is ultimately serviceable to morality in one's relationship to oneself and other people. Yet, aren't underground fight clubs or street fights the 'real deal'? Isn't MMA just a show designed to facilitate hyper-real spectacles? Are these fights not merely there to entertain an audience and give them what they believe or want to think a real fight looks like? We do not hold this view since there is a big difference between the theatrical performances of professional wrestling and two fighters who try to beat each other with any available techniques and skills to prove who is the better fighter. But it need not be black-and-white. Perhaps MMA lies on a continuum somewhere between a 'real' underground match and a scripted performance. If this is the case, we'd be willing to bite the bullet and accept the conclusion that true MMA is only found in the *Untergrund*. Since this issue is largely empirical and raises its own challenges unrelated to institutionalized MMA matches, we will leave this issue unsettled here. It is nevertheless an interesting one that should be explored in future work.

Conclusion

Mixed martial arts have been admired since the Ancient Greeks. Zeus himself, according to the mythos, grappled with his own father in order to rule Mt. Olympus (see Gross 2016). Gross argues that mortals could themselves become 'godlike if they found success' in the ancient Olympic games (ibid.: 20) Myths aside, the present chapter aims to show that engaging in MMA fights is far from an intrinsically immoral activity, an act of violence that fails to respect other people as ends in themselves. It is instead a virtuous and praiseworthy activity that fosters our natural inclination to see our bodies as ends in themselves, something that is ultimately serviceable to morality in one's relationship to oneself and other people. In order to realize these ends, we will have to change the negative public perception of these events. Indeed, studies have shown that the typical viewers of such fights are 'far from the sadistic spectators represented in mainstream media reports on fight pages' (Wood 2018: 36).

There is, indeed, something 'god-like' in MMA fights, in seeing two people face off in their struggle to become the best, the strongest, and most skilled. Unlike any other sport, MMA requires fighters to stay mentally alert at all times, to endure pain and nevertheless calculate their best moves in every situation. Here, MMA is more demanding than in any other fighting competition, requiring fighters to anticipate a wider range of possible techniques than any other sport. The unparalleled physical and mental challenges of MMA make it unique as an activity that promotes one's connection to one's own body and thus to truly treat oneself as an end rather than merely a means. This activity, like no other, fosters our natural moral inclination to treat not only ourselves, but also our opponents, and ultimately humanity itself, as an end in itself. It is for this reason that MMA is not only (contrary to Dixon 2015) a permissible activity, but one which is morally praiseworthy.

Notes

1 See Notopoulos (1939).
2 The show is the fighting equivalent of *America's Next Top Model*.
3 There have however been previous similar treatments of the ethics of boxing (Herrera 2002; Schneider et al. 2001; Davis 1993).
4 Some Italians may object.
5 Griffin with Krauss (2009).
6 While initially claiming that he is not making any empirical judgements, Dixon (2015) suggests that MMA is more problematic than professional boxing partially because there is no 'count' once a fighter has been downed. In actuality, the lower number of head injuries in MMA Dixon himself cites, are the very result of the lack of a down count in MMA. In the case a fighter is not able to defend themselves from a barrage of strikes after being knocked down, the referee will jump in and instantly end the fight. This is why knock-downs in MMA result in a win. In boxing on the other hand, a fighter is given 10 seconds to stand up, after which he has to live through a barrage of strikes with a brain that has already sustained substantial damage. What is dismissed as a brutal street-fighter mentality that has no place in a serious sport is thus upon closer inspection an actual safety precaution.
7 See Ngai et al. (2008).
8 The paternalistic version of Dixon's argument is discussed in more detail in another chapter of this volume.
9 In his paper, Dixon (2015) does not seek to make any policy recommendations regarding the legal status of MMA. After all, there might be many behaviors we deem immoral yet do not think require legal action: consider for instance someone lying to their partner or someone using their right to protest to advocate for the unequal treatment of different racial groups. Nevertheless, if someone were to succeed in making a case for the intrinsic immorality of MMA, then it seems justified to conclude that it should be prohibited.
10 Here citing the UFC fighter Mark Hunt as an example (Kershnar and Kelly 2020: 108).
11 Here, Green (2011) notes that in particular it is more affluent men who have searched to engage in extreme sports to feel alive again; see Le Breton (2000).
12 Titled: Grappler Baki.
13 See Russell (2004).
14 A weaker version of the argument we present here, may treat other physical activities, such as rock-climbing, as somewhere on a continuum.
15 We thank our editors for emphasizing this nuance in Dixon's argument.
16 The first female champion in the UFC.
17 While Velija et al. (2013) only interview 11 fighters, and one may thus consider the study non-representative, one should not underestimate the evidential support that can be gained through anecdotes, especially when they all point in one direction (see Browning 2017).
18 Though this may be possible if one considers, for instance, the bygone practice of dueling, which proceeded according to a strict set of rules (though often included weapons).
19 See Russell (2004).
20 Under the assumption that neither is compromised by the influence of alcohol.

References

Acevedo, W. and Cheung, M. (2010) 'A Historical Overview of Mixed Martial Arts in China', *Journal of Asian Martial Arts* 19(3): 30–45.

Boichi (2012) *Sun-Ken Rock* (Vol. 8), Tokyo: Young King.

Brent, J. J. and Kraska, P. B. (2013) '"Fighting is the Most Real and Honest Thing": Violence and the Civilization/Barbarism Dialectic', *British Journal of Criminology*, 53(3): 357–377.

Browning, H. (2017) 'Anecdotes Can Be Evidence Too', *Animal Sentience: An Interdisciplinary Journal on Animal Feeling*, 16(13), https://www.wellbeingintlstudiesrepository.org/cgi/viewcontent.cgi?article=1246&context=animsent, accessed 17 November 2020.

Davis, P. (1993) 'Ethical Issues in Boxing', *Journal of the Philosophy of Sport* 20(1): 48–63.

Dixon, N. (1999) 'On Winning and Athletic Superiority', *Journal of the Philosophy of Sport*, 26 (1): 10–26.

Dixon, N. (2001) 'Boxing, Paternalism, and Legal Moralism', *Social Theory and Practice*, 27(2): 323–344.

Dixon, N. (2015) 'A Moral Critique of Mixed Martial Arts', *Public Affairs Quarterly*, 29(4): 365–384.

Downey, G. (2014) '"As Real as It Gets!" Producing Hyperviolence in Mixed Martial Arts', *JOMEC Journal*, 5: 1–28.

Furinji, H. (2014) *Kenichi: The Mightiest Disciple* (Vol. 3), S. Matsuena (trans.), Tokyo: Shonen Sunday Comics.

Green, K. (2011) 'It Hurts So It Is Real: Sensing the Seduction of Mixed Martial Arts', *Social & Cultural Geography*, 12(4): 377–396.

Gregory, S. (2013) 'Women in Combat: Ronda Rousey Kicks Female Fighters into Mixed Martial Arts', *Time Magazine*, 25 February, 48–50.

Griffin, F., with Krauss, E. (2009) *Got Fight! The 50 Zen Principles of Hand-to-Face Combat*, New York: HarperCollins.

Gross, J. (2016) *Ali vs. Inoki: The Forgotten Fight That Inspired Mixed Martial Arts and Launched Sports Entertainment*, New York: BenBella Books.

Herrera, C. D. (2002) 'The Moral Controversy over Boxing Reform', *Journal of the Philosophy of Sport* 29(2): 163–173.

Kant, I. (1996) *Immanuel Kant: Practical Philosophy*, Cambridge: Cambridge University Press.

Kantowski, R. (2007) 'Q+A: Lorenzo Fertitta & Dana White', *Las Vegas Sun*, 21 April, https://lasvegassun.com/news/2007/apr/21/qa-lorenzo-fertitta-dana-white/, accessed 17 November 2020.

Kershnar, S. and Kelly, R. (2020) 'Rights and Consent in Mixed Martial Arts', *Journal of the Philosophy of Sport*, 47(1): 105–120.

Kerstein, S. J. (2008) 'Treating Oneself Merely as a Means', in M. Betzlerr (ed.), *Kant's Ethics of Virtue*, New York: de Gruyter, pp. 201–218.

Le Breton, D. (2000) 'Playing Symbolically with Death in Extreme Sports', *Body & Society*, 6 (1): 1–11.

MacDonald, J. (2012) 'MMA: Are Honor and Respect Just Empty Buzzwords in Today's MMA World?', *Bleacher Report*, 3 October, https://bleacherreport.com/articles/1357469-mma-are-honour-and-respect-just-empty-buzzwords-in-todays-mma-world, accessed 17 November 2020.

Merleau-Ponty, M. (1962) *Phenomenology of Perception*, New York: Routledge.

Merleau-Ponty, M. (1983) *The Structure of Behavior*, A. Fisher (trans.), Pittsburgh: Duquesne University Press.

Monroe, J. (2005) 'Women in Street Prostitution: The Result of Poverty and the Brunt of Inequity', *Journal of Poverty*, 9(3): 69–88.

Ngai, K. M., Levy, F., and Hsu E. B. (2008) 'Injury Trends in Sanctioned Mixed Martial Arts Competition: A 5-year Review from 2002 to 2007', *British Journal of Sports Medicine*, 42(8): 686–689.

Notopoulos, J. A. (1939) 'The Name of Plato', *Classical Philology*, 34(2): 135–145.

Nussbaum, M. C. (1995) 'Objectification', *Philosophy & Public Affairs* 24(4): 249–291.

O'Neill, O. (1989) *Constructions of Reason: Explorations of Kant's Practical Philosophy*, Cambridge: Cambridge University Press.
Reid, H. (2010) 'Aristotle's Pentathlete', *Sport, Ethics and Philosophy*, 4(2): 183–194.
Russell, B. (2004) *History of Western Philosophy*, New York: Routledge.
Schneider, A. and Butcher, R. (2001) 'Ethics, Sport, and Boxing', in W. Morgan, K. Meier, and A. Schneider (eds.), *Ethics in Sport*, Leeds: Human Kinetics, pp. 357–369.
Stenius, M. (2013) 'The Legacy of Pankration: Mixed Martial Arts and the Posthuman Revival of a Fighting Culture', *The International Journal of Combat Martial Arts and Sciences*, 13(5): 40–57.
Svare, H. (2006) *Body and Practice in Kant*, New York: Springer.
Velija, P., Mierzwinski, M., and Fortune, L. (2013) '"It Made Me Feel Powerful": Women's Gendered Embodiment and Physical Empowerment in the Martial Arts', *Leisure Studies*, 32 (5): 524–541.
Weaving, C. (2014) 'Cage Fighting Like a Girl: Exploring Gender Constructions in the Ultimate Fighting Championship (UFC)', *Journal of the Philosophy of Sport*, 41(1): 129–142.
Weimer, S. (2017) 'On the Alleged Intrinsic Immorality of Mixed Martial Arts', *Journal of the Philosophy of Sport*, 44 (2): 258–275.
Wood, M. A. (2018) '"I Just Wanna See Someone Get Knocked the Fuck Out": Spectating Affray on Facebook Fight Pages', *Crime, Media, Culture*, 14(1): 3–40.

12 Gender, pain, and risk in women's mixed martial arts

Audrey Yap

Women's MMA had a breakthrough moment in the public eye when the UFC introduced a women's bantamweight division in 2012. Despite the presence of women professional fighters in other organizations such as Invicta and Strikeforce, Dana White, the UFC's President, had previously (and famously) declared that women would never compete in the organization. Though women have clearly proved their skill as fighters to White and the general public, there remains a certain background ambivalence about the sight of women hurting each other in public. In 2019, White was prompted to revisit his earlier comments, saying,

> There's always going to be this, it's changing rapidly, but there's always going to be this chauvinist side to men that men don't want to see women getting pinned up against the cage and hit with elbows and getting cut, things like that. So I thought. It's very popular now. The difference is, the reason that the women's MMA has taken off and it's so big is because these women are legit. Really good, very technical, and it's amazing and I never saw it coming.
>
> (Martin 2019)

I certainly agree with White that many women in MMA are extremely talented, strong, and technically excellent fighters. This will simply be taken for granted in this chapter. And while he specifically claims that men are reluctant to see women being injured, I do take his remarks to reflect a more general social reluctance to see women injured in these particular ways. An easy explanation for this attitude is that it is a kind of benevolent sexism, reflecting the fact that women are often stereotyped as less physically capable than men, and more fragile. Under such a view, this attitude might seem patronizing or irritating, but ultimately it is born of the impulse to protect those physically weaker from harm. The basic argument of this chapter is that if we consider the larger context of how women's bodies are treated, the story becomes much more complicated. I will argue that there are many tensions in the way women's bodies are imagined to function, and are thereby treated. So the attitude that White expresses, of a general social discomfort at seeing women injured in the cage, actually stems from the broader ways in which women's bodies, and what women do with their bodies, are subject to social control.

If we take for granted that the reluctance White identifies is a genuine tendency, then it raises several puzzles about our society's relationship to women's pain. After all, there is no shortage of media portrayals of women in pain, generally. Whatever chauvinist tendency there is still permits a wide range of police procedurals and horror movies

DOI: 10.4324/9781003122395-13

featuring variously victimized women. The media also does not shy away from releasing photographs of injured women, such as a picture of two women injured after a homophobic attack in London (BBC News 2019). Similarly, while their franchises might not be as large of as those of their male counterparts, there are many portrayals of heroic women in the media seen causing pain. Whatever squeamishness there might be does not seem to extend to Wonder Woman beating up Nazis, or to many women in comics being harmed in a variety of ways (Simone 2000). So it seems, at least on the face of it, to be socially acceptable to show women causing pain and to show women in pain.

The argument I give in this chapter will parallel one that Marilyn Frye (1983) gave about the widespread tendency for men to open doors for women. Frye notes that while the door-opening ritual purports to remove a barrier to women's movement throughout the world, various contradictions and tensions arise when we look at the larger picture. For example, men will sometimes try to open doors for women even when it makes no practical sense, for instance when the men are loaded down with packages and the women are physically unencumbered (ibid.: 5). In addition,

> These very numerous acts of unneeded or even noisome 'help' occur in counterpoint to a pattern of men not being helpful in many practical ways in which women might welcome help. What *women* experience is a world in which gallant princes charming commonly make a fuss about being helpful and providing small services when help and services are of little or no use, but in which there are rarely ingenious and adroit princes at hand when substantial assistance is really wanted either in mundane affairs or in situations of threat, assault or terror. There is no help with the (his) laundry; no help typing a report at 4:00 a.m.; no help in mediating disputes among relatives or children.
>
> (Frye 1983: 6)

Ultimately, Frye argues, the detachment of these supposed acts of male gallantry from the concrete reality of women's needs, demonstrates that they are simply part of a larger social reality in which women's own interests are considered irrelevant. What is important is that such rituals are performed; whether women actually benefit from their performance ends up being secondary.

My argument is that an analogous case can be made for a social reluctance to see women injured in fighting sports. I will argue that when we look at the bigger picture, and consider cases in which women's bodies are imagined to be delicate and in need of protecting, as well as many cases in which they are not, we will find analogous contradictions. I will argue that protective attitudes towards women engaging in risky sports like MMA can be contrasted with many ways in which women in sports are genuinely at risk of harm and such protective attitudes do not seem forthcoming.

One feature of women's MMA is that whatever pain or bodily damage people incur is the result of an activity in which they are an enthusiastic participant, that is primarily for their own sake, and in which they transgress gendered norms of behavior. Though some sports, like figure skating and gymnastics, are much more compatible with norms of feminine conduct, many other women's sports, like ice hockey and rugby, also share this particular feature, and I would expect this argument to generalize to those cases as well. I will argue in this chapter that one of the central reasons behind people's ambivalence about women in fighting sports are the gender-transgressive circumstances in which they might become injured. I will not argue that this is the only reason why people might find it objectionable. Some people, after all, find mixed martial arts immoral generally, regardless of the fighter's gender (Dixon 2015). Instead, I will focus on some of the contradictions in our gendered social attitudes towards bodily pain. And I will show that the gendered differences in attitudes towards participation in combat sports are just part of a wider social context in which women are not seen as fully entitled to bodily autonomy.

Gender and risk in sport

It is a common social stereotype that women are less physically capable than men in sports, particularly when it comes to sports that rely on physical strength or significant risk. We can see these stereotypes in players' attitudes, in media coverage of such sports, as well as in the sport regulations themselves. Stereotypes about women being inherently less capable arguably lead to a variety of negative outcomes. In some cases, women and girls automatically defer to their male teammates at practice, or accept without question that the boys will be more capable than them. In other cases, women are patronized or excluded from full participation or community membership. All of this generally leads to women's marginalization in many athletic contexts (Davies and Deckert 2020; Kavoura et al. 2018; Merritt et al. 2018; Follo 2012). Since this territory is relatively well covered in existing literature, I will focus primarily on social attitudes towards women who purposely take on physically risky challenges in the pursuit of sport.

Admittedly some women in martial arts are treated differently, particularly when they have achieved great success. Polish former strawweight champion Joanna Jędrzejczyk, who dominated the division for several years, was often described as exceptional in ways that implied her opponents stood no chance. Of course, her opponents were sometimes described in sexist and objectifying terms. Jakubowska et al. (2016) survey a great deal of Polish media coverage of Jędrzejczyk, and while there is surprisingly little in the way of sexism around the former champion herself, at least one journalist they quote expresses dismay at her 'macabre battering' of another conventionally attractive woman, Carla Esparza (ibid.: 417). However, quite a lot of Polish coverage of Jędrzejczyk's fights makes much of her dominance over her opponents, and highlights the sheer damage that she has been able to inflict (ibid.: 419–20). But this is in line with the ways in which some successful women athletes are portrayed as exceptional, or as naturals, in ways that imply a division between them and 'ordinary' women.

At least some women fighters – and media coverage of them often reinforces this – are portrayed as exceptional in ways that make them more closely aligned with masculine characteristics. For instance, one study that interviewed successful female judoka found that

> They differentiated themselves from ordinary women by performing the self-image of exceptional beings, born with masculine qualities, such as competitiveness, tolerance to pain, and the ability to fight. The participants constructed themselves as naturally born fighters who never complain and are dedicated to their sporting goals.
>
> (Kavoura et al. 2018: 248)

But while this self-portrayal as exceptional may have enabled the women to better make sense of their own identities and place within the martial arts world, it does little to advance the cause of gender equality. After all, this attitude does nothing to challenge the default presumption of women's physical inferiority, as it simply casts the successful athletes as exceptions to the general rule. This means that it is entirely possible to view some women as capable of great athletic success, even in male-dominated sports, while in general maintaining the attitude that most women are physically unsuited for such activities. Women who can be viewed as exceptional in these ways are likely to be seen as superheroes of a sort.

While there are exceptions – *Atomic Blonde* and *Old Guard* are two movies in which we see a visibly wounded Charlize Theron struggle through fights that she ultimately wins – women heroes in comic books and action movies rarely seem to show any bodily signs of having even been in fights in the first place. In contrast, many classic and contemporary action movies show obviously bloodied and battered men heroically fighting their way through to the end. The fact that most women in such media are either brutalized by the violence they encounter or seem virtually impervious to it, with almost no in-between, makes it very easy to draw at least implicit divisions between successful women fighters and all other women. So, if a woman fighter does sustain an obvious injury, as most fighters do, it becomes a very natural move to take that injury as evidence that she is not one of the exceptional superhero types who belongs in such spaces.

Gendered attitudes of disapproval about women's athletic participation are not exclusive to martial arts, nor are expressions discomfort about women being injured in the pursuit of risky sports. Many women athletes have been on the receiving end of public skepticism about their capabilities. For example, Maya Gabeira, one of very few women big wave surfers in the world, almost drowned in an attempt to ride an 80-foot wave. Such near-death experiences are relatively commonplace among elite big wave surfers, and fatal accidents are not a rarity either. But many detractors singled Gabeira out in ways that they had not singled out male surfers who had undergone similar experiences, calling her 'unprepared' and suggesting (unjustifiably) that she was lacking in skill (Skenazy 2014). Now, the patronizing remarks and dismissal of her expertise are not by themselves noteworthy, in light of the stereotypes that have already been discussed. Many women find their talents similarly undervalued. What is noteworthy is the contrast between social attitudes towards risky athletic behavior of the kind in which Gabeira engaged, and in which many women fighters engage, and the risky athletic behavior of women athletes in other sports.

The female athlete triad is the name for a syndrome characterized by disordered eating, osteoporosis, and amenorrhea. It is particularly common among female athletes in sports like distance running, dance, figure skating, or gymnastics, in which a low body mass is seen as desirable. Matzkin et al. (2015) review a range of studies estimating the frequency of the female athlete triad among high school and college aged athletes. Many studies found that somewhere between 15% and 40% of the athletes surveyed had or were at risk of at least one of the major features of the triad. A lot of the health issues related to the female athlete triad can be connected to women and girls attempting to have the kind of physique the sport considers ideal. For women in sports that valorize thinness, the overall social pressures to be thin coincide with at least the perceived demands of their sport. But then women and girls who are risking their health by adopting diets that cannot support their calorie expenditures are not transgressing gender norms, but acting in accordance with them. And as Susan Bordo (2004: 147–8) argues, anorexia can often lead to a person feeling a sense of perceived struggle between the mind or will, and the body or their appetites. The thinness often associated with anorexia then comes to represent a triumph of the will over the body.

Given all this, it is unsurprising that there is no major concerted effort in athletic circles to counteract disordered eating. The literature on the female athlete triad largely suggests educational solutions. Matzkin et al. (2015) seem primarily concerned with raising awareness among athletes and coaches about the triad itself, and the potential for long term damage. But in athletics more broadly, despite the ways in which practices such as weight cutting[1] in fighting sports can encourage disordered eating patterns and cause other kinds of health concerns over the long term, it remains widespread and relatively unchallenged. Moreover, the perceived strength of will that Bordo observes associated with anorexia, and in the self-conception of many anorectics, is exactly the kind of quality that is often encouraged in athletic contexts. It is absolutely routine among competitive athletes to be told (or to tell themselves) to 'suck it up' and force their body to keep going through a difficult training session. The triumph of mind over body is something that is thoroughly valorized in sports, combat and non-combat. And yet, despite the fact that many young women athletes must deal with musculoskeletal injuries brought on by aspects of the female athlete triad, the pressures to be thin nevertheless remain.

In other words, the risks to women's bodies from the female athlete triad seem arguably as significant as the obvious risks to women's bodies from participating in fighting or other contact sports. Yet while women in fighting sports might face surprise or concern, the concern for risk does not seem to be so prevalent for women runners, for example, despite some studies which have found a rate of 20% for bone stress injuries among middle- and long-distance runners (Tenforde et al. 2015). Sports, after all, are frequently gendered, where some, such as gymnastics and dance, are seen as primarily appropriate for female participation, and others, such as ice hockey and boxing, are seen as primarily appropriate for male participation.

To sum up, we can see a clear contrast between social attitudes towards women who take public and highly visible risks in masculine-coded environments (like Gabeira), and women who take much more private risks that primarily impact their long-term health in feminine-coded environments (like many gymnasts, skaters, and ballet dancers). What this means is that there cannot be a *general* social attitude towards protecting women from risk, as might be suggested if we just look at cases like Gabeira's, and at the attitude suggested by Dana White in the introduction to this chapter. After all, were there a genuine interest in protecting women from risky pursuits in sports across the board, it seems likely that there would be more attention paid to protecting women and girls in sports in which significant injuries are commonplace, but less acute. If a female kickboxer breaks her wrist in a match, I think she could easily expect friends and family members to encourage her to give up the sport for something less dangerous, and perhaps implicitly nudge her towards things for which she might be more 'suitable'. Perhaps similar things could happen to a female ballet dancer who sustains a stress fracture in her ankle, but barring the interference of discrimination on the basis of race, body size, or class, it seems unlikely that people would take the injury as a sign that she did not belong there in the first place.

Women in martial arts do often need to struggle in these gendered spaces in order to prove that they belong. But as in the cases of the judoka who tried to distinguish themselves as 'natural born fighters' in ways suggesting that ordinary women are not naturally suitable for these kinds of pursuits, some women's attempts to belong in masculine spaces can further reinforce the assumption that most women are naturally physically inferior to men. But as I will argue in the next section, this presumption of physical inferiority is tightly linked to a view of women's bodies as subject to social regulation and control.

Pain, risk, and control

The presumption of women's physical inferiority is longstanding. It is linked as well to biological essentialist views about sex and gender, and relatively recently to bigoted views about trans people as deceivers. This came to the forefront in professional MMA with controversy around Fallon Fox, a trans woman and professional fighter. Commentary surrounding Fox is often explicitly transphobic. But even her supporters often fall back on sexist and cissexist lines of defense. For example, some have defended her right to fight in the women's division by pointing out that she is a relatively unexceptional fighter by cis women's standards, and that her victories are well within the range of what cis women have accomplished. In other words, her lack of clear physical superiority is taken as evidence that she is not in fact a man. Others have defended her by falling back on an implicit association between testosterone and maleness, and correspondingly between estrogen and femaleness. The hormone therapy that Fox undergoes means that her testosterone levels are quite plausibly lower than those of many of her cis opponents. This, for some, suffices to show that she is no longer in possession of the advantages she might have had prior to her transition (McClearen 2015: 86–7). Now, issues of gender essentialism pose their own set of problems, but the opposition Fox faced in her MMA career points to a clear set of shared social attitudes about the biological nature of women's supposed inferiority.

Consequences of this presumptive feminine weakness have been observed by many who write about gendered treatments of pain in clinical contexts. Many women have self-reported on their treatment by medical professionals who dismissed their claims to be in pain. Such treatments range from a basic lack of attentiveness and a failure to take patients' claims sufficiently seriously, to more serious dismissals and behavior that undermined patients' sense of self-knowledge. The source of this gendered behavior is sometimes attributed to stereotypes of women's physical weakness and propensity for hysteria. Yet many women report suffering serious harms as a result of medical practitioners' failures to understand their pain as genuine (Freeman and Stewart 2018; Culp-Ressler 2015; Foreman 2014; Enson 2014).[2]

But again, there are tensions between this presumption of women's delicacy and the ways in which women are treated in certain contexts like pregnancy. These tensions also reveal that the presumptive social attitude that women ought to be protected from risk only extends to risks of certain kinds. At least in the United States, rates of maternal morbidity are high and steadily increasing (Centers for Disease Control and Prevention 2020; Ellison and Martin 2017). One professor of community health services that Ellison and Martin interviewed said,

> The nature of our system is to focus on these women while they're pregnant. And then if there are difficulties later, they get lost to the larger system that doesn't particularly care about women's health to a great degree unless they're pregnant.
> (Ellison and Martin 2017)

This is entirely consistent with a culture that polices health during pregnancy largely in terms of how the ingestion of substances, exercise habits, or unhealthy environmental conditions, will affect the fetus (Kukla 2005: 106–7). In other words, the treatment of women in particular during pregnancy is largely a function of their being a kind of passive receptacle for a fetus. This often justifies the implementation of systems of control for the sake of the fetus, particularly for racialized or otherwise marginalized women who are seen as prone to 'risky' behavior.

It is worth pausing, though, to note that focussing this discussion on pregnant *women* is not meant to suggest that only women can become pregnant. Certainly, people of a variety of genders can become pregnant, reproductive systems allowing. But since we are in a cissexist society, most discussion of women in general takes cis women to be the paradigm case. The kinds of discrimination that trans and non-binary people face does not frequently imagine them as the kinds of people who might become pregnant, nor are they frequently portrayed as in need of protection. And the situation does in fact become more complicated when we consider the transmisogyny that trans women face. Indeed, as we can see in the case of Fallon Fox, trans women are frequently portrayed as deceivers, and as people who hide their 'real nature' for some kind of predatory end (Bettcher 2007; Serano 2016: 36–8). As such, much of the conversation around Fox centres on the question of whether she should be 'allowed' to fight other women, to the point where she has been subjected to deeply vitriolic remarks for wanting to fight in the category that matches her gender (Noble 2013). So in this particular case, the portrayal of cis women (presented by Fox's detractors as the 'real' women) as delicate and in need of protection serves to control trans women's bodies rather than cis women's. Regardless, the presumption of women's fragility still serves as a pretext for social control.

Yet to return to the discourse on maternal risk, is that it is not clear that women's bodies are treated as fragile and delicate in *all* contexts. As Kukla points out, in many representations of pregnancy, the pregnant body all but disappears; many depictions, some purporting to describe 'What You Might Look Like' during a particular month of pregnancy, feature depersonalized torsos where only the fetus and reproductive system appears in detail (2005: 122–5). In other words, it does not seem as though presumptions of feminine weakness are at play here. There seems to be relatively little concern that a maternal body will succumb to its inherent fragility. Maternal bodies are strictly regulated, with prescriptive regimes outlining diet and exercise, and strict prohibitions against substances like alcohol, despite there being little concrete evidence that light to moderate drinking will be detrimental (ibid.: 129–30). So the concern seems to be that maternal bodies will be unruly and that women will display a lack of discipline, not that they will be too physically weak to sustain a fetus. But if, as is suggested by some of the literature on pain, women are too weak and emotional to be reliable self-reporters about their own bodily sensations, why are such bodies treated as generally trustworthy vessels when pregnant? After all, the accounts of women's treatment during and post-pregnancy suggest very little concern for damage to the maternal body, except insofar as it might affect the health of the fetus.

So while there are many ways in which society purports to try to protect women from risk (such as restricting or socially sanctioning their participation in physically dangerous sports like MMA), the tensions I have highlighted between various ways in which women's bodies are socially imagined suggests that this is more than just a matter of benevolent sexism. To revisit the two points of contrast that I have raised so far, we have (1) a tendency to step in and tell women they should not engage in risky pursuits like fighting or big wave surfing, but little beyond a push towards increased awareness about the more common risky realities of women athletes, like the female athlete triad; and (2) a tendency to dismiss women's claims of pain based on stereotypes of bodily weakness and propensity towards hysteria, but very little concern about a pregnant woman's body itself, treating it as something that the woman can and ought to strictly regulate for the sake of the fetus it contains.

What this suggests, to return to the original guiding analogy, is that social attitudes do not indicate genuinely protective attitudes towards women, but controlling ones. The contexts I have described in which women's risk seems acceptable (or at least is not widely socially challenged) are those in which women are acting in accordance with gender norms. Women who are harmed in the pursuit of thinness, or who risk death in the course of pregnancy, are pursing ends socially sanctioned ends. Even if women athletes are not necessarily endorsing *beauty* ideals that value thinness, and see themselves to be dieting solely for the sake of their athletic success, the ends and methods largely coincide.

In contrast, women who risk life and limb by trying to surf giant waves, climb mountains, or test their skills in the octagon, may do so only for the thrill of it all, just like many men who do the same. But thrill-seeking is not something that is generally socially endorsed for women, and so we might be pushed to discourage women from engaging in it in the name of protecting them. But there does not seem to be any reason to believe that elite women in risky sports are any less prepared or more in danger than elite men in risky sports. Now that women have been competing professionally in MMA for over a decade in promotions like Strikeforce, Invicta, and the UFC we regularly see women headlining main cards and featuring in event promotion. There is no question that many women are extremely skilled mixed martial artists, who do sustain regular injuries from fighting and training, but recover just as many men do. Of course, we are right if we see MMA as a dangerous sport for women. But this is just because fighting sports are endeavors in which we punch, kick, elbow, and otherwise manipulate our opponents' bodies in ways they do not want us to. MMA is a dangerous sport for women because it is a dangerous sport for people of any gender. Yet background assumptions about women's (biological) physical inferiority shape social attitudes about women's participation. And when we also take into account the background acceptability of regulating what women do with their bodies, arguments that women ought to be protected from the dangers of fighting sports become entirely unsurprising.

Conclusion: bodies to be controlled

Marilyn Frye's (1983) argument about door-opening, with which this chapter began, points out that the widespread social practice of men opening doors for women should not be seen as entirely benign. While many individual acts of door-opening are likely just motivated by simple courtesy, the ritual itself is part of an overall social system in which women are constructed as inferior. And so participation in the ritual can have significance that goes beyond an individual door-opener's intentions. Frye argues that when viewed in a larger social context, women tend to be offered assistance by men primarily in cases such as these, when it is often of little genuine benefit. In contrast, women seem to be offered much less assistance with more weighty tasks like childcare or housework, both of which fall into the private sphere and have largely been seen as women's primary responsibility. Her conclusion, then, is that door opening is not best seen as a matter of assisting women, but reveals a further way in which the image of women as physically incapable is reinforced.

The argument I have made here runs parallel to Frye's. Even though Dana White, in his initial quote, admitted that the reluctance to see women being beaten up in the cage is chauvinist in its origins, many women in martial arts have experienced people telling them, often with at least the appearance of concern, that they might be better off with a less dangerous pastime. What I have argued here is that, even when these expressions of concern are genuine, and come from a real desire to protect the woman in question, they are still part of an overall social system that sees women's bodies as sites of control.

Women do face genuine risks in sport, and some of those risks, like the female athlete triad, are gendered. But the risks that women face in virtue of their gender rarely get as high a profile as the risks they face simply because fighting in the octagon, surfing in the ocean, or climbing up the side of a cliff are just dangerous things for anyone to do. So just as the door-opening ritual does very little to improve the lives of most women due to its insensitivity to women's gendered needs, a social concern over women's risk of injury in MMA is insensitive to the gendered risks that women do in fact face in sports. As such, it also reinforces a sexist social order – not only by its tacit endorsement of women's physical inferiority, but also by its support for restricting women's activity.

The bottom line is that we do not live in a society that is overly concerned with the protection of women, but we do live in a society in which women's behavior is subject to a variety of methods of social control in the name of protection. The phenomenon I have been describing in this piece, of seeing women as less suitable for MMA and other kinds of risky masculine-associated sports, is continuous with many other messages that women receive throughout their lives. When I teach Frye to undergraduate students, I often ask them what pieces of advice they might have received about protecting themselves when going out at night. Answers generally fall along predictably gendered lines. Women students, as well as non-binary students who are frequently read as women, will often have an array of examples come to mind, such as avoiding wearing their hair in a ponytail, holding their keys between their fingers, and only walking in well-lit or relatively populated areas. Some men will also have received this kind of advice and some women will not, but in general women are raised with the message that gendered violence, particularly from a stranger, is a distinct possibility if they find themselves alone in the city at night. Also, the steps that they are prescribed to avoid being victimized by such violence will often noticeably restrict their free movement throughout the world – avoiding certain places entirely, or at least avoiding them if they will be alone. Some women may have taken self-defense classes, or been advised to, for their protection, but it seems rare to find a young woman whose concerned family members have sent her to their local MMA gym so she can most effectively fight off a potential attacker. Tongue-in-cheek as that suggestion might be, the point nevertheless stands that advice to promote women's safety is generally given to women themselves, and also takes the form of constraints that women should impose on their own behavior. Generally the only cases in which men's movement is restricted or tightly controlled for the protection of others, are situations in which the men in question face racism, ableism, or some other kind of oppression that portrays them as inclined towards criminal behavior.[3]

Notes

1 This is the process of losing a great deal of weight, often water weight, in a very short time in order to make weight (and so qualify for their division). Athletes might sit in saunas or go for runs in the heat while wearing heavy clothing or garbage bags in order to produce more sweat. This is often extremely unhealthy.
2 Dismissals of pain are not just gendered; they are also racialized. Harmful stereotypes about Black people's physicality contribute the ways in which they are treated by a variety of social institutions, including the medical system. The fact that Black people are often given inadequate pain treatment is relatively well documented (Hoffman et al. 2016), but there is also some evidence that many people have a harder time even *perceiving* Black people as being in pain in the first place (Mende-Siedlecki et al. 2019). Obviously factors such as race and gender cannot be cleanly separated in anyone's life, but I will still focus the majority of my arguments on gendered treatments of pain.
3 Thanks to Quill Kukla, Chris Goto-Jones, and Dan Steinberg for extremely helpful conversations each of which helped me work out different sections of this piece. Thanks also to Jason Holt and Marc Ramsay for their editorial comments and feedback.

References

BBC News (2019) 'London Bus Attack: Arrests after Gay Couple Who Refused to Kiss Beaten', BBC News, 7 June, https://www.bbc.com/news/uk-england-london-48555889, accessed 28 November 2020.

Bettcher, T. M. (2007) 'Evil Deceivers and Make-Believers: On Transphobic Violence and the Politics of Illusion', *Hypatia*, 22(3): 43–65.

Bordo, S. (2004) *Unbearable Weight: Feminism, Western Culture, and the Body* (2nd Ed.), Berkeley, CA: University of California Press.

Centers for Disease Control and Prevention (2020) 'Severe Maternal Morbidity in the United States', Centers for Disease Control and Prevention, 31 January, https://www.cdc.gov/reproductivehealth/maternalinfanthealth/severematernalmorbidity.html, 1 October 2020.

Culp-Ressler, T. (2015) 'When Gender Stereotypes Become a Serious Hazard to Women's Health', *ThinkProgress*, 11 May, https://archive.thinkprogress.org/when-gender-stereotypes-become-a-serious-hazard-to-womens-health-f1f130a5e79/, accessed 30 September 2020.

Davies, S. G., and Deckert, A. (2020) 'Muay Thai: Women, Fighting, Femininity', *International Review for the Sociology of Sport*, 55(3): 327–343.

Dixon, N. (2015) 'A Moral Critique of Mixed Martial Arts', *Public Affairs Quarterly*, 29(4): 365–384.

Ellison, K. and Martin, N. (2017) 'Nearly Dying in Childbirth: Why Preventable Complications Are Growing in US', *National Pain Report*, 22 December, https://www.npr.org/2017/12/22/572298802/nearly-dying-in-childbirth-why-preventable-complications-are-growing-in-u-s, accessed 1 October 2020.

Enson, P. (2014) 'Women in Pain Report Significant Gender Bias', *National Pain Report*, 12 September, http://nationalpainreport.com/women-in-pain-report-significant-gender-bias-8824696.html, accessed 30 September 2020.

Follo, G. (2012) 'A Literature Review of Women and the Martial Arts: Where Are We Right Now?', *Sociology Compass*, 6(9): 707–717.

Foreman, J. (2014) 'Why Women Are Living in the Discomfort Zone', *Wall Street Journal*, 31 January, https://www.wsj.com/articles/escape-from-the-chronic-pain-trap-1391220523, accessed 30 September 2020.

Freeman, L. and Stewart, H. (2018) 'Microaggressions in Clinical Medicine', *Kennedy Institute of Ethics Journal*, 28(4): 411–449.

Frye, M. (1983) *The Politics of Reality: Essays in Feminist Theory*, New York: Crossing Press.

Hoffman, K. M., Trawalter, S., Axt, J. R., and Oliver, M. N. (2016) 'Racial Bias in Pain Assessment and Treatment Recommendations, and False Beliefs about Biological Differences between Blacks and Whites', *Proceedings of the National Academy of Sciences of the United States of America*, 113(16): 4296–4301.

Jakubowska, H., Channon, A., and Matthews, C.R. (2016) 'Gender, Media, and Mixed Martial Arts in Poland: The Case of Joanna Jędrzejczyk', *Journal of Sport and Social Issues*, 40(5): 410–431.

Kavoura, A., Kokkonen, M., Chroni, S., and Ryba, T. V. (2018) '"Some Women Are Born Fighters": Discursive Constructions of a Fighter's Identity by Female Finnish Judo Athletes', *Sex Roles*, 79: 239–252.

Kukla, Q. (writing as Rebecca) (2005) *Mass Hysteria: Medicine, Culture, and Mothers' Bodies*. Lanham, MD: Rowman & Littlefield.

Martin, D. (2019) 'Dana White Addresses Equality in Sports for Women, Champions the UFC as "An Even Playing Field"', *MMA Fighting*, 1 July, https://www.mmafighting.com/2019/7/1/18761466/dana-white-addresses-equality-in-sports-for-women-champions-the-ufc-as-an-even-playing-field, accessed 28 November 2020.

Matzkin, E., Curry, E. J., and Whitlock, K. (2015) 'Female Athlete Triad: Past, Present, and Future', *Journal of the American Academy of Orthopaedic Surgeons*, 23(7): 424–432.

McClearen, J. (2015) 'The Paradox of Fallon's Fight: Interlocking Discourses of Sexism and Cissexism in Mixed Martial Arts Fighting', *New Formations: A Journal of Culture/Theory/Politics*, 86: 74–88.

Mende-Siedlecki, P., Qu-Lee, J., Backer, R., and Van Bavel, J. J. (2019) 'Perceptual Contributions to Racial Bias in Pain Recognition', *Journal of Experimental Psychology: General*, 148(5): 863–889.

Merritt, M., Yap, A., Comley, C., and Diehl, C. (2018) 'Stereotype Threat and the Female Athlete: Swimming, Surfing, and Sport Martial Arts', in M. L. Cappuccio (ed.) *Handbook of Embodied Cognition and Sport Psychology*, Cambridge, MA: MIT Press, pp. 485–510.

Noble, M. (2013) 'UFC's Matt Mitrione Says Transgender Fighter Fallon Fox Is a "Disgusting Freak"', *Bleacher Report*, 8 April, https://bleacherreport.com/articles/1597393-ufc-matt-mitrione-says-transgender-fighter-fallon-fox-is-a-disgusting-freak, accessed 5 October 2020.

Serano, J. (2016) *Whipping Girl: A Transsexual Woman on Sexism and the Scapegoating of Femininity*, Berkeley, CA: Seal Press.

Simone, G. (2000) 'Women in Refrigerators', https://lby3.com/wir/, accessed 1 December 2020.

Skenazy, M. (2014) 'Maya Gabeira Takes a Breath', *Outside*, 3 September, https://www.outsideonline.com/1925936/maya-gabeira-takes-breath, accessed 1 December 2020.

Tenforde, A. S., Nattiv, A., Barrack, M., Kraus, E., Kim, B., Kussman, A., Singh, S., and Fredericson, M. (2015) 'Distribution of Bone Stress Injuries in Elite Male and Female Collegiate Runners', *Medicine & Science in Sports & Exercise*, 47(5S): 905.

13 Gender and ethics

Thoughts on the case of transgender athlete Fallon Fox

Nancy Kane

In 2014, transgender MMA fighter Fallon Fox won her fight against Tamikka Brents, breaking Brents' skull in the process. The press, as well as other MMA athletes, reacted with swift and vituperative rhetoric. Fox, who had undergone gender reassignment surgery in Bangkok in 2006, had been a topic of controversy since being forced to 'come out' as a transgender athlete. Some fellow MMA fighters supported her right to fight as a woman, but other fighters and sports commentators decried her participation in the sport, effectively calling for transgender discrimination. This chapter is an introductory consideration of the rights and duties associated with the participation of transgender athletes in MMA, with a focus on Fallon Fox as a case study in gender identity and the ethics of transgender athletic participation in MMA.

In recent years, the literature on the philosophy of transgender participation in sport has included arguments for and against physiological testing and application of such standards as a means of ensuring fair competition between cisgender and transgender athletes (Coggon et al. 2008; Devries 2008; Kahrl 2015; Karkazis et al. 2012; Sykes 2006; Teetzel 2006; Wahlert and Fiester 2012). Some, like Martínková (2020), have gone so far as to suggest the creation of new unisex sports to obviate the necessity for physiological gender testing. On the theoretical philosophical side, depending on the approach one follows toward ethical considerations of transgender competitors, it is quite possible to arrive at different conclusions as to the morality of allowing transgender athletes to compete in categories other than their natal gender. Given the rise in questions of inclusiveness for transgender athletes during the 21st century, with a few notable exceptions in the 20th century, we seem to be in the beginning stages of a normative change. For example, at this point in the early 21st century, philosophers following Morgan (2020) and Posner (1999) might call convention-challenging athletes like Fallon Fox moral entrepreneurs, and with a nod to Rorty (1991), might see Fox's example as one step toward a redescription of norms that may well lead to greater inclusivity and moral progress among members of the community of mixed martial arts practitioners.

In the case of Fox, the questions of gender, identity, and ethics are understandably complex. For example, Fox initially fought opponents without revealing her gender identity, which led to a review and confirmation of the legality of her fighting license by the Florida State Boxing Commission (FBC). Critics overtly or implicitly examined Fox's intersectional identities: her race, gender identity, and sexual orientation were openly discussed, with emphasis on the question of whether or not she should have been acknowledged as a woman. Underlying issues of paternalism and subtle racism factored into the discussions, along with a paradoxical view that Fox could best prove herself to be female by failing to overcome her opponents in fights.

DOI: 10.4324/9781003122395-14

Questions regarding Fox's career have continuing philosophical and regulatory impact. What are the rights and duties of individual fighters, compared to the rights and duties of gender classes of fighters? How and by whom are these classifications, rights, and duties determined? Which authoritative entity bears responsibility for fair competition, the safety of fighters, and the determination of suitable opponents for matches?

At the nexus of ethics and law, transgender athletes face uncertainty, aversion, and hostility in their efforts to compete. As the sports world struggles to come to grips with the question of nonbinary gender classification, crucial ethical questions face athletes in MMA and beyond. The answers to these questions are not definitive, but looking back at the career of Fallon Fox and the implications it presented for participation of transgender athletes may help guide future decision-making in MMA organizations and beyond.

Background

The woman born as Boyd Burton in 1975 began feeling that she was a woman well before adolescence. Born a year before transgender tennis star Renee Richards was denied the right to play in the US Open, and two years before Richards won a US Supreme Court decision allowing her to play professionally against women, young Burton was raised in a strict religious home. At one point, her father placed her in gay-conversion therapy because he was convinced that she was a gay man in need of counseling.

She married her then-pregnant girlfriend after graduating from high school, and although they were later divorced, she raised their daughter. Following stints in the US Navy and at the University of Toledo, she worked as a long-haul truck driver to earn money for gender reassignment surgery. Post-surgery, she moved to Chicago, Illinois, where she began training at the Midwest Training Center in an attempt to lose weight (Stets 2013).

She began fighting competitively as a woman, in 2011, without public disclosure that she was a transgender athlete. In the cage, she became known as 'The Queen of Swords' for her victory celebration move, in which she spun an imaginary sword and sheathed it (ibid.). After winning an exhibition match against Elisha Helsper in 2012 with a TKO/RSC (the referee stopped the fight, and Fox won in a technical knockout), her first official American Boxing Commission fight was against Ericka Newsome on March 2, 2013. The fight ended in a knockout after just 39 seconds. On March 5, upon being called by a reporter who told her that her transgender status was going to be revealed, Fox decided to take control of her story and came out in an *Outsports* interview (Zeigler 2013a).

The public response to the revelation was a mix of outrage and support. Some critics insisted Fox had been deceptive, and that she should have revealed her gender identity in advance of any fights (Popper 2013; Stets 2013; Zeigler 2013b). Others decried the fact that a male-to-female (MTF) transgender competitor was allowed to fight against cisgender women (women whose gender identity matched their birth sex). Challenging Fox's status as a woman, some cited medical studies that alleged size, strength, muscle mass, and bone density advantages did not diminish after gender-altering surgery, so fights against her were unfair and less safe for female opponents (Chiapetta 2013; Noble 2013b).

UFC color commentator Joe Rogan and fighter Matt Mitrione were among the most vociferous in their attacks, with Mitrione calling her a 'disgusting freak' – a comment for which he was suspended from fighting under the UFC's code of conduct (Noble 2013a). Rogan's statements asserted that Fox was a 'f***ing man.... I don't care if you don't have a dick anymore' (Noble 2013b) and similar objections. That sentiment was echoed shortly afterward by UFC fighter Ronda Rousey, who said, 'She can try hormones, chop her pecker off, but it's still the same bone structure a man has.... It's an advantage. I don't think it's fair' (Samano 2013). Following fights with Fox, Ashlee Evans-Smith, Rosi Sexton, and Tamikka Brents all said in interviews that Fox was too strong and should not be allowed to fight other women (MMA Interviews 2013; Murphy 2014; Popper 2013).

Some of the criticism was less direct, but made similar points, as for example when Allana (also known as Al-Lanna or Allanna) Jones entered the ring to fight Fox, using Aerosmith's 'Dude Looks Like a Lady' as her walkout song (McClearen 2015), or when UFC President Dana White repeatedly referred to Fox as 'he' in an interview (MMA Junkie Staff 2013). A subtle racism due to Fox's ethnicity and former identity as a powerful black man was implicit in some of the rhetoric (Crowder 2013).

It should be noted that Fox also had her share of supporters in the MMA world. In a *Bleacher Report* article, MacDonald (2013) cited peer-reviewed medical journals to debunk critics' claims that chromosomes determine gender and that physical advantages are not diminished by the use of surgery and hormone treatments. Jorge De La Noval, founder and president of the Championship Fighting Alliance (CFA), said, 'My reaction from the get-go was we're going to support her. In CFA, we don't discriminate against anybody' (Stets 2013). The issue of discrimination brings questions of cissexism, racism, sexism, paternalism, and transphobia into the discussion, but the root of the controversy remains the question of whether or not the world accepted Fox as a woman, since the sports world maintains a binary classification system in which competitors must be either male or female. The first issue, then, is biological in nature.

Sex testing

Sex testing in sport has a history going back to the 1930s, and notable examples of so-called 'gender fraud' in the Olympics (e.g., Dora Ratjen, also known as Heinrich or Hermann) and the Boston Marathon (Kathrine Switzer) combine with examples of intersex and gender non-conforming athletes like Indian runner Santhi Soundarajan and South African runner Caster Semenya to form a complicated tapestry of gender expectations and regulatory complications (Heggie 2010; Singh and Singh 2011). The International Olympic Committee (IOC) decision on May 27, 2004 to allow transsexual athletes to compete in the Olympic Games came with requirements concerning surgery, legal recognition of the assigned sex, hormonal therapy, and waiting periods. One of the authors of the IOC guidelines, Eric Vilain, worked with the Association of Boxing Commissions' (ABC) medical advisory chairwoman Dr. Sherri (Sheryl) Wulkan to devise the regulations for transgender athletes in 2012. If an MTF athlete is two years post-gonadectomy, with a documented record of medically supervised hormone therapy during that time, and has a letter from a board-certified physician, she is considered eligible to fight in the women's division (Palmquist 2013a).

If a fighter is medically cleared to compete against women, the arguments against her doing so do not automatically dissipate. Fighter Peggy Morgan and her trainer John Fain referenced Fox's lack of disclosure of her transgender status, and indicated that concern for Fox's 'feelings' should not outweigh the risk to the safety of fighters, given Fox's early decisive successes in matches. Morgan flatly refused to consider fighting Fox, with a cissexist statement: 'Like Fallon, I am a semi-finalist in the CFA tournament. Unlike Fallon, I was born with a vagina' (Palmquist 2013b).

Nevertheless, during the years in which Fox was fighting professionally (2012 to 2014), there was a growing international acceptance of the Statement of the Stockholm Consensus on Sex Reassignment in Sports, which stated that 'individuals undergoing sex reassignment of male to female before puberty should be regarded as girls and women' (IOC Medical Commission 2003). In its wording, this statement implies a binary gender normativity, and retains a focus on the perspective of others, rather than on the desires or gender identification of the athlete. Even the binary designation, MTF, ignores the possibility that the individual may have a range of gender expression and/or identity. When Dana White and John Fain repeatedly referred to Fox as 'he,' they denied that Fox had a right to self-determination and identity.

The fighters, writers, and commentators who denounced Fox's participation in MMA reinforced stereotypes of the female as inherently weaker, smaller, and in need of paternal protection from males, especially from a non-white male. The scholarly literature has plentiful examples of feminist, biopolitical, bioethical, and queer theory discussing the unique problems that contribute to gender oppression of transgender athletes (Dworkin and Cooky 2012; Fischer and McClearen 2020; Kamasz 2018; Lenskyj 2018; Love 2014; Maskalan 2019; McClearen 2015; Phipps 2021; Sykes, 2006; Wahlert and Fiester 2012). Given the nature of MMA as a violent contact sport, its male-oriented audience and history, and the continuing struggle of women for equality in that and other sports, the question of fairness in fights between females and MTF transgender athletes consists of a network of interlocking biases, interests, and other discourses.

Whereas arguments concerning many of those perspectives have already been presented in the literature, now that Fox's fighting career is a matter of historical record and the IOC in 2019 abandoned its reliance on the Stockholm Consensus, it is time to reconsider the ethical questions raised by Fox's experience, because transgender athletes are still struggling for recognition. In 2020, for example, the U.S. Department of Education's Office of Civil Rights informed the state of Connecticut that federal education would be cut if MTF athletes were allowed to compete against females in high school sports (Ennis 2020). Generally speaking, if youth are not able to complete gender reassignment surgery and then wait for two years until their testosterone levels are considered to be within normal female range before being allowed to compete (following the scientifically questionable assumption that testosterone is *the* decisive factor in athletic ability), transgender youth would effectively be barred from high school sports. The deleterious effect on physical and mental health combines with the lack of access to sports participation, leading to potentially devastating ramifications that could create disadvantages in terms of higher education and beyond. What light can Fox's experience shed on the continuing issue of rights, duties, and respect for transgender and gender nonconforming athletes?

Rights and theories

Rights and duties quickly became part of the controversy surrounding Fallon Fox's outing. The right to privacy of medical records was invoked within days of the revelation in a *Sports Illustrated* article:

A transgender athlete's medical privacy is also a continuing concern, though this falls more into the legal realm. Most specifically, is a commission required to notify a transgender athlete's opponent of their medical history prior to a bout? The answer is no.

'Discussions involving the medical history of the opponent would not typically take place, and would not be legally required to take place,' said Nick Lembo, Legal Committee Chair for the ABC.

(Hunt 2013a)

That seems to define Fox's right to privacy and her right to compete in bouts, as well as the limits of other fighters' rights to her medical information and history, at least as far as the ABC is concerned. Eylon and Horowitz note that 'There is an important difference between the legal realm and games' (2017: 12). However, the locus of Fox's rights, versus those of her opponents and prospective opponents, is still not clear. Do the rights obtain from the people involved, or from the authorities, including the ABC, the FBC, the Florida Department of Business and Professional Regulation (FDBPR, regulators of the state's athletic commission), the CFA, the California State Athletic Commission (CSAC, which Fox believed had granted her a fighting license before she applied for one in Florida), or some other person or persons?

According to sources, Fox was either mistaken when she told the FBC that she was licensed in California, or she falsely claimed that she had been licensed. She listed herself as female on applications, in accordance with her gender identity. She was not asked to list surgeries or similar medical information on her forms (Hunt 2013a, 2013b; Pugmire 2013). Was she under any obligation to disclose her surgery and medical information, either to licensing agencies or to opponents? This could be considered a moral issue, but moral reasoning of basic deontological or teleological models in this case is insufficient to answer the question. The obligation to disclose one's medical history is countermanded by current Health Insurance Privacy and Portability Act (HIPAA), and the utilitarian stance overwhelmingly favors a group's desires and happiness over those of any given individual. Combining a Kantian categorical imperative in her truthful disclosure of her gender identity, and behaving according to the FBC rules (a Hegelian *Sittlichkeit*), Fox obeyed the requirements of the commissions charged with assessing her eligibility to fight.

Kreft (2019) has argued that, within the commoditized world of sport, the Olympic ideal of equality masks a structure designed to perpetuate gender hierarchy, but that ethical behavior of individual athletes contains a duty of respect alongside an ongoing fight against discrimination of all kinds. Kant's *Critique of Judgment*, Kreft implies, calls on athletes to exercise free will in moral decisions. If Fox identified as a woman, and saw no obligation to disclose her medical history based on the applications for licenses, it could be said that her self-identification as a female before engaging in amateur or professional bouts stemmed from her desire both to maintain the privacy to which she is entitled, and also to engage in the freedom of pursuing her life while living her authentic reality. Her decision to continue fighting despite the controversy surrounding her identity was also, therefore, a moral choice in favor of the human choice of culture over happiness, in that she accepted her role as an openly transgender athlete in the interest of greater equality for others of that community (a form of moral entrepreneurship).

That perspective, however, ignores what may be considered the right of other fighters to whatever degree of safety can be expected in a sport of violent confrontation, if the comments by other fighters concerning Fox's strength and abilities are to be believed. Did Fox owe any duty of disclosure to other fighters, even if they did not have a right, as such, to that information? For insight into that aspect of the case, we must go deeper into modern discussions of rights and duties.

Hohfeld's writing on legal conceptions in judicial reasoning is sometimes cited as the bedrock upon which the foundation of the logic of legal rights is built (Hohfeld 1917; Schaab 2018). But there are also conventional and moral rights, as well as other kinds of rights, in varying degrees and configurations, as described by Hart (1961), Feinberg (1979), Scanlon (1998, 2003), Wenar (2013a, 2013b), and many others. Space constraints preclude delving into all of these in depth, but a few examples will help to outline some elementary discussion of rights theories.

Hart's will theory, following from Hohfeld and also further explicated by Steiner (1994), indicates that 'X has a right that Y do φ if and only if X can legitimately waive or enforce Y's duty to do φ' (Schaab 2018: 99). Note that rights are not the same as claims. A claim might be made without a valid basis, and therefore would not be a right, which is why some theorists specify rights as valid, justifiable, or recognized claims, also known as claim-rights. Following this, if we consider an opponent's (X) claim-right to make Fox (Y) divulge her medical history (φ), we must believe that X can either waive *or* enforce that duty. Under current medical privacy law, X cannot enforce that duty, nor can she legitimately waive it on behalf of Y.

Therefore, under the will theory, a given opponent would not have the right to make Fox disclose her medical history. Her claim on Fox would be invalid. As Feinberg (2014) would say, 'To have a right is to have a claim against someone whose recognition as valid is called for by some set of governing rules or moral principles' (155). The agency of enforcement would be the ABC, FBC, CFA, or some other interested power of authority, and their decision was to allow Fox to compete, as a woman. Fox was in compliance with the requirements of the relevant regulatory structures. At the time Fox was competing, those authoritative agencies had a claim to her medical information, whereas her opponents did not have a valid claim to her medical information under the sport's regulations. For her part, Fox did not claim a right to access to the medical records of all her opponents (e.g., to know when or if they had ever been pregnant, or when they were menstruating and perhaps more susceptible to ligament damage), nor should she have had a right to such information. Claims may be against such invasions of privacy, or they may be to preserve one's privacy.

By contrast, Raz's interest theory (following Bentham's beneficiary theory) states that '"x has a right", if and only if x can have rights, and other things being equal, an aspect of x's well-being (his interest) is a sufficient reason for holding some other person(s) to be under a duty' (Raz 1984: 195). Is the interest of opponent x's well-being sufficient reason to consider Fox to be under a duty to disclose a previous gender identity? Or is Fox's right to medical privacy inviolate? If a question arises as to which fighter's rights should take precedence, which agency, or which individual, gets to decide whether (and whose) rights will be preserved, to what extent, and with what means of enforcement, if any? One approach to resolution of such ethical questions is described below, with an appeal to the kind-desire theory. That theory offers one resolution for the question of balancing opposing interests and making decisions about rights in conflict, *provided* the competitors are willing to accept the authority of a governing body, as they generally do in order to be allowed to compete.

However, an isolated decision by a governing body still does not resolve the underlying issue of preservation of the essential rights of each party. A governing body's decisions in questions of rights may be final, but they may also be influenced by biases, deference to conventions, or other mitigating factors. Granting full deference to each fighter's rights and duties, if we consider each to be equally valid from their perspective, the losing party in a decision by an enforcing agency will most likely believe that their rights were not preserved.

This problem goes well beyond the gender considerations under discussion in this chapter, of course. Arguably, the governing body's overarching duty to provide conditions to preserve the safety of the competitors in the sporting community adds a paternalistic layer to their decisions. Public comments by Rogan (Noble 2013b) and others go so far as to imply that allowing Fox to fight against women is akin to condoning male-on-female domestic abuse. However, since MMA fighters are accustomed to sustaining physical harm as part of the sport, the notion of arguing rights from the ordinary standpoint of interest in well-being (i.e., the normal right not to be physically attacked) is somewhat skewed. Are such duties absolute? The answer is no, because the sport is a combat sport, at its essence. Nevertheless, historically, the sport *has* evolved, and governing bodies such as the UFC have made significant adjustments to the sport since the 1990s. Back then, UFC fighter Gary 'Big Daddy' Goodridge has said, 'It was meant to be a no-holds-barred freakshow, a spectacle' (Bateman 2020).

As Kramer and Steiner (2007) would have it, Fox's duty to an opponent 'necessarily involves the protection of some aspect of [x's] situation that is generally beneficial for any typical human being or collectivity' (290). The *necessity* of protection of x's physical well-being would be in the interest of any *typical* human being, or Fox's opponents as a collectivity. If one accepts the arguments concerning residual strength and other physical advantages in MTF fighters, the nature of violent contact sport might constitute a valid interest on the part of x in knowing any possible advantages an opponent might have, even though the opponent herself may have no enforcement authority to preserve her interest, nor any way to prove that the physical abilities of Fox were insurmountable in competitions.

In that case, Fox would have to lose a fight to prove that she did *not*, in fact, have superior or unfair physical advantages. In essence, she had to fail in order to prove her vulnerability, to align with what might be seen as a stereotypically 'feminine' characteristic. That, in effect, is what happened when she lost her CFA fight against Ashlee Evans-Smith in October of 2013 with a TKO/RSC decision. It was Fox's only professional loss, but it was enough to prove that she was not inherently invincible. Were an opponent to argue against Fox's right to compete, or for the right to know her medical history, it would be particular difficult to claim that Fox had a duty not to compete against other women or a duty to reveal her previous gender status, once a cisgender female had dominated a fight to the extent that the referee had to stop it. Without placing normative gender expectations on a MTF fighter and setting up a paradox in which she must fail in order to disprove a claim upon her under the interest theory, there can be no absolute duty of disclosure that does not violate the transgender athlete's rights.

Contractualism, or as another theorist would have it, 'what we owe to each other' (Scanlon 1998) has been posited as an alternative to the will theory and the interest theory. This theory of mutual respect and care, promulgated by Kumar (1999, 2003) and Darwall (1977, 2014) dovetails with Wenar's kind-desire theory:

> Consider a system of norms S that refers to entities under descriptions that are roles, D and R. If and only if, in circumstances C, a norm of S supports statements of the form:
>
> 1 Some D (qua D) has a duty to *phi* some R (qua R); where '*phi*' is a verb phrase specifying an action, such as 'pay benefits to,' 'abstain from searching through the notes of,' 'shoot,' and so on;
> 2 R (qua R) want such duties to be fulfilled; and
> 3 Enforcement of this duty is appropriate, ceteris paribus;
>
> then: the R has a claim-right in S that the D fulfill this duty in circumstances C.
> (Wenar 2013b: 219)

Under the kind-desire theory, an entity D can be a group of entities, such as those fulfilling the role of FTM athletes (also known as a Kind). If, in circumstance C, R (opponents of the kind 'cisgender female fighters', for example) want to lay claim to something promised or due from D, R will only have a claim-right in S (under the system of norms established by MMA) if enforcement of this duty is appropriate, *ceteris paribus*, in circumstances C. As with other theories of rights, the interaction between two entities is dependent upon a third entity, a repository of power such as the ABC, the FBC, the FDBPR, the CFA, and the CSAC.

Under any of these theories of rights, an MTF fighter who meets the terms of the governing body's requirements for competition as a female has the right to fight as a female. Fox's right to self-determination in terms of gender representation only falls under the auspices of these authorities when the question of her rights and duties, and those of other fighters, is in question. Other fighters did not have the right to access Fox's medical records under the kind-desire theory, but conversely, Fox did not have the right to demand that others fight her, either as a female or as a transgender athlete. Her rights were limited in that respect, as were some of her opportunities. On the other hand, her opponents retained the options of waiving their claim to disclosure, or declining to fight her on the basis of her gender status. As Eylon and Horowitz noted, 'one may always quit the game, but not the law.... it is up to the participants to accept or reject the formal rules of a game' (2017: 12). When potential opponents definitively stated that they would not fight Fox, they may have been within their rights, yet in violation of a duty toward a member of their kind: respect.

The duty of respect

Respect may take different forms, according to Darwall. *Recognition respect* is that which is given to something (an athlete's feelings) or a person or a person's role. *Appraisal respect*, on the other hand, is a positive estimation for someone, such as a gifted athlete (Darwall 1977). Returning to the second part of the kind-desire theory model, D has a duty to *phi* R if Rs (qua Rs) want that duty to be fulfilled. Suppose we suggest that D (other fighters) have a duty to respect transgender athletes (R) if Rs want that duty to be fulfilled. It is possible that Fox, in the role of R, did not necessarily desire that the duty of respect be paid to her by other fighters, and she did not have the means to enforce that duty.

There may also be a contractualist argument to be made that a duty of respect exists such that fighters owe each other mutual respect, qua fighters. It could be considered a sign of disrespect for an MTF fighter to decline to fight a cisgender female based on their respective gender identities. Likewise, a duty of benevolent concern for someone's well-being could morph into a form of paternalism, setting up a conflict between the will to achieve success in a fight with the impulse to refrain from interfering with an opponent's welfare. Fox's initial decision not to focus on her identity as a transgender MMA fighter, but rather to meet opponents as equals (female fighters) would be seen as a mark of what Darwall would call *second-person recognition respect* toward them. Her strenuous efforts to win her fights are indicative not only of self-respect, but also of appraisal respect for her opponents, because to give less than her greatest effort would be a form of disrespect toward them. Treating opponents as worthy of one's efforts is a form of *honor respect*, in Darwallian terms (Darwall 2014).

Fox had the right to fight as a female, and critics' expressed desires to deny her that right were inherently disrespectful. Duties are not enforceable in the way rights are. Fox could not force other fighters, commentators, and MMA personnel to respect her. According to Cruft (2013), respect is not a *directed duty* precisely because of the lack of enforceability. Meanwhile, could it be said that Fox was in any way wronged by the disrespect shown her during her career? Kumar, referencing what Parfit (1984) called the *non-identity problem*, wrote that 'the legitimacy of a person's claim to have been wronged requires that the psycho-physical identity of the wronged not be what it is because of the wrongdoing' (Kumar 2003: 99–100). Fox's gender expression, her psycho-physical identity, was not essentially changed by her outing; it was only exposed, albeit in a way that had ramifications for her life and fighting career.

Affronts to her personal dignity made in statements by White, Rogan, Crowder, and Mitrione were examples of the opposite of *honor respect*, in that they revealed paternalism toward cisgender female fighters while disdaining Fox. Comments by other fighters including Rousey, Morgan, and Jones were also disrespectful. As Darwall wrote, 'We disdain someone when we refuse to recognize the self-presentation he projects' (2014: 100). Or, to be more inclusive, we respect others when we honor their self-presentation.

Conclusion

From the moment Fox's gender identity became known, her quest for recognition as an MMA fighter was thwarted: she was never able to compete in the elite UFC and ended her career after a few years with a 5-1-0 record. Her right to compete as an equal based on her gender, skills, and abilities was sustained by the powers of the MMA, but she was subject to disrespect from her peers and critics from the moment she exerted agency by making the choice to come out rather than be outed by a reporter.

What do we owe transgender MMA fighters like Fallon Fox? By extension, what do we owe to boxers like Patricio Manuel, kathoey (preoperative transsexual) Muay Thai transgender fighters like Parinya Charoenphol, and transgender athletes of all sports, ages, and levels of competition? For now, if these athletes meet the requirements for competition under the rules of their sports, they have the right to compete. However, for the future, we will need ongoing discussion about the fairness of those gender-normative rules, which reinforce the binary gender categories of competition rather than expanding opportunities for the spectrum of gender identities. Different competition classes based on physiological capacity or experience levels might be possible, for example, or a new version of the sport may emerge in which rules, environments, and practices mitigate against physical differences as they do in many other martial arts. In any event, whatever the future may hold for the mixed martial arts sports community, we owe respect for the identities of all participants in the sport, and we have a duty to refrain from disrespect. The case of Fallon Fox is past, but it is not necessarily prologue.

References

Bateman, O. L. (2020) 'The Early Years of MMA Were a "No-Holds-Barred Freakshow" That Couldn't Be More Different from Today', *MEL*, https://melmagazine.com/en-us/story/the-early-years-of-mma-were-a-no-holds-barred-freakshow-that-couldnt-be-more-different-from, accessed 30 October 2020.

Chiapetta, M. (2013) 'Fallon Fox Bout Set as Allanna Jones Accepts Matchup, but Commission Review Still Looms', *MMA Fighting*, 2 April, https://www.mmafighting.com/2013/4/2/4175766/fallon-fox-bout-set-as-allanna-jones-accepts-matchup-but-commission, accessed 30 October 2020.

Coggon, J., Hammond, N., and Holm, S. (2008) 'Transsexuals in Sport – Fairness and Freedom, Regulation and Law', *Sports, Ethics and Philosophy*, 2(1): 4–17.

Crowder, S. (2013) 'Dear Transgender Fallon Fox: No, You Don't Get to Beat up Women….', *Louder with Crowder*, 21 March, https://www.louderwithcrowder.com/mixed-martial-arts-fighter-fallon-fox-shouldnt-allowed-beat-women, accessed 30 October 2020.

Cruft, R. (2013) 'Why Is It Disrespectful to Violate Rights?', *Proceedings of the Aristotelian Society*, 113(2): 201–224.

Darwall, S. L. (1977) 'Two Kinds of Respect', *Ethics*, 88(1): 36–49.

Darwall, S. L. (2014) 'Respect, Concern, and Membership', in D. Thomä, C. Henning, and H. B. Schmid (eds.) *Social Capital, Social Identities: From Ownership to Belonging*, Boston: de Gruyter, pp. 93–104.

Devries, M. C. (2008) 'Do Transitioned Athletes Compete at an Advantage or Disadvantage as Compared with Physically Born Men and Women: A Review of the Scientific Literature, Canadian Association for the Advancement of Women and Sport and Physical Activity', https://athletescan.com/sites/default/files/images/do-transitioned-athletes-compete-at-an-advantage-or-disadvantage-as-compared-with-physically-born-men-and-women-a-review-of-the-scientific-literature2.pdf, accessed 30 October 2020.

Dworkin, S. L., and Cooky, C. (2012) 'Sport, Sex Segregation, and Sex Testing: Critical Reflections on This Unjust Marriage', *American Journal of Bioethics*, 12(7): 21–23.

Ennis, D. (2020) 'Betsy DeVos Tells Connecticut: Ban Transgender Athletes, or Say Goodbye to Your Federal Funding', *Forbes*, 29 May, https://www.forbes.com/sites/dawnstaceyennis/2020/05/29/betsy-devos-tells-connecticut-ban-transgender-athletes-or-say-goodbye-to-your-federal-funding/#1ee3bcb21793, accessed 30 October 2020.

Eylon, Y., and Horowitz, A. (2017) 'Games, Rules, and Practices', *Sport, Ethics and Philosophy*, 12(1): 1–14.

Feinberg, J. (2014) 'The Nature and Value of Rights', in J. Feinberg, *Rights, Justice, and the Bounds of Liberty: Essays in Social Philosophy*, Princeton: Princeton University Press, pp. 143–158.

Fischer, M., and McClearen, J. (2020) 'Transgender Athletes and the Queer Art of Athletic Failure', *Communication & Sport*, 8(2): 147–167.

Hart, H. L. A. (1955) 'Are There Any Natural Rights?', *The Philosophical Review*, 64(2): 175–191.
Hart, H. L. A. (1961) *The Concept of Law*. Oxford: Oxford University Press.
Heggie, V. (2010) 'Testing Sex and Gender in Sports: Reinventing, Reimagining and Reconstructing Histories', *Endeavour*, 34(4): 157–163.
Hohfeld, W. N. (1917) 'Fundamental Legal Conceptions as Applied in Judicial Reasoning', *The Yale Law Review*, 26(8): 710–770.
Hunt, L. (2013a) 'How Fallon Fox Became the First Known Transgender Athlete in MMA', *Sports Illustrated*, 7 March, https://www.si.com/mma/2013/03/07/fallon-fox-profile, accessed 30 October 2020.
Hunt, L. (2013b) 'Transgender MMA Fighter Faces Licensing Problems', *Sports Illustrated*, 5 March, https://www.si.com/mma/2013/03/05/fallon-fox-transgender-mma, accessed 30 October 2020.
IOC Medical Commission (2003) Statement of the Stockholm Consensus on Sex Reassignment in Sports, https://stillmed.olympic.org/media/Document%20Library/OlympicOrg/News/20040517-IOC-Approves-Consensus-With-Regard-To-Athletes-Who-Have-Changed-Sex/EN-report-905.pdf#_ga=2.236881281.1002555743.1591829486-273148662.1591829486, accessed 30 October 2020.
Kahrl, C. (2015) 'IOC Opening Field of Competition to Trans Athletes with New Policy', *ESPN*, 28 January, http://espn.go.com/olympics/story/%5f/id/14626858/olympics-opening-field-competition-transgender-athletes-updated-policy, accessed 30 October 2020.
Kamasz, E. (2018) 'Transgender People and Sports', *Journal of Education, Health and Sport*, 8 (11): 572–582.
Karkazis, K., Jordan-Young, R., Davis, G., and Camporesi, S. (2012) 'Out of Bounds? A Critique of the New Policies on Hyperandrogenism in Elite Female Athletes', *The American Journal of Bioethics*, 12(7): 3–16.
Kramer, M. H., and Steiner, H. (2007) 'Theories of Rights: Is There a Third Way?', *Oxford Journal of Legal Studies*, 27(2): 281–310.
Kreft, L. (2019) 'From Kant to Contemporary Ethics of Sport', *Synthesis Philosophica*, 68(2): 253–265.
Kumar, R. (1999) 'Defending the Moral Moderate: Contractualism and Common Sense', *Philosophy and Public Affairs*, 28(4): 275–309.
Kumar, R. (2003) 'Who Can Be Wronged? ', *Philosophy & Public Affairs*, 331(2): 99–118.
Lenskyj, H. J. (2018) *Gender, Athletes' Rights, and the Court of Arbitration for Sport*, Bingley: Emerald Publishing Limited.
Love, A. (2014) 'Transgender Exclusion and Inclusion in Sport', in J. Hargreaves and E. Anderson (eds.) *Handbook of Sport, Gender and Sexuality*, New York: Routledge, pp. 376–383.
MacDonald, J. (2013) 'Fallon Fox and the Culture of Ignorance: A Response to Controversy', *Bleacher Report*, 20 March, https://bleacherreport.com/articles/1575170-fallon-fox-and-the-culture-of-ignorance-a-response-to-controversy, accessed 30 October 2020.
Martínková, I. (2020) 'Unisex Sports: Challenging the Binary', *Journal of the Philosophy of Sport*, 47(2): 248–265.
Maskalan, A. (2019) 'Sporting the Glass Jaw: Views on Women in Sports', *Synthesis Philosophica*, 68(2): 285–300.
McClearen, J. (2015) 'The Paradox of Fallon's Fight: Interlocking Discourses of Sexism and Cissexism in Mixed Martial Arts Fighting', *New Formations*, 86: 74–88.
MMA Interviews (2013) 'Ashlee Evans-Smith Says She Feels Fallon Fox Shouldn't Be Able to Fight Women', *MMA Interviews*, 18 November, https://www.youtube.com/watch?v=TRBGnjoWdo8&feature=youtu.be, accessed 30 October 2020.
MMA Junkie Staff (2013) 'Dana White on Transgender Fighter Fallon Fox: Not Even Close to UFC-ready', *MMA Junkie*, 13 March, https://mmajunkie.usatoday.com/2013/03/dana-white-on-transgender-fighter-fallon-fox-not-even-close-to-ufc-ready, accessed 30 October 2020.
Morgan, W. J. (2020) *Sport and Moral Conflict: A Conventionalist Theory*, Philadelphia: Temple University Press.

Murphy, A. (2014) 'Exclusive: Fallon Fox's Latest Opponent Opens up to #WHOATV', *WhoaTV*, 17 September, http://whoatv.com/exclusive-fallon-foxs-latest-opponent-opens-up-to-whoatv/#sthash.pf5lAbaq.dpuf, accessed 30 October 2020.

Noble, M. (2013a) 'UFC: Matt Mitrione Suspended for Fallon Fox Rant, "Code of Conduct" Breach', *Bleacher Report*, 8 April, https://bleacherreport.com/articles/1597646-ufc-matt-mitrione-suspended-for-fallon-fox-rant-code-of-conduct-breech, accessed 30 October 2020.

Noble, M. (2013b) 'UFC's Joe Rogan to Transgender MMA Fighter Fallon Fox: "You're a F***ing Man"', *Bleacher Report*, 19 March, https://bleacherreport.com/articles/1573044-ufc-joe-rogan-to-transgender-mma-fighter-fallon-fox-youre-a-man, accessed 30 October 2020.

Palmquist, C. (2013a) 'Official ABC Policy on Transgender Fighters', *The Underground*, 8 March, https://www.mixedmartialarts.com/news/Official-ABC-policy-on-transgender-fighters, accessed 30 October 2020.

Palmquist, C. (2013b) 'Peggy Morgan: Why I Won't Fight Fallon Fox', *The Underground*, 27 March, https://www.mixedmartialarts.com/news/Peggy-Morgan-Why-I-wont-fight-Fallon-Fox, accessed 30 October 2020.

Parfit, D. (1984) *Reasons and Persons*, Oxford: Oxford University Press.

Phipps, C. (2021) 'Thinking Beyond the Binary: Barriers to Trans* Participation in University Sport', *International Review for the Sociology of Sport*, 56 (1): 81–96.

Popper, B. (2013) 'Fighting Fallon Fox: The Controversial Science of Transgender Athletes in Combat Sports', *The Verge*, 21 March, https://www.theverge.com/2013/3/21/4131174/fallon-fox-mma-science-transgender-fighting-athletes, accessed 30 October 2020.

Posner, R. (1999) *The Problematics of Moral and Legal Theory*, Cambridge: Harvard University Press.

Pugmire, L. (2013) 'Transgender MMA Fighter Fallon Fox Puts California Panel on the Spot', *Los Angeles Times*, 7 March, https://www.latimes.com/sports/la-xpm-2013-mar-07-la-sp-sn-mma-transgender-fallon-fox-20130307-story.html, accessed 30 October 2020.

Raz, J. (1984) 'On the Nature of Rights', *Mind*, 93(370): 194–214.

Rorty, R. (1991) *Objectivity, Relativism, and Truth*, Cambridge: Cambridge University Press.

Samano, S. (2013) '"Ronda Rousey: "I Don't Think It's Fair" Transgender Fighter Fallon Fox Faces Women', *USA Today*, 11 April, https://www.usatoday.com/story/gameon/2013/04/11/ufc-ronda-rousey-transgender-fighter-fallon-fox/2072937/, accessed 30 October 2020.

Scanlon, T. M. (1998) *What We Owe to Each Other*. Cambridge: Belknap Press.

Scanlon, T. M. (2003) *The Difficulty of Tolerance*, Cambridge: Cambridge University Press.

Schaab, J. D. (2018) 'Why It Is Disrespectful to Violate Rights: Contractualism and the Kind-Desire Theory', *Philosophical Studies*, 175: 97–116.

Singh, B., and Singh, K. (2011) 'The Hermeneutics of Participation of Transgender Athletes in Sports – Intensifying Third Force', *Physical Culture and Sport Studies and Research*, 52(1): 44–48.

Steiner, H. (1994) *An Essay on Rights*, Oxford: Blackwell Publishing.

Stets, M. (2013) 'Transgender Fighter Fallon Fox Speaks on Her Journey to the Cage', *Bleacher Report*, 23 May, https://bleacherreport.com/articles/1648786-transgender-trailblazer-fallon-fox-talks-jason-collins-x-men-being-a-pioneer, accessed 30 October 2020.

Sykes, H. (2006) '"Transexual and Transgender Policies in Sport', *Women in Sport & Physical Activity Journal*, 15(1): 3–13.

Teetzel, S. (2006) 'On Transgendered Athletes, Fairness and Doping: An International Challenge', *Sport in Society: Cultures, Commerce, Media, Politics*, 9(2): 227–251.

Wahlert, L., and Fiester, A. (2012) 'Gender Transports: Privileging the "Natural" in Gender Testing Debates for Intersex and Transgender Athletes', *The American Journal of Bioethics*, 12(7): 19–21.

Wenar, L. (2013a) 'Rights and What We Owe to Each Other', *Journal of Moral Philosophy*, 10 (4): 375–399.

Wenar, L. (2013b) 'The Nature of Claim-Rights', *Ethics*, 123(2): 202–229.

Zeigler, C. (2013a) 'Erika Newsome Appealing MMA Loss to Fallon Fox', *Outsports*, 11 March, https://www.outsports.com/2013/3/11/4090738/ericka-newsome-appealing-mma-loss-to-fallon-fox, accessed 30 October 2020.

Zeigler, C. (2013b) 'Fallon Fox Comes out as Trans Pro MMA Fighter', *Outsports*, 5 March, https://www.outsports.com/2013/3/5/4068840/fallon-fox-trans-pro-mma-fighter, accessed 30 October 2020.

Index

Page numbers followed by 'n' refer to notes.

Abbott, Tank 95–96
action-packed fighting 22
aesthetic apology for MMA 78–85, 85n1; *see also* utility-based aesthetic, for MMA
agency in stabilization 56–58
aikido, techniques of 84
Aikikai 37
Ali-Frazier fight, first 88, 91, 101
Allen, Barry 70–71
anorectics, concept of 154
anorexia 153–154
'anything goes' assault 49
Aquinas, Thomas 67
archery 25
arguing rights, notion of 167
Aristotle 6, 67, 111, 123
armbar 135
art of defense 7
Asian martial arts, classical mess of 31; *see also* Chinese martial arts; Japanese martial arts
Association of Boxing Commissions (ABC) 59, 163
athletic combat, violence of 46, 165
athletic superiority, concept of 141
Atomic Blonde 153
attention-demanding cognitive task performance 57
Augustine of Hippo 67
Aurelius, Marcus 123, 125, 129
autonomic arousal 83

'bad boy' images, in MMA 39
bar brawling, constraints/rules of 48–49
battle dance 7
beauty, perception of 68–69
being in the zone, notion of 141
Beneath the Planet of the Apes 83
Bentham's beneficiary theory 166
Best, David 79
biological de-powerment, sense of 142

Black Belt Magazine 24
Bloodsport 39, 40n5, 86n9
blood sports 22, 43, 141–142, 144
blows to head, ban on 89
body–mind integration 58
'body's learning' 58
bondage, domination, sadism, and masochism (BDSM) 105, 107, 114–115
Bowman, Paul 7, 9, 32, 100
Bordo, Susan 153–154
boxing 12, 31, 47, 60; Ali-Frazier fight 88, 101; comparison with gladiatorial matches 100; critics of 88; 'dirty-boxing' counters 59; diseases associated with 59; ethics of 105; female boxer 145; knockout 125; legal ban on 88–89; medical associations' recommendation to ban 105; moral objections to 96–101; risk factor associated with 93–94
brain damage: effects of 106; long-term 93, 101; paralleling death in arena 100; risk of 89, 92; slavery/brain damage analogy 92
brawling 17, 48
Brazilian Jiu-Jitsu (BJJ) 13, 31, 47–48, 49, 83, 98, 125, 135; distinction between *jutsu* and *do* 122; enjoyment of 100; practitioners, dynamical representation of 57; *see also* Gracie Jiu-Jitsu
Brents, Tamikka 161, 163
brotherhood, sense of 117, 143
Buddhism 25, 32, 58
budō 12
Burke, Edmund 68, 76n6
Burton, Boyd 162
Bushido (code of the samurai) 25

cage fighting 9, 106, 107
California State Athletic Commission (CSAC) 165
capoeira (Brazil) 7
carcinogen, exposure to 95

Cejudo, Henry 82
character traits, of expert martial artist 26
Chinese martial arts 18–19, 25, 32
Chojun, Miyagi 40n4
choke holds: in Jiu-Jitsu 49; losing consciousness through 8, 116, 135
chronic traumatic encephalopathy (CTE) 89, 93–96, 100
cissexist society 156
cis women, portrayal of 155, 156
claim-rights 166, 168
close combat 4, 5, 10–11
closed hand strikes to head, permissibility of 60
close-quarter combat tools 59
clutter aesthetic 80
code of conduct 35, 163
cognitive impairments 93, 99
combat sports 1, 5, 7, 33, 126; aesthetic appeal of 84; constitutive violent skills and sub-optimal constraints 46–49; constraint theory of 44–46; decision-making process in 74; in-house sparring sessions 50, 51n7; maximization of skill and creativity in 50; MMA and 12–13, 43, 48; potential of contests in 79; practice of 'ground and pound' 48–50; rationally training in 50; *Ulysses and the Sirens* 44; utility-based aesthetic for 66
community health services 155
competitive sports 46, 79, 112; constraints/rules in 45; pursuit of excellence in 51n5
competitors, intention of 74
Confucius, teachings of 25
constitutive skilled violence of martial art 43, 46–49
constrained maximization, of skill and creativity 45, 50
constraint theory, for philosophy of sport 44–46, 49
Cooper, Anthony Ashley 68
corticospinal commands, sport-specific 57
COVID-19 pandemic 53; ethical representation of MMA during 63–64; UFC events during 62
Covington, Colby 39
craft-expert 17, 25
crafts 16–17; difference with martial knacks 20; of fighting 26
cult of celebrity, in MMA 39
cultural association, between martial arts and moral philosophy 122
Cusson, Jason 22

dangerous sport 13
Daoism 25, 32
Davidson, Donald 71

Davie, Arthur 20, 22
Davis, Paul 114, 137
death: doctor-assisted 109; as public entertainment 100; threat of 99; *see also* gladiatorial death-matches
decision-making processes 57; all-things-considered decisions 89; in combat sports 74
deference, practices of 35–38
dementia puglistica 93
dichotomy of control (DOC) 123, 125–126
dim mak (death touch) 24
dirty boxing, martial art forms of 59
disinterestedness, aesthetic principle of 68–69
disordered eating, issue of 153–154
distributed cognition, of stabilization 53, 56–58
diversity of techniques 79, 81–82
Dixon, Nicholas 89, 95, 114, 116, 136, 138; analogy with J. S. Mill's rejection of slavery contracts 92; appeals to legal moralism 90; approach to legal restrictions on MMA 102n4; argument about intrinsic immorality of MMA regarding cage fighters 107, 134; case against boxing and MMA 89; consent/rights-based arguments 110; cumulative paternalistic case against boxing 90; demand for an 'even distribution' of fighters among socioeconomic classes 91; downplaying of moral significance of servility 98; economic coercion argument 91–92; on Feinberg's worries concerning excessive paternalism 92; and his critics 105–110; Kantian argument 97–98; 'Moral Critique of Mixed Martial Arts, A' 135; moralistic comparison between boxing and gladiatorial matches 100; moral objections to MMA and boxing 96; pre-emptive paternalism 89, 92–96; on professional boxing without headstrikes 101; slavery/brain damage analogy 92; soft paternalism approach 90
doctor-assisted death 109
dominance, concept of 84
Dōshu (Master of the Way) 37
double effect, doctrine of 98, 100–101
Downey, Greg 27, 95, 145
ducking and weaving technique 54
Dux, Frank 39
dwarf-tossing 97, 106–107
Dworkin, Gerald 93

Eastern martial arts, perspective of 25, 48
economic coercion 2, 89, 91–92
'Elements of Sport, The' 46
elite-level MMA 92
Elster, Jon 43–45, 49

Index

emotional-biasing signals 57
Enter The Dragon 32, 57
Epictetus, Stoic 123–124, 126, 128, 130–131
epistemic stabilization, notion of 53, 64
Esparza, Carla 152
'essentially competitive' activities 5
estrogen 155
ethics of mixed martial arts 25, 134–147; embodied practices in MMA and UFC 38–40; intrinsic immorality 137–138; intrinsic praiseworthiness 138–144; masculinity, gender-norms, and feminism 142–144; moral revulsion, assessment of 135; representation of 64; respect, means, and ends in MMA 139–142; self-cultivation and 40
eudaimonia 123
experimental stabilization, to development of MMA 53
eye-gouging 80, 144

Fain, John 163–164
Fédération Internationale d'Escrime (FIE) 72
Feinberg, Joel 89, 92
female athlete triad 153–154
female *judokas* 152
female MMA fighters 142–143; benevolent sexism 156; challenge to traditional gender-norms 143; disordered eating 154; gender and risk in sport 152–155; hormone therapy 155; media portrayals of 150; as natural born fighters 154; pain, risk, and control 155–157; Polish coverage of Jędrzejczyk's fights 152; portrayals of heroic women in media 151; presumption of women's physical inferiority 155; weight cutting in fighting sports 154; *see also* female athlete triad
Fighter in the Wind 40n4
fight-or-flight response, in situations of extreme conflict 83
fish-hooking 80
fitness, concept of 72–73
Florida Department of Business and Professional Regulation (FDBPR) 165, 168
Florida State Boxing Commission (FBC) 161
flow states 57–58
folklore, concerning MMA's relative safety 90
formal sports 79
Fox, Fallon 155, 161–164; fights against women 167; identity as a transgender MMA fighter 169; right to compete in bouts 165; right to privacy 165–166; right to self-determination 168
freedom of movement 58
'free-floating' evils, bans on 89, 99, 109

friendship between MMA fighters: camaraderie after fighting 109; for moral defense of MMA 105; nature of 114–118; respect between MMA fighters 109
friendship in sport 110–114, 120; *see also* friendship between MMA fighters
frontoparietal attention network 57–58
Frye, Marilyn 151, 157–158

Gabeira, Maya 153–154
gay-conversion therapy 162
gear, permissible in a fight 60
gender: classes of fighters, rights and duties of 162; equality 153; fraud, in Olympics 163; gendered violence 158; identity 161–162, 164–166, 169; reassignment surgery 161–162, 164
Gentry, Clyde 23
Gichin, Funakoshi 25, 35, 40n4
gladiatorial death-matches 2, 53, 88, 96, 99–100
gladiatorial entertainment 5
gong-fu 32–33
Gracie Jiu-Jitsu 20–22
Gracie, Rorion 20
Gracie, Royce 31
grappling (open-fingered) knuckle pads 48
greatness, sense of 145
Greco-Roman clinches 59
ground and pound, practice of 48–50, 83, 126

Harrison, Kayla 82
Hart's will theory 166
headbutts 59, 80, 90
Health Insurance Privacy and Portability Act (HIPAA) 165
Hellenistic schools of philosophy 123
higher education 164
Hirokazu, Kanazawa 36
Hobbesean war of 'all against all' 47
Hogshead-Makar, Nancy 142
Holm, Holly 127–128
Holt, Jason 70
honbu dōjō (head dojo) 38
Hongjia 31
honor respect 169
hormone therapy 155, 163
human cockfighting 17
human mortality 85
Hume, David 69–70, 79
Hutcheson, Francis 68
hybrid sports 48, 79
hypermasculine sports 78

informed consent, of rational agents 145
intentionality in sports, concept of 71
intention, problem of 73–75

interception, concept of 58
International Olympic Committee (IOC) 163
intersex and gender non-conforming athletes 163
intrinsic immorality, of MMA 137–138
intrinsic praiseworthiness, of MMA 145

Japanese martial arts 25, 37
Japan Karate Association (JKA) 36
Jeet Koon Do 31–33
Joslin, Gabby 34
judicial reasoning 166
judo 12, 36–37; evolution of 55, 57; *ippon* (full-point) 61, 125; kata (combative throws) 25; methodology of competing in 61; *ne waza* (ground grappling) 61; practice of 55, 57; principles of 25; *waza-ri* (half-points) 61
judokas (practitioners of judo): female *judokas* 152; iterative representation and technique manipulation 55; *randori* session 60; representational stability by practicing kata 55, 60; techniques in response to specific opposing movements 60

Kano, Jigoro 19
Kant, Immanuel 106, 137; Categorical Imperative 144; *Critique of Judgment* 165; dictum of treating others 'always as an end' 109; principle of treating others 'as a means only' 110; respect for persons 97–98; view of sublime, applied to martial arts 84
karate 33, 132; '21 precepts of karate' calligraphy of Funakoshi Gichin 35; aim of 25; code of conduct 35; Kyokushin 40n4; Shotokan 35
Karate Kid, The 122
kata (combative throws) 55
kendo (Japan) 7, 12
kenjutsu (close combat) 4
Kerstein, S. J. 140
kickboxing 23, 36, 47, 60–61, 83, 143
kind-desire theory 166, 168
kinesthetic learning 55
knacks (*empeiriai*) 17–18, 20
knockdown in MMA 49, 83
knockouts, importance of 98, 125, 135
Kodokan judo 19
Kristol, Irving 88–90, 99
Kyokushin karate 40n4

Lee, Bruce: attempt to transform traditional martial arts into more flexible and effective fighting systems 32; *Dao of Jeet Koon Do* 32–33; *Enter The Dragon* 32, 57; *gong-fu* 32–33; Jeet Kune Do 58, 59; 'oblique' kicks 59; representation of a technique 'throwing itself ' 53; views on traditional martial arts 31–32
legal moralism 89, 90
Li, Chong 40n5
linear sports 79
Long, Kathy 23
Lopez, Jean 34
Lopez, Steven 34
Lorge, Peter 18–19
loyalty and deference, issue of 2, 35–38

macabre battering 152
Machida, Lyoto 82
Maia, Demian 98–99
male-to-female (MTF) domestic abuse 167
male-to-female (MTF) transgender competitors 162
Mark Hunt *vs.* António Silva event 86n16
martial activities: categories of 4–5; genealogies of 8; objections to categorization of 5–9; purpose of 5
martial aristocratic social class, emergence of 91
martial art control, representational principles of 55
martial artists 25, 122; character traits of 26
martial arts 11–12, 33; craft of 17–20; definition of 6, 19; determination of real martial art 16–20; difference with martial sports/combat sports 7; ethical values of 25; films, popularity of 23; Kant's view of sublime and 84; meaning of 4, 10; MMA and; moral character traits 26; moral teachings of 24; moral virtues of 25; 'no holds barred' MMA and 20–26; sport-oriented 37; techniques of 14; training in 19; Western conceptions of 7
martial craft ('real' martial arts) 16, 20, 23
martial entertainment and display 5
martial knacks (imitation martial arts) 16, 20
martial path (kendo) 4–5, 33
martial practices, classification of 4
martial sports 4, 7, 33; meaning of 10; purpose of 5
martial techniques 53, 54, 55, 57
masculine-associated sports 158
material stabilization, complexity of 55
McCain, John 2, 88
McGregor, Conor 32, 127
medical associations, recommendation to ban boxing and MMA 105
medical records, right to privacy of 164
Miller, Rory 8–9
Million Dollar Baby 145
mindsets, notion of 8–9
minimalist aesthetic 80–81
Miocic, Stipe 54

178 Index

Mitrione, Matt 162
mixed martial arts (MMA): acceptance as a legitimate sport 16; cage fighting 9; championship contests 48; character of 12; and close combat 10–11; as combat sport 1, 12–13; comparable to death penalty 138; competitive aspect of 16; complex hybridity of 47; contemporary 26–28; criticism of 17; dangerousness of 13; determination as craft or a knack 18; development of 53, 58; difference with BDSM 115; difference with traditional martial arts 2; discrediting of 17; 'ground and pound' moves 48, 50; grounding aesthetic interest in 72–73; harmful outcomes related to 106; impoverished version of Muay Thai 48; interdisciplinarity of 47; Kantian criticism of 2; and martial arts 11–12; meaning of 1, 9–14; mental challenges of 147; moral defense of 105; moral distinction with American football 100; morality of 106; no holds barred spectacle 16, 26; octagonal cage for 11; origin of 12; participation of transgender athletes in 161; philosophical treatment of 135; philosophical treatments of 138; popularity and hype-based matchmaking 27; rise in popularity of 27; risk of cumulative brain damage 90; as rule-constituted skilled violence 43; rules of 10–11; safety parameters and time limits 98; spectacle objection 21–22; stabilization at many scales in 58–62; stabilization of 2; superstar culture 40; techniques in 11; as testing ground for fighting techniques 96; three-phase combat sequence of 49; use of Jiu-Jitsu in 48; utility-based aesthetic for 2; vision devoid of cultural norms and values 32; what's wrong and what's right about 49–51; see also objection, to craft status of MMA
MMA see mixed martial arts (MMA)
MMA fighters 143; dwarf-throwers 106–107; female fighters 143; infliction of pain between partners 105; injury rates 94; levels of brain volume loss in 94; modern MMA superstars, behavior of 39; objectification of 106, 110; objectionable attitude toward each other 109; Simple Theory for assessment of CTE risk in 90, 92, 94; see also friendship between MMA fighters
MMA's rules, development of 96
'Moral Critique of Mixed Martial Arts, A' 135
morality/moral: campaign, against MMA 89; critiques, of MMA 134–137; conservatism 89, 90; defense of MMA based on concept of friendship between MMA fighters 105; good, perception of 68; objections, to MMA and boxing 96–101; praiseworthiness, of MMA 138, 146; revulsion, assessment of 135, 139; teachings, of martial arts 24; virtues, of martial arts 24–26
Morgan, Peggy 163–164
Morihei, Ueshiba 35, 37
MPFC 57
Muay Thai 60, 135; as combat sport 47–48; defense technique 54; headbutts, permissibility of 59; Submission Grappling 126
Mumford, Stephen 68, 75, 78, 81, 85

National Collegiate Athletic Association (NCAA) wrestling 92
neurofibrillary tangles 93
NFL, risk reduction policies for 94–95, 101
non-egoistic ethics, attitude of 68
Norris, Chuck 22, 80
no-rules competition 80
Nurmagomedov, Khabib 9, 61, 127
Nussbaum, Martha 137–138

objection, to categorization of martial activities 5–9; dogmatic 6; as fossilization 7–8; Miller's 'practical' approach and 8–9; as ontological exercise 6–7; as social construction 8; as universalistic 6
objection, to craft status of MMA 23–26, 27
'oblique' kicks 59
Octagon, The 22
Old Guard 153
Ōsensei (great teacher) 37
Overeem, Alistair 54
Oyama, Mas (Ōyama Masutatsu) 40n4

panantuken (Filipino martial arts) 59
Pancrase 2, 53, 59–60, 62
pankration (Greek amateur sport) 47–49, 125, 141, 145
philosophy of martial arts 57
physical force, intentional use of 82
physical skill training 39
physiological gender testing 161
pitting of different fighters/styles, against one another 86n9
Plato 67, 111, 134; account of craft and knacks 16–17; Gorgias 16, 17; Symposium 112
Praying Mantis 31
primary motor cortex, excitability of 57
privacy in sports, norms of 113
Pseudo-Dionysus the Areopagite 67
psychological suffering 126

punch-drunkenness, signs of 136
purposive sports 79

Qawi, Dwight Muhammad 54
Qinna 31, 40n1
qualitative sports 79
quality of life 136
quantitative sports 79
queer theory 164

Raz's interest theory 166
real fight, notion of 24, 27, 95–96, 144, 146
real-life fighting 5, 10–13
real-world fighting 83
Reid, Anna 88, 90–91
repeated head trauma (RTH) 93–94
respect: as an integral part of MMA 139–142; duty of 168; Kant's respect for persons 97–98; of selfhood 106
Respect Fighting Championship (RFC) 139
rivalries between fighters, promotion of 39
rock-climbing 147n14
Rock, Sun-Ken 143
Rogan, Joe 83, 162
Roman gladiators 88, 91, 99
Ronda Rousey *vs.* Holly Holm event 81
roundhouse-kicks 54
Rousey, Ronda 9, 81–82, 127, 128, 142, 163, 169
Russell, Gillian 36

SafeSport 34
'safetified' martial techniques 5
samurai, code of 25
self-determination 106, 168
selfhood 106, 141
self-reference 53, 57–58
self-restraint 12, 118, 120
self-worth, sense of 78
Semenya, Caster 163
sex testing, in sport 163–164
sexual abuse, in martial arts 30, 33–35
Shotokan Karate International Federation (SKIF) 36
side-kicks to knees *see* 'oblique' kicks
Simple Theory, for assessment of MMA's CTE risk 90, 92, 94, 100
Sityodtong, Chatri 26
skill in fighting 19–20, 22, 27
slavery/brain damage analogy 92
Slice, Kimbo 82
Smith, Anthony 63–64
social construction, of martial activities 8
Socrates 16, 17, 112, 134
soft paternalism, notion of 90
sonnet-making, rules of 51n4
Soundarajan, Santhi 163

Southern Mantis 31
spectator-less fights 64
spirit of martial arts 16, 26
sport: aesthetics 70, 81; Kupfer's threefold typology of 79
sport-oriented martial arts 37
stabilizing intervention systems: agency in 56–58; excitement, safety, and stabilization 62–64; modes of spectating 61–62; from science to martial art 54–56; techniques that are deployed in a particular fight 60–61
stance-independent excellences 16
stand-up fighting techniques 23
Statement of the Stockholm Consensus on Sex Reassignment in Sports 164
stillness in motion 58
Stockholm Consensus 164
Stoicism: antagonism of MMA and reimagining obstacles 128–129; chaos of MMA and dichotomy of control 125–128; difficulty of MMA and gaining freedom 130–131; philosophy of 123–125; three lessons of 125–131
St-Pierre, Georges 80
street-fighting 10, 16, 82, 141, 144–146
studying a fighter 54
submission fighters 23
Submission Grappling 126
suitable opponents for matches, determination of 162
Suits, Bernard 46
supplementary motor area, excitability of 57

taekwondo 12, 30, 32–35, 37, 39, 132
tai chi 4, 132
taijiquan 7, 31
Tate, Miesha 128
tau proteins 93
technical knockout 81, 135, 162
technical proficiency at MMA events 16, 26
Teixeira, Glover 64
Telfer, Elizabeth 110–111, 114, 119
testosterone 155, 164
Thai Boxing 135, 143
Theron, Charlize 153
three-phase combat sequence, of MMA 49
'throwing itself' technique, representation of 53
traditional martial arts (TMA) 16, 23, 26, 30–33, 35, 36, 38, 40; 'bad boy' exception 40n4; difference with mixed martial arts 2; negative public image of 39
traditional mixed martial art (TMMA) 32
training, in martial arts: of both mind and body 19; in combat sport 50; intention,

problem of 74; physical skill 39; traditional martial arts (TMA) 33
transgender athletes, in MMA: background of 162–163; discrimination against 161; duty of respect 168–169; ethics of 161; fair competition with cisgender athletes 161; gender oppression of 164; male-to-female (MTF) transgender competitor 162; non-identity problem 169; in Olympic Games 163; rights and theories 164–168; sex testing of 163–164; struggling for recognition 164
transgender participation in sport, philosophy of 161
trans women, challenges faced by 156

ultimate fighter 80, 135; *Ultimate Fighter, The* 135
Ultimate Fighting Championship (UFC) 31; blood sport 22; code of conduct 163; events during COVID-19 pandemic 62; female fighters clash 142; formation of 16; goal of 22; Hall of Fame 143; Light Heavyweight Champion 143; marketing for 22; Mark Hunt *vs.* António Silva event 86n16; no holds barred 20; 'no technique' objection 23–24; permissibility of headbutts in 59; prohibition on biting and gouging 95; pro wrestling 22; Ronda Rousey *vs.* Holly Holm event 81; spectacle objection 21–22; spectatorship of 63; tagline of 16; towards ethical embodied practices 38–40; Vale Tudo-style fighting tournament 20; women's bantamweight division 150
Ulysses and the Sirens 44
unarmed fighting, structured contest of 1, 81
unconscious competence, action of 71
underground fight clubs 146
unisex sports, creation of 161
usefulness, concept of 72
utility-based aesthetic, for MMA: aesthetic flaws and 85; beauty, perception of 68–69; categories of 66; concept of 66, 71; counterarguments in 69–70; determinant of 73; disinterestedness in 67–69; draw of diversity 81–82; effectiveness of movement and qualities of 70; empathetic sublime 83–84; as fitness and usefulness 72–73; four major facets of 80–81; Holt's five-level analysis and 70; Hume's theory of 67; intention, problem of 73–75; levels of analysis 79–80; minimalism in 80–81; movement and performance as objects of beauty 70–72; perception of 73–75; setting and significance of 75–76; social virtues and 69–70; theory of 69–70; translating utility into beauty 75–76; transpersonal aesthetic judgment 78; unconscious competence, action of 71; utility of technique 70–72, 74; value of 83; violence as definitive 82–83

Vale Tudo (Brazilian sport) 20
values, of traditional martial arts 26
Vilain, Eric 163
violence of MMA 83–84
violent sports 47, 88, 105
virtues 12, 124

Wallace, Bill 21
warrior arts 4, 5
Wei, Lei 31
White Crane 31
White, Dana 154, 158, 164
Whittaker, Robert 59
wide weaving technique 54
winner of a sporting contest, precondition for determining 10
women in risky sports 157
women's physical inferiority, presumption of 155–156
wrestling 47, 54, 92, 135

Xu, Xiaodong 31

Yongchun 31, 33
Yoshimune, Tokugawa 24

Zampetti, Nina 34
zanshin 12
Zen Buddhism 58
Zeno of Citium 123

Printed in the United States
by Baker & Taylor Publisher Services